Family and Identity in Contemporary Cuban
and Puerto Rican Drama

Florida A&M University, Tallahassee
Florida Atlantic University, Boca Raton
Florida Gulf Coast University, Ft. Myers
Florida International University, Miami
Florida State University, Tallahassee
University of Central Florida, Orlando
University of Florida, Gainesville
University of North Florida, Jacksonville
University of South Florida, Tampa
University of West Florida, Pensacola

Copyright 2004 by Camilla Stevens
Printed in the United States of America on recycled, acid-free paper
All rights reserved

09 08 07 06 05 04   6 5 4 3 2 1

Library of Congress Cataloging-in-Publication Data
Stevens, Camilla.
Family and identity in contemporary Cuban and Puerto Rican drama /
Camilla Stevens.
p. cm.
Includes bibliographical references and index.
ISBN 0-8130-2707-1 (cloth : alk. paper)
1. Cuban drama—20th century—History and criticism. 2. Puerto Rican drama—
20th century—History and criticism. 3. Family in literature. 4. Identity (Psychology)
in literature. 5. Literature and society—Cuba. 6. Literature and society—
Puerto Rico. 7. Cuba—Civilization. 8. Puerto Rico—Civilization. I. Title.
PQ7381.S74   2004
862'.6093552—dc22   2003070502

The University Press of Florida is the scholarly publishing agency for the State
University System of Florida, comprising Florida A&M University, Florida Atlantic
University, Florida Gulf Coast University, Florida International University, Florida
State University, University of Central Florida, University of Florida, University
of North Florida, University of South Florida, and University of West Florida.

University Press of Florida
15 Northwest 15th Street
Gainesville, FL 32611-2079
http://www.upf.com

Program

For Mike

•◆•

Acknowledgments

The generous support of many individuals and institutions has immensely facilitated the writing of this book. In the early stages of researching and writing at the University of Kansas, Danny Anderson, Mary Karen Dahl, Sharon Feldman, Vicky Unruh, and George Woodyard provided encouragement and guidance. I wish to recognize especially the extraordinary mentoring I have received from Vicky Unruh and George Woodyard. Their scholarship, professionalism, and sound advice have played an invaluable role in my development as a scholar and a teacher. I am very grateful as well to Susan Martin-Márquez, Yolanda Martínez-San Miguel, Kirsten Nigro, and Alberto Sandoval-Sánchez for carefully reading any part or version of the manuscript and offering thoughtful feedback that greatly benefited this book. My friends, colleagues, and students at Rutgers University have been constant sources of inspiration and support. In particular, I would like to thank Larry La Fountain-Stokes, Yolanda Martínez-San Miguel, Ben. Sifuentes-Jáuregui, and Brenda Werth, who were cheerfully bribed to help me with translations and editing. Thanks, too, to Amy Gorelick and Jaqueline Kinghorn Brown at the University Press of Florida, for their interest in the project and for patiently fielding my questions. Finally, I would like to thank my family, whose love of dialogue has instilled in me a thirst for inquiry and investigation. Above all, I extend my deepest gratitude to Mike, who weathered with me the most challenging moments of realizing this project.

Two publishers have graciously granted permission to reproduce materials that appeared in earlier forms. Portions of Act II, Scenes 1 and 2, appeared in my articles "Ties That Bind: Staging the New Family in Revolutionary Cuba" in *Gestos* 16.32 (November 2001): 89–104 and "Traveling Troupes: The Performance of Puerto Rican Identity in Plays by Luis Rafael Sánchez and Myrna Casas" in *Hispania* 85.2 (May 2002): 240–49.

two countries. While it has become commonplace to expect any cultural history of Latin America and the Hispanic Caribbean to identify the role of writing in the project of constructing and defining nationhood, the place of performance in the cultural politics of representing the nation has been less rigorously investigated. Thus the aim of this book is to present a genealogy of modern Cuban and Puerto Rican drama that reveals how theater and performance constitute a special site and activity for imagining communities.

Throughout the twentieth century, sociopolitical, economic, and cultural transformations in Cuba and Puerto Rico have profoundly changed the ways their national communities have envisioned themselves. The following contextualized analysis of two key periods of the production of family drama—the mid-1950s to the mid-1960s and the mid-1980s to the mid-1990s—charts historical changes in the modes of representing families as a metaphor for national community and, consequently, significant changes in long-standing identity debates in Cuba and Puerto Rico. The onstage family quarrels between husbands and wives, between parents and children, and among siblings embody divergent views of national experience and provide insight into how communities are defined and by whom, as well as how visions of national culture change over time.

Family and theater have been intimately related since the beginnings of Western drama. Aristotle, commenting on Greek tragedy, observed that the best plots dealt with famous mythical houses and the messy affairs among family members (Haliwell 44–45, ch. 13). In the Roman period, domestic entanglements often took a comic turn in plays by well-known authors such as Terence and Plautus. Family matters in the plays of the English Renaissance by Shakespeare and his contemporaries, in the *comedias* of the Spanish Golden Age, and in the neoclassic comedies of seventeenth-century France helped produce the modern subject by dramatizing the (un)acceptable behavior for monarchical communal life. At the turn of the twentieth century, dramatists including Henrik Ibsen, Anton Chekhov, August Strindberg, and George Bernard Shaw exposed the social problems of the bourgeoisie by oftentimes looking at the details of ordinary, domestic life. Their legacy of dramatic realism has informed generations of American playwrights, from Arthur Miller, Eugene O'Neill, and Tennessee Williams, to Sam Shepard, August Wilson, and Marsha Norman. Even a cursory review of the Western dramatic tradition shows that the family play, whether it be tragic or comic, realist or experimental, reactionary or progressive, serves as a basic locus for examining wider social dramas. As we will see, in contemporary Cuban and Puerto Rican theater the specific themes of generational and marital conflict lead to broad inquiries into problems of national and cultural identity.

Contemporary researchers of the family insist that no definition of family fits the reality of all cultural groups and historical periods.[2] Perhaps the best way to allow for the diverse forms of this social institution is to draw attention to its constructed character. In *The Making of the Modern Family* (1975), Edward Shorter asserts that family is "a state of mind rather than a particular structure or set of household arrangements" (205), and in another classic on the family, *Haven in a Heartless World* (1977), Christopher Lasch affirms that "the family, like society in general, is held together by the power of imaginative identification, by ideas and 'sentiments' and by the development of clearly defined social roles which alone have the power to evoke sentiments and sympathy" (31). In this study, what I refer to as a "family drama" is a staged play that contains "any group of two or more persons who engage in ongoing intimacy and obligation, whether they do so because of birth, marriage, adoption or choice" (Coontz 19). In other words, this definition envisions the family as a group of people who imagine themselves as one. Such an elastic definition of the family allows me to analyze texts that include traditional intergenerational families created by marriage, families bound by fraternal bonds, and groups unrelated by blood who create familial relationships, such as a military organization or a troupe of circus performers. Although the image of the nuclear family composed of parents and children and headed by a male haunts many of the characters of the plays in this study, almost none of the families represented in these works form this sort of family unit. As I have suggested, the unconventional arrangements of family and their attendant complicated relationships signify unresolved questions of the national body politic.

Most of these families, however, are associated with the traditional domestic space, the house. Unless otherwise noted, I use "house" and "home" to denote a place; a home is situated in space, most often in a house but not necessarily designed or represented as such (nor is it automatically assumed to be a fixed place). In twentieth-century theater, house and family inevitably invoke dramatic realism, and while not every play in this study is representative of realism, many are linked to this mode of theatrical expression. The connection between the domestic sphere and the nation we will see in many of the plays analyzed in this book has its roots in the late-nineteenth-century realist drama of Ibsen, Chekhov, and Shaw.[3] These playwrights introduced to the stage controversial subjects such as the position of women in society, social justice and economic exploitation, and the problems of rigid social mores. Their plays frequently approach these themes by way of the family, making paradigmatic the representation of the private space of the family as a microcosm of society.

The plays included here also manifest typically realist conventions by dramatizing ordinary human experiences in which psychologically complex characters confront social problems in an onstage world that reflects the real one. Many also employ realistic stage techniques such as creating an illusionist set and situating the spectator as an eavesdropping observer behind an imaginary fourth wall created by the proscenium arch. In contrast, due to their use of metatheater, the plays frequently contradict one gauge of realism, the minimalization of theatricality; I would also argue that the plots do not always follow realism's characteristic linear dramatic structure that leads to the resolution of the problems posed by the play. Central to all of the works, however, is the foregrounding of the social background of the play's action, that is, a specific cultural context. Realism accents what Roland Barthes would call the referential or cultural code of textual signification (20). In dramatic realism, the references to the various social discourses that mediate and organize cultural knowledge about reality assume a shared sociocultural background between the audience and the text. In conjunction with the code of reference, Barthes explains that texts construct a symbolic code based on familiar patterns of antitheses that articulate meaning in a particular culture (19). Ideology plays a part in deciphering these codes. For Baz Kershaw, performance is an ideological transaction, ideology being "the source of the collective ability of performers and audience to make more or less common sense of the signs used in performance, the means by which the aims and intentions of theatre companies connect with the responses and interpretations of their audiences" (137). As the following play analyses will show, Cuban and Puerto Rican audiences, ideologically interpellated as subjects by the dramatic text, understand their national cultural imaginary through differential coordinates—such as colonialism and nationalism, tradition and modernity, revolution and resignation, nostalgia and present reality, utopia and skepticism, machismo and feminism, and heterosexuality and homosexuality—that are frequently deconstructed by the works themselves.[4] The domestic stories enacted in these plays can thus be read allegorically as stories about broader social issues.

If family has been a dominant motif in the history of Western drama, since the nineteenth century family sagas have provided a cardinal metaphor for addressing the enduring themes of nation and identity in Latin American letters and the literature of the Hispanic Caribbean. Drawing on Michel Foucault's studies on sexuality and Benedict Anderson's theory of nation, in *Foundational Fictions: The National Romances of Latin America* (1991) Doris Sommer examines the connections between narrative romances (fiction) and nation-building (politics) in the postindependence era in Latin America. The romantic relationships in these "foundational fictions" attempt to cross racial and class boundaries, forming "part of a general bourgeois project to hegemonize a culture in formation" (Sommer, *Foundational Fictions* 29). Heterosexual love and marriage, in other words, would ideally strengthen bourgeois interests by reconciling racial, regional, economic, and gender conflicts. Read allegorically, the young lovers of these novels represent different national constituencies, and their private passions reflect a public desire to build the nation.

Nineteenth-century Latin American dramas have never been as widely disseminated as the romantic national novels. Reading the treatment of the education and marriage of women in plays by Fernando Calderón (Mexico), Manuel Ascencio Segura (Peru), and Felipe Pardo y Aliaga (Peru) as an allegory of the project of nation building, however, could reveal the theater's distinct style of imagining the nation. In Pardo y Aliaga's *Los frutos de la educación* [The rewards of education] (1830), for example, a young woman's passion for the *zamacueca*, a popular Peruvian dance, alienates her from a promising English marriage partner. From the play's perspective, the potential romance would have strengthened the nation by forming an English and criollo connection. Consequently, Pardo y Aliaga teaches his audience that the deficient education of women is detrimental to building the national family.

The period of massive European immigration and urbanization that took place at the turn of the century through the 1930s in the Río de la Plata region constitutes another intense moment of exploring collective identity in Latin American drama. Plays by Florencio Sánchez and Armando Discépolo dramatize these demographic shifts and the cultural conflicts created by them through the theme of the family. In Sánchez's *La gringa* (1904), for example, a wedding between a family of gaucho origins and a newly immigrated Italian family registers the changing composition of Argentine national identity. The unions depicted in both foundational novels and plays, however, are not always easily obtained. Sommer points out that the conflicts the couples face in the course of their romances serve to create the reader's desire for their relationship to succeed (*Foundational Fictions* 49).[5] The dynamic of this desire in the context of the collective and live theater event could very well be one area that distinguishes theatrical representations of national romances from novelistic ones.

Like the aforementioned nineteenth- and early-twentieth-century plays mentioned earlier, the detailed cultural specificity of the Cuban and Puerto Rican family plays examined in this study and the historical circumstances of their staging implicitly assert a connection to a context shared by their audiences that invites an allegorical interpretation. Although none of the dramatists explicitly declare their writings as allegories, their works encourage audiences to draw a correlation between the two apparently distinct narratives of family plots and the discourses of national identity. In this sense, my use of the term "allegory" builds on Angus Fletcher's minimal definition: "in the simplest terms, allegory says one thing and means another" (2). The domestic plays I analyze allegorically perform a political desire to (re)tell a national identity story. The private family story refers implicitly to another story, a public discourse on collective identity.

The double narrative of allegory lends itself to thinking about the categories of the public and the private spheres, concepts central to discussions of the family and the nation, as well as to the function of theater in society. Liberal political philosophy has traditionally presented the family as a private realm—a haven of intimate, familial relationships separate from the political and economic relationships that define the public space. In a different context, Barbara Johnson mentions a public/private tension inherent in allegory that I find suggestive for thinking about family and nation: "Allegory is speech that is other than open, public, direct. It is hidden, deviant, indirect—but also, I want to emphasize, public. It folds the public onto itself. It names the conflictuality of the public sphere and the necessity of negotiating those conflicts rhetorically" (61). Interestingly, in the dramas I will examine here, playwrights choose the "hidden," private sphere of the home to signify indirectly public conflicts: the unsettled state of Cuban and Puerto Rican collective identities. As opposed to the more traditional view of allegory as a producer of metaphoric and parallel meanings, Sommer envisions allegory's double narrative as metonymic and interlocking. Thus she reads romantic plots in Latin American national novels as allegories of state formation, narratives "in which one line is a trace of the other, in which each helps to write the other" (*Foundational Fictions* 42). Like the sentimental novels studied by Sommer, in the plays I critique, allegory's dual stories—family and nation—fold back and forth onto themselves in a complex relationship not characterized by a one-to-one correspondence.

Consequently, these plays enable us to see the interconnectedness of the family and the nation and of the public and the private spheres. For playwrights, the family provides a convenient trope that lends itself to the consideration of society at large because family structures and dynamics often mimic those of the nation. The male-dominated patriarchal family, for example, evokes the hierarchies of a larger collectivity: the paternalist political leader/father who implicitly assigns hierarchical roles to members of the national family. Similarly, the conflicts within families that develop among couples, siblings, and different generations parallel the multiple points of view at play in considering the issues of race, class, and gender in constructions of national identity. What I would like to highlight here, though, is that by casting the family as the nation, these playwrights contest the separation of the public and the private spheres that tends to present practices and ideologies associated with each as natural, constant, and universal. The dramatic representations of the family help show the gendered differentiation between the public and the private worlds and the entry of what Jacques Donzelot calls "the social" into the family (xxvi, 7). Donzelot's notion of "the social" includes the many public institutions (such as medicine, government legislation, and education) and services (philanthropy and public charity) that have produced and controlled the family household.[6] If the daily activities of the private sphere are regulated in relation to other social organizations and the larger processes of production, reproduction, and consumption that characterize the public sphere, then domestic relationships form a basic part of a society's political organization. Simply stated, the personal is

most illusionist productions, those in the audience are aware that the actors play a role and that they are watching a representation, however much it may approximate the real. Homi Bhabha writes that the discourse of the nation provides an ambivalent image of cultural authority "because it is caught, uncertainly, in the 'act' of composing its powerful image" (3). Staging nationalist discourse can only accentuate its ambivalence because the theatrical context underscores how identities come into being through repetitive performances. Furthermore, works that flaunt their theatricality oftentimes expose the performativity of the roles that constitute us as subjects. Theater, as a character in Luis Rafael Sánchez's play *Quíntuples* affirms, is risky because its artifice suggests that all forms of identity are human-made representations that must be constantly (re)performed. Performance, then, paradoxically implies the possibility of transformation at the same time that it may attempt to lead the audience to envision the nation in a particularly set way.

An Overview

Contemporary Cuba and Puerto Rico provide abundant examples of family dramas that enact problems of national identity, due in large part to the historical commonalties shared by the islands, including their late-nineteenth-century independence from Spain and their ensuing struggle against North American colonialism.[12] This study focuses on thematically and aesthetically similar family plays by playwrights from two significant historical periods: the mid-1950s to the mid-1960s and the mid-1980s to the mid-1990s.[13] The family stands out as a particularly strong theme in plays from both countries in the 1950s because these years constitute a period of intense self-reflection for Puerto Ricans and Cubans. Puerto Rican history throughout the first half of the twentieth century was marked by its evolving semicolonial condition, which culminated in the island's permanent status as a Commonwealth in 1952. Although Cuba had gained its independence in 1898, political authoritarianism and North American interventionism trapped the island in an unproductive cycle. By the 1950s, the conditions under the dictatorship of Fulgencio Batista led intellectuals to express frustration with the reality that Cuba had never really achieved national sovereignty.

The Marxist orientation of the 1959 Cuban Revolution strongly differentiates the histories of these countries during the latter half of the twentieth century, but in both Cuba and Puerto Rico the family emerges as a central image in the theater of the 1980s and 1990s. The discussion about the nature of Cuban identity in the 1960s and 1970s, sparked by the task of implementing and institutionalizing the Revolution, was the subject of many Cuban plays from the 1980s. The breakup of the Soviet bloc (1989–91) and subsequent loss of Soviet support have again made the issue of self-definition a national concern in the 1990s. In Puerto Rico, the 1968 elections reopened old ideological divisions by breaking the political hegemony of the party in favor of the Commonwealth. By the 1980s, however, the debate over the political identity of Puerto Rico was less urgent than facing social and economic crises. As a result, during this decade the focus on nationalism and colonialism shifts to consider new approaches to defining national community.

The clusters of plays that presented themselves during two particular decades largely determined the temporal framework of this book.[14] Rather than beginning with such foundational family plays as *La cuarterona* [The quadroon] (Alejandro Tapia y Rivera, 1867) in Puerto Rico or *Tembladera* [Tremor] (José Antonio Ramos, 1917) in Cuba and attempting to sketch a literary history of the family play in each country, I have chosen to explore why certain moments in the Cuban and Puerto Rican traditions are so densely populated by images of the family. That is, my approach to the corpus of plays outlined below is genealogical rather than teleological. Foucault, reading Nietzsche, describes a historical inquiry that advocates treating the past not as a continuous or progressive development, nor as a search for origins. He writes:

> Genealogy does not pretend to go back in time to restore an unbroken continuity that operates beyond the dispersion of forgotten things; [. . .] Genealogy does not resemble the evolution of a species and does not map a destiny of a people. On the contrary, to follow the complex course of descent is to maintain passing events in their proper dispersion; it is to identify the accidents, the minute deviations—or conversely, to complete reversals—the errors, the false appraisals, and the faulty calculations that gave birth to those things that continue to exist and have value for us; it is to discover that truth or being do not lie at the root of what we know and what we are, but the exteriority of accidents. ("Nietzsche" 146)

In this spirit, I do not present unifying, linear histories from the 1950s to the 1990s of two dramatic traditions; instead, my "course of descent" weaves back and forth between countries looking for discrete examples of canonical and noncanonical family plays that, read comparatively across geographical and temporal borders, yield a broad picture of how the stage participates uniquely in the cultural politics of representing the nation.

The exploration of family and identity in Cuban and Puerto Rican drama that follows draws on a variety of cultural texts—from histories and national identity essays to revolutionary documents and film—in order to place theater and performance within the broad cultural dialogue of which they are a part. Thus each chapter begins by situating the plays in the historical, sociopolitical, economic, and intellectual contexts in which they were produced. In Act I, scene 1, I demonstrate how a series of plays staged between 1958 and 1960—*Vejigantes* [Masks] (1958) by Francisco Arriví, *Los soles truncos* (1958) and *Un niño azul para esa sombra* [A blue boy for that shadow] (1960) by René Marqués, and *Cristal roto en el tiempo* [Glass broken in time] (1960) by Myrna Casas —participate in a public discussion on Puerto Rico's failure to gain independence and on what constitutes the island's identity. I argue that, in these works, a desire to found the nation through a national family romance characterizes Puerto Rico's search for identity. The family quarrels and failed romances portrayed in these plays evoke the contrasting stances on Puerto Rican political and cultural identity debated on a national level and the use of the space of the house raises questions about what kind of family should embody the nation.

In contrast to romances among peers falling apart, in Cuban plays produced between the mid-1950s and the mid-1960s the vertical tension between generations signifies a desire for national self-determination and social justice. In Act I, scene 2, I look at how the conflict between parents and children in Rolando Ferrer's *Lila, la mariposa* [Lila, the butterfly] (1954), Virgilio Piñera's *Aire frío* [Cold air] (1962), Abelardo Estorino's *El robo del cochino* [The theft of the pig] (1961), and José Triana's *La noche de los asesinos* (1966) highlights Cuba's struggle to define itself in a stifling authoritarian and neocolonial context. In all of these plays, escaping parental authority and the oppressive space of the family home implies the restructuring of the institution of the family and implicitly asks what kind of national family should replace the Republican model.

In the 1980s and 1990s, rather than positing a fixed vision of national community, plays examine instead the formation of subjectivities that challenge former constructions of the nation and the family. New studies from the post-1968 era that center on the issues of race, class, gender, and immigration in Puerto Rico reveal how the debate on national character has moved beyond the nationalist/colonialist framework that had defined many intellectuals from the first half of this century. In this context, Act II, scene 1 discusses how *Hotel Melancolía* [Melancholy hotel] (1989) by Antonio García del Toro and *Callando amores* [Silencing loves] (1995) by Roberto Ramos-Perea expose a need for new national identity stories, while *Quíntuples* [Quintuplets] (1984) by Luis Rafael Sánchez and *El gran circo eukraniano* [The Great USkrainian Circus] (1988) by Myrna Casas present novel ways of understanding Puerto Rican identity. Although these four plays contest many representations of the national family from the 1950s, they paradoxically display a nostalgic desire to preserve the cultural traditions of a seemingly more stable past.

In the final scene of this study, I explore how the family play in post-1959 Cuba plays a role in a national movement to instill revolutionary values. *La emboscada* [The ambush] (1978) by Roberto Orihuela and *Ni un sí ni un no* [No arguments] (1980) by Abelardo Estorino participate in a national discussion on the role of family in a socialist society. These plays represent the challenges confronted by the evolving conception of a new Cuban family in the mid-1960s and mid-1970s. In the 1990s, by comparison, due to the economic and ideological crises provoked by the disintegration of the Soviet bloc, plays have become less didactic and more critical of the new family and the nation. Thus *Manteca* [Lard] (1993) by Alberto Pedro Torriente and *Vereda tropical* [Tropical path] (1994) by Joaquín Miguel Cuartas Rodríguez dramatize a new, fragmented revolutionary family arising from the loss of paternalist state support.

The marriage between family and drama in contemporary Cuban and Puerto Rican drama foregrounds the complexity of representing collective identities. The abundance of family plays in this region and the identity stories they bring to life before an audience add a unique dimension to a cultural dialogue that critics have tended to examine through narrative. In performance, the spoken word and other sounds, the image, and the body and its gestures constitute a countermemory that registers views of national identity that otherwise remain unilluminated in discursive constructions of the nation.[15] A genealogy of the performance of the family also discerns patterns—continuities and changes—in how playwrights use family plots and identifies ideological shifts in conceptualizations of the family and the nation over time. Theatrically constituted through the trope of the family, national identity emerges as historically specific and contextually variable, thus putting into question any claim that presents the family and the nation as self-evident or immutable.

Act I

1950s and 1960s

ships between race and class and between men and women. The plays take place in the paradigmatic family space, the house, which comes to be identified with the nation, and the material condition of the houses and the characters' perceptions of their place within them highlight different interpretations of the national community. Tensions among husbands and wives and brothers and sisters and the spaces they inhabit become metaphors for a society in transition, one marked for some by disorientation and loss and characterized for others by the forging of a new kind of Puerto Rican family.

To explain my use of the term "family romance," I must return to *Foundational Fictions*, Doris Sommer's study of the link between romantic novels and nation building in nineteenth-century Latin America. In these tales of the origins of national identity, erotics and politics are inseparable, for the desire that joins men and women to form families is part of the political scheme to consolidate the Republic. In the Hispanic Caribbean, the salient characteristic in the foundational national allegories, including the Cuban novels *Sab* (1841) and *Cecilia Valdés* (1882) and the Dominican novel *Enriquillo* (1882), is the quest for racial synthesis. In the Cuban novels, however, racial tensions are not effaced by love relationships, and the island's quest for nationhood is complicated by the issue of slavery; in *Enriquillo*, the novel's image of a national family founded by a romance between whites and Indians refutes the nineteenth-century historical reality that blacks constituted the majority of the Dominican population. The drama *La cuarterona* [The quadroon] (1867) could also be read in the context of Caribbean romances. In this play by Puerto Rican Alejandro Tapia y Rivera, an aristocratic white man wishes to marry a humble quadroon, but the (false) threat of incest thwarts their romance and keeps different classes and races from forging a nation-building alliance. In contrast, the Puerto Rican novel *La peregrinación de Bayoán* [The pilgrimage of Bayoán] (1863) by Eugenio María de Hostos attempts to cross geographical borders. In this work, the allegorical protagonists represent Cuba, Puerto Rico, and the Dominican Republic, and their relationships constitute an effort to form a pan-Antillean family. History shows, however, that the cultural heterogeneity of the region and the experience of colonialism have never permitted the realization of Hostos's vision of a united Antillean archipelago. Caribbean nations gained their independence much later than their Latin American counterparts, and in the case of Puerto Rico, it never obtained it at all. My reading of

Puerto Rican failed romances thus expands Sommer's nineteenth-century model to include the complex struggle for self-definition in twentieth-century Puerto Rico.

As we will see in contemporary dramatic works by Marqués, Arriví, and Casas, frustrated Puerto Rican family romances have their roots in the nineteenth-century failure to develop a strong sense of national community. Puerto Rico gained autonomy from Spain in November 1897 only to become a pawn in the Spanish-American War and the first experiment in colonial expansion by the United States. The origins of this lost opportunity for nationhood go beyond the events of 1898, however, and are important in contextualizing the plays examined in this chapter. Under Spanish rule, the Puerto Rican peasant economy was fairly diversified, and compared to Cuba, where large sugar plantations dominated, a relatively significant portion of the population owned some land (Rogozinski 207). Consequently, Puerto Rican peasants, the *jíbaros*, were cautious in demanding changes that could jeopardize their situation. In addition, two waves of immigration had a deleterious effect on the growth of a bourgeois class with strong nationalist sentiments. First, during the South American wars of independence (1810–25), Spanish royalist partisans migrated to the island in order to flee the conflicts. Second, to bolster the island's economic development (and in hopes of "whitening" the population), the 1815 Real Cédula de Gracias declared that any Catholic subject of an allied nation could settle in Puerto Rico (González Valés 93). The foreigners—mainly English, Dutch, French, Corsicans, Majorcans, and Catalans—generally took sides with the Liberal Conservatives who wanted to preserve colonial status with Spain. The other elite political group, the Liberal Reformists (made up of criollo landowners), favored political reforms and broader autonomy. In brief, although in the course of the nineteenth century some nationalist sentiments did develop, these did not coalesce around the idea of a strong, independent nation.[2]

Much like the failure of nineteenth-century Puerto Rico to define itself as a nation independent of Spain, its twentieth-century social, political, and economic relationships with the United States created a situation in which the question of national identity is a perennial topic of debate. Consequently, the constant search for self-definition has maintained the family as an important metaphor in contemporary literature, particularly during the periods of cultural nationalism in the 1920s and 1930s and in the 1950s. Throughout the first third of the century, the Puerto

Rican semifeudal hacienda economy was transformed into one dominated by capitalist plantation agriculture. The process of mechanization and concentration of land in fewer hands began before 1898, but under U.S. occupation, the sugar industry came to dominate the island's economy until the Second World War. The development of large North American sugar and tobacco companies created a rural proletariat and dislocated the criollo hacendado class from their hegemonic position in the agrarian sector.[3] This profoundly changed social relations on the island. The paternalist bond between the hacendados and their workers was broken, and the proletariat class became politically active through the creation of unions and political parties, while the criollo landowning classes faced the loss of economic power and their seignorial way of life.[4]

The cultural crisis brought on by capitalist modernization affected far more than Puerto Rico's class structure and economy, for the United States sought to instill new cultural values by refashioning local institutions based on Spanish traditions, such as the educational system.[5] Consequently, the institutionalization of an official national culture became an important project in academic circles at the end of the 1920s and into the early 1930s. The establishment of the department of Hispanic studies at the University of Puerto Rico and the founding of important cultural magazines such as *Revista de Estudios Hispánicos* (1928), *Índice* (1929), and *Revista del Ateneo Puertorriqueño* (1935) exemplify this project. In response to North American political and economic domination, many intellectuals, some of whom belonged to the displaced criollo class, adopted ideologically defensive, traditional Hispanic values in an attempt to bolster Puerto Rican cultural identity in the face of North American influence. Many of the Generation of 1930 writers, in particular Tomás Blanco in his *Prontuario histórico de Puerto Rico* [Inventory of Puerto Rican history] (1935) and Antonio S. Pedreira in his long essay *Insularismo* [Insularism] (1934), sought to define an essential Puerto Rican national culture.

In *Insularismo*, Pedreira responds to the questions "What are we and how are we?" posed by the editors of *Índice* in 1929. His interpretation of Puerto Rican national identity examines geography and climate, the varied groups that inhabit the island, and the island's customs and literature to conclude that the Puerto Rican peasant, the *jíbaro*, is the true root of Puerto Rican culture (Pedreira 149). This would seem to be a contradiction since, as many critics have noted, Pedreira's view of national culture is framed by his own class formation, and his definition of the Puerto Rican "soul" clearly rejects popular culture in favor of high culture.[6] For example, in his survey of Puerto Rican literature, Pedreira dismisses the importance of the *décima*, a folk verse literary tradition (67). In contrast, he chooses the *danza*, a formal ballroom dance with a Spanish rhythm, as Puerto Rico's national music and dance (153–54). He is able to appropriate the *jíbaro*, an icon of the popular classes, as the symbol of *puertorriqueñidad* only because this figure has already passed into history. That is, Pedreira bases much of his vision of Puerto Rico on a mythologized past that reflects the nostalgia of his class for its hegemonic position in society. His treatment of race and gender also reveals a hierarchical conception of Puerto Rican identity. Pedreira's interpretation of Puerto Rican culture, which privileges Hispanocentricism, high culture, and a paternalist agrarian lifestyle, became a foundational building block for a Puerto Rican nationalist discourse to which writers continue to respond today.

The growing nationalist sentiment of the 1920s and 1930s manifested itself politically as the Partido Popular Democrático [Popular Democratic Party] (PPD), founded in 1938 and led by Luis Muñoz Marín. The PPD, which dominated Puerto Rican politics between 1944 and 1969, initially put the political status issue on hold in order to launch new economic and social policies. According to historian Arturo Morales Carrión, "No other period in the history of the island saw such a dramatic transformation or such an alteration in the social horizon. The hard crust of an agrarian economy was permanently broken, and the rural character of culture was changed by new population shifts and distribution. Puerto Rico became urbanized and increasingly industrialized with new social classes of fluid mobility" ("The PPD" 256). As the agrarian sugar-based economy declined, North American postwar development programs in conjunction with the PPD's Operation Bootstrap (1947) put into effect economic policies to promote industrial capitalism. The United States encouraged investments in Puerto Rico through tax exemptions and other benefits, which made Puerto Rico increasingly dependent on American capital. The question of political status could no longer be skirted, since American companies did not want to invest in the island if it became independent. In contrast to independence or statehood, the PPD promoted the middle-of-the-road alternative of an Estado Libre Asociado [Associated Free State], a status that was granted in 1952. Similar to a Commonwealth, Puerto Rico is neither a colony nor a state; it is self-governing in local affairs, but the United States handles all foreign relations and defense matters.

From the PPD's perspective, Commonwealth status has economic advantages, and it allows the island to retain its distinct identity by placing education, health, and justice (all of which played an important role in the attempt to Americanize the island) under local control (Silvestrini 160). As a counterpoint to Operation Bootstrap's economic development plan, the PPD's Operation Serenity instituted cultural policies intended to strengthen cultural pride and curb resistance to the new political status of the island. According to Arlene Dávila, Operation Serenity "aimed to provide a sense of spiritual balance to a society threatened by the rapid social change caused by the new economic policies" (34). Staff from the División de Educación de la Comunidad [Division of Community Education] (DIVEDCO) traveled to rural areas to help the island's transition to modernity by providing educational workshops and pamphlets about budgeting, family planning, diet, and emigration (Dávila 36–37). With the establishment of the Instituto de Cultura Puertorriqueña [Institute of Puerto Rican Culture] (ICP) in 1955, the PPD adopted an even more explicit role in promoting Puerto Rican culture. Through festivals, conferences, exhibitions, contests, the creation of museums, and the restoration of historical buildings, the ICP's goal was to circulate and preserve Puerto Rican cultural values. By promoting the cultural uniqueness of the island, government agencies such as the ICP and DIVEDCO helped "the PPD legitimize Puerto Rican nationality within the new semi-independent yet mostly contingent commonwealth status" (Dávila 38).[7]

Some groups, however, rejected Muñoz Marín's populist and conciliatory brand of nationalism and lashed out against the island's continuing colonialist relationship with the United States.[8] The founding of the Partido Independentista Puertorriqueño [Puerto Rican Pro-Independence Party] (PIP) in 1946 and the release from jail of nationalist leader Pedro Albizu Campos the following year contributed to a renewal of nationalist fervor. Between 1950 and 1954 there were assassination attempts on President Harry Truman and Governor Muñoz Marín, as well as a shooting attack in the U.S. House of Representatives. Clearly, the tremendous social, political, and economic transformations brought about during the 1944–69 democratic hegemony of the PPD did not silence dissenting voices. In addition to the nationalists who used violence to make their point, intellectuals, many of whom identified with the *independentista* cause, pondered what they saw as the negative effects of Puerto Rico's permanent association with the United States.

In the context of these turbulent events, the prominent intellectual voice of the 1950s was essayist, short story writer, novelist, and dramatist René Marqués. Much like Pedreira, who responded to the social and economic changes of the 1930s from an ideologically conservative perspective, Marqués's entire body of work nostalgically laments the loss of the paternalist agrarian world of the landed criollo class (Díaz-Quiñones, *El Almuerzo* 146; Barradas, "El machismo" 69). His essay "El puertorriqueño dócil (Literatura y realidad psicológica)" [The docile Puerto Rican (Literature and psychological reality)] (1960) explores Puerto Rican national characteristics from a more pessimistic perspective than does Pedreira's 1934 essay, *Insularismo*. While Pedreira blames the island's *"aplatanamiento"* (46), or docility and lack of direction, on political destiny (the 1898 invasion and subsequent North American dominance) and on geographical determinism, his essay provides the components necessary to build a Hispanic Puerto Rican identity: "Mi propósito es más bien señalar los elementos dispersos que pueden dar sentido a nuestra personalidad" (30) [My intent is rather to identify the disperse elements that may lend sense to our personality]. In contrast, Marqués's essay focuses on a major national flaw, docility, which he considers the result of Puerto Rico's colonial condition.

Writing in the late 1950s, Marqués finds proof of Puerto Rican docility in contemporary Puerto Rican literature. He argues that the constant acts of violence and self-destruction depicted in Puerto Rican literary works, in his own and in others'—such as Emilio Díaz Valcárcel's "El soldado Damián Sánchez" [The soldier Damián Sánchez] (1956) and Pedro Juan Soto's collection of stories *Spiks* (1956)—tragically reveal a colonial guilt complex created by the dependent and "inferior" condition of Puerto Ricans. For Marqués, these acts are neither heroic nor a sign of healthy aggression. Instead, they arise from the "desesperación de seres débiles y dóciles acorralados en el último reducto de la dignidad humana" ("El puertorriqueño" 156) [desperation of weak and docile beings, cornered in the last redoubt of human dignity]. Politically, Marqués sees Muñoz Marín and his party's creation, the Estado Libre Asociado, as the essence of compromise between nationalism and annexationism; it is the expression of the "peaceful" and "democratic" or, not so euphemistically, docile Puerto Ricans who are resigned to their dependent condition ("El

ary phenomenon is the result of the devastating introduction of a foreign cultural pattern: the matriarchy ("El puertorriqueño" 170). The appearance of the matriarchy, he laments, marks the disappearance of machismo, the last national characteristic that might have been summoned to combat docility. In Marqués's view, gender roles in Puerto Rico have become distorted by the 1950s; men have taken on the feminine characteristic of docility, and women's new active role fosters this weakness. In other words, the growing importance of women's contributions to Puerto Rican society, especially in the burgeoning middle class, cannot be seen as a positive development, for it provides evidence that the patriarchal agrarian world in which Marqués was raised is disappearing.

Significantly, the identity debates of the 1930s and 1950s and the institutionalization of "official" Puerto Rican culture coincided with the consolidation of Puerto Rico's national theater movement. In the first third of the twentieth century, theatrical activity was limited and mostly dominated by foreign authors and traveling troupes. In 1938, the oldest cultural institution of the island, the Ateneo Puertorriqueño [Puerto Rican Athenaeum], helped initiate an autochthonous theater movement by holding a contest for native playwrights and producing the winners. The three winning plays, *Esta noche juega el jóker* [The joker plays tonight] by Fernando Sierra Berdecía, *El clamor de los surcos* [The clamor of the furrows] by Manuel Méndez Ballester, and *El desmonte* [The clearing] by Gonzalo Arocho del Toro, can be loosely defined as social realist. They treat the problems of rural displacement and emigration that resulted from North American imperialism. Also in 1938, the Ateneo Puertorriqueño's president, Emilio Belaval, delivered a manifesto entitled "Lo que podría ser un teatro puertorriqueño" [What a Puerto Rican theater could be]. He predicted: "Algún día tendremos que unirnos para crear un teatro puertorriqueño, un gran teatro nuestro, donde todo nos pertenezca: el tema, el actor, los motivos decorativos, las ideas, la estética" (qtd. in Arriví, *Areyto* 245) [One of these days we will have to unite to create a Puerto Rican theater, a great theater we can call our own in which the theme, the actor, the decorative motifs, the ideas, and the aesthetic all belong to us].

The contest and the manifesto sparked a serious theater movement that created a Puerto Rican audience for plays addressing island realities written by native playwrights. Subsequently, throughout the 1940s and early 1950s a variety of short-lived theater groups such as Belaval's

Areyto, Arriví's Tinglado Puertorriqueño, Marqués's Teatro Nuestro, and the Ateneo Puertorriqueño's Teatro Experimental developed new stage techniques and stimulated awareness of a national theater tradition. Alternatively, it is important to note that throughout the first half of the century, authors such as Ramón Romero Rosa, José Limón de Arce, Luisa Capetillo, and Nemesio R. Canales produced plays outside of the dramatic circle with ties to major cultural and state institutions. From the working-class world himself, Romero Rosa wrote plays for the proletariat with clear socialist intentions, such as *La emancipación del obrero* [The emancipation of the worker] (1903), and in the 1920s Capetillo, also an advocate for the working class, called for female liberation by addressing taboo subjects like female sexual desire and by critiquing the institution of marriage.[12] Through their work in the theater, these and other authors staged a discourse on national identity different from the concerns of the dominant classes.

In the university context, Leopoldo Santiago Lavandero, director of the Teatro Universitario, taught modern techniques of acting, staging, and directing and produced many classics of world drama. In fact, between 1944 and 1956 no plays by national authors were produced by the Teatro Universitario (Pilditch 7). For political reasons, the university administration privileged Western culture in hopes of assimilating local Puerto Rican culture and discouraging nationalist or proindependence sentiments. As we have seen, however, with the creation of the Estado Libre Asociado in 1952, the PPD and Muñoz Marín began to promote national heritage.[13] The collective forum of the theater was one area in which the PPD could implement its project of preserving national cultural patrimony and legitimizing certain visions of national community. Consequently, in 1958, twenty years after the Ateneo Puertorriqueño's call for national playwrights, the ICP sponsored its first annual festival of Puerto Rican theater. The event brought actors, directors, and technicians trained in the Teatro Universitario together with Puerto Rico's most influential playwrights. The performances, well publicized and reviewed, took place in Puerto Rico's national theater, Teatro Alejandro Tapia y Rivera in Old San Juan, in front of capacity houses (Dauster, "Drama" 182).

The plays performed at the 1958 festival were by four playwrights whose work was fundamental in the development of theater on the island: *Los soles truncos* by René Marqués, *Vejigantes* by Francisco Arriví,

Hacienda de cuatro vientos [The house of four winds] by Emilio Belaval, and *Encrucijada* [Crossroads] by Manuel Méndez Ballester. With the exception of *Encrucijada*, which exhibits naturalist-realist characteristics, the plays go beyond the social realism of the 1938 Ateneo Puertorriqueño contest to examine the island's crisis of identity from a more subjective, psychological, and poetic perspective typical of the literature of the post–World War II period (Phillips 90). In each play from the festival, as well as in *Un niño azul para esa sombra* (1960) by René Marqués and *Cristal roto en el tiempo* (1960) by Myrna Casas, the family unit provides a crucial entrée to the widespread discussion on the character of the nation during the 1950s. In the theater, the failure to create a national family with a hegemonic vision of Puerto Rican collective identity plays out as ruined or unrealized romances. The following pages will show how each play enacts love relationships incapable of resolving tensions between people of differing origins. The repeating scenario of love matches made and unmade onstage, however, reflects a continued desire to imagine a nation-building romance that would represent Puerto Rican identity in the face of North American imperialism. But in these plays, family members embody different positions on the island's identity, and the disagreements among them attest to the dissension on a national level on what should constitute *puertorriqueñidad*.

Vejigantes: Unmasking Black Puerto Rican Identity

As a playwright, a chronicler of the development of drama in his country, and, for many years, supervisor of the theater wing of the ICP, Francisco Arriví (b. 1915) was instrumental in promoting a national theater from the 1940s through the 1960s. Unlike many writers of the 1930s and 1950s, Arriví does not base Puerto Rican identity on Hispanic criollo roots. In contrast, *Vejigantes* (1958), Arriví's best-known play, argues that the mixing of African and Spanish traditions forms the foundation of Puerto Rico's national identity. In this regard, he contests Pedreira's suggestion that miscegenation created "una pugna biológica de fuerzas disgregantes y contrarias que han retardado la formación definitiva de nuestros modos de pueblo" (38) [a biological struggle resulting from disintegrating and contrary forces that have hampered the definitive formation of the character of our people]. From Pedreira's perspective, the superior Spanish race absorbed the weaker indigenous groups, and the mix between the Spaniards and the inferior Africans created a national psychology that is "mezclada y equívoca" (38) [mixed and obscure]. Arriví's play, in contrast, examines a national psyche damaged by not endorsing a mixed cultural heritage. The play portrays the effects of cross-cultural romances between Mamá Toña, who is of African descent, and a Spaniard; between her daughter, Marta, and another Spaniard; and between her granddaughter, Clarita, and a North American. The three generations of relationships represent what Matías Montes Huidobro calls the erotic synthesis of Puerto Rican history (*Persona: Vida y máscara en el teatro puertorriqueño* 151; hereafter referred to as *Teatro puertorriqueño*).[14] Because of the refusal to recognize African heritage as an integral part of the Puerto Rican identity, however, the unions fail to form a national family. Clarita comes to understand this through her relationship with Bill, a North American, and when she exclaims, "¡Si tuviéramos el valor de afirmar nuestra alma!" (64) [If we had the courage to affirm our soul!], she calls for the audience to recognize a long-suppressed part of Puerto Rican identity.

In its study of cross-racial romances, *Vejigantes* recalls *La cuarterona*, Tapia y Rivera's nineteenth-century play that also issued a challenge to its audience by confronting the unspoken theme of race. The fact that *La cuarterona* was staged in Puerto Rico in 1877, a decade after it was written, and that Tapia y Rivera situated the dramatic action in Cuba suggests that the play's delicate theme was vulnerable to censorship.[15] The play offers several romantic possibilities: the hero, Carlos, could enter into a loveless marriage with Emilia, which would wed his noble family to her family's wealth (they represent the nouveau riche) and thereby strengthen the island's upper class. Or Carlos could marry his true love, Julia, who is poor and racially mixed, which would bring together different classes and races in a union that represents the consolidation of a new society. In romantic fashion, Julia tragically dies when Carlos, horrified to discover that Julia is his sister, is convinced by his mother to marry Emilia. The threat of incest is false, however, and through his loss and the pain of having to live with a marriage built on lies, the audience is led to identify with Carlos's progressive position on race. The play ultimately suggests that Puerto Rico (and Cuba) must abolish slavery and embrace its racial heritage as it creates a national consciousness.

Tapia y Rivera's play breaks the silence of racism and makes visible what some sectors of Puerto Rican society during the late nineteenth century did not want to see or hear. The play's themes and action parallel this tension between concealment and revelation. Julia's romance with Carlos would draw attention to her race, or "condición" [condition], and break the invisibility and silence that surround her family heritage and the subject of race in general. Julia is white in appearance, and as long as she does not do anything that might challenge societal norms, no one calls attention to her race. She states: "En general los de mi clase, la niegan o la disimulan; yo no lo publico, pero Dios me ha dado una compensación; la conformidad, y por eso manifiesto mi condición sin humillarme" (64–65) [In general those of my class deny or try to hide it; I don't make it public, but God has compensated me with resignation, and for that reason I assume my condition without humiliating myself]. The mere mention of her "condición"—her rival, Emilia, refers to her as a *mulata*—causes Julia to faint (113). The stain, the metaphorical racial marker Julia insists she sees in her delirious, dying state, is only made perceptible when referenced verbally: "Una mancha que debe ser muy visible, porque todos la ven, todos me la echan en la cara. ¡Cuando todos lo dicen!" (138) [A stain that must be very visible, because everyone sees it, everyone throws it in my face. They must know what they say!]. Tapia y Rivera's words, when embodied and enacted onstage, refuse the conformity of silence and expose the "mancha" of racism in Puerto Rico.

Nearly a century later, Arriví's play takes up the tensions between racial concealment and revelation and employs the motif of the *vejigante* to unmask Puerto Rico's African heritage. Literally, *vejigantes* are monsterlike devil masks worn during the carnivalesque celebrations of Santiago (Saint James) in Loíza, a predominantly black region on the north coast of the island. The feast day is a hybrid and paradoxical celebration because Santiago was also the Spaniards' "Saint of Conquest" in the wars against the Moors and the conquest of the Americas. Dressed as *vejigantes* (masked forces of mischief), caballeros (the Spanish knights), and *locas* (men dressed as women who behave as a chorus in the ritual battles between the caballeros and the *vejigantes*), Puerto Ricans of Spanish, African, and Indian descent perform their own conquest. On a metaphorical level, the *vejigantes* mask underscores the theme of disguise and deception; that is, the denial of African heritage as a part of national identity is a psychological block, or *vejigante*.[16] In the play's climax scene, Clarita insists that her family face the reality of Puerto Rico's racial diversity and take off the mask of whiteness: "Mamá, vivamos de frente a esa realidad puertorriqueña. Sin los disfraces que convierten al país en una pesadilla de máscaras. Nos sobrarán fuerzas para vencer este embrujo de vejigantes y buscar una dicha real" (106) [Mother, let's face this Puerto Rican reality without the disguises that turn the country into a nightmare of masks. We have plenty of strength to defeat the curse of these *vejigantes* and seek true happiness]. The tension between concealment and revelation that leads to Clarita's appeal is highlighted by the characters' relationships to the different spaces constructed onstage.

In some respects, *Vejigantes* is a typical well-made play. The first act presents a problem that is developed in the second act and resolved in the third. However, props, lighting, and music establish a variety of spaces and periods that transcend the unities of time and space and re-create the island from a symbolic and poetic perspective. Act 1 takes place in 1910 in a palm grove in Loíza on the feast day of Santiago. The sexual union between Toña, a young mulatto woman, and Benedicto, a Spaniard disguised as a *vejigante*, introduces the theme of miscegenation. The second and third acts take place forty-eight years later, primarily in the living room of a home in an upper-middle-class San Juan neighborhood, el Condado.

Act 2 centers on Marta, Toña's daughter, who denies her African origins by covering her head with a turban. Marta's greatest desire is to further "whiten" her appropriately named daughter Clarita by marrying her to an American businessman, Bill. Marta knows there has been a falling out between the two, and hoping for reconciliation, she has invited Bill over for a drink. Marta does not know, however, that the tension between her daughter and Bill stems from an outing to Luquillo beach during which, to Clarita's chagrin, Bill makes clear his racism. Bill's visit in the third act leads the play to its climax in which Clarita reveals what her mother has tried so desperately to conceal: her family's African heritage. In a final symbolic scene, Clarita dares her mother and grandmother to step outside their home to walk in their garden: "Ese jardín pertenece a todas. Tenemos el mismo derecho a disfrutar de los flamboyanes" (124) [This garden belongs to all of us. We all have the same right to enjoy the *flamboyanes*]. The red color of the *flamboyán* flower, a symbol of *puertorriqueñidad*, embodies the mixed blood of the Puerto Rican people. To walk freely in the garden is to assert their mestizo identity and to "unmask" themselves. This affirmation is spatially reinforced as the walls of the house begin to disappear, and the Condado scene merges with the scene from Loíza in which caballeros are engaged in killing *vejigantes*.

The dissipating walls of the house at the end of the play are significant because the space of the house in *Vejigantes* constitutes a sign for the psychological entrapment that the nation suffers for not confronting the problem of racial prejudice. With respect to the construction of character subjectivity and theatrical space, Charles Lyons argues that "the spectator sees the character in space and observes the character perceiving the scene and conceptualizing his relationship to that site" (37). In my view, witnessing this process of constructing identity through the theatrical space of the house leads spectators, in turn, to contemplate their relationship to the nation and to evaluate (consciously or subconsciously) their own position on collective identity. In *Vejigantes*, each generation of women is linked to a different space within the house/nation, and the female characters' voiced perceptions of that space convey different views on the racial identity of the island. Throughout the course of the play, the audience sees the three women negotiate their identity in a variety of spaces: outside on beaches in Loíza and Luquillo and inside a San Juan, urban middle-class home. References to offstage spaces such as Clarita's workplace and the southern United States are also important in shaping character subjectivity.

In 1910, during the celebration of Santiago, Toña takes center stage outdoors in a palm grove while dancing to the beat of the *bomba* "Joyalito," the musical motif of the play. Unlike Pedreira, who in the 1930s chose the formal *danza* to represent Puerto Rican culture, Arriví selects the percussive, African-derived *bomba*.[17] While dancing to the *bomba*, Toña becomes Benedicto's object of desire, and he seduces her on the beach, a space that brings to mind the conquest of the Americas. The Spaniard's imperialist cry "Santiago y cierra España" (13) and his syncretic "Viva Alfonso XIII y Toña de Loíza" (12) make explicit the union as a metaphor of the colonization of Puerto Rico. It is clear, however, that Toña is not a completely unwilling party. First, a dream reveals her subconscious desire to give birth to a son or daughter physically lighter then herself, and second, her disappointment when Benedicto proposes that she be his servant by day and lover by night conveys her hopes for a legitimate relationship. She does give birth to a lighter child, but the only space in Benedicto's life is in a small wooden shack behind his store.

In the second act, Toña (now Mamá Toña) is further relegated to the back room of her race-conscious daughter Marta's home in the affluent San Juan neighborhood the Condado. The anxiety produced by racial miscegenation recalls Fortunato Vizcarrondo's popular poem in which the poetic voice asks: "Mi mai se sienta en la sala /¿Y tu agüela, a'onde ejtá?" (77) [My mother sits in the living room/ And your grandmother, where is she?]. By playing a record of the *bomba* in the living room, Mamá Toña creates a contrast between her youth in Loíza and her current life in San Juan. Marta turns the music off and says, "Mamá Toña. Vivimos en el Condado. (*Señalando hacia el jardín.*) Los vecinos aborrecen esta música. La asocian con . . ." (35) [Mama Toña. We live in the Condado. (*Pointing toward the garden.*) The neighbors hate this music. They associate it with . . .]. Mamá Toña completes her sentence with "gente de color" (35) [people of color]. Highly aware of her marginalization, she laments that "Yo era feliz en el palmar de Loíza. Jugaba en las arenas blancas, corría suelta frente al mar azul y podía bailar la bomba bajo las flores del flamboyán. [. . .] Nadie me encerraba en el cuarto de atrás" (35– 36) [I was happy in the palm groves of Loíza. I played in the white sands, ran free along the blue sea, and I could dance the *bomba* beneath the flowers of the *flamboyán* tree. [. . .] Nobody kept me closed up in the back room]. In *Vejigantes*, as in many realist plays, the living room constitutes the public space of the house. Not surprisingly, the living room is the only space the audience is allowed to see, as the back rooms are associated with the private, or in Marta's case, what is being suppressed from public life. At one point, Mamá Toña even describes herself as living "entombed" because of her daughter's extreme efforts to conceal her (49). Mamá Toña knows that Marta fears Bill will discover Clarita's African heritage if he sees her and constantly offers to move into a retirement home. Mamá Toña manipulates Marta's sense of guilt, and although she is displaced, her presence in the living room—Puerto Rican public life—cannot be fully concealed.

Mamá Toña asserts her sense of identity and cultural roots through folkloric language replete with nature metaphors. For example, in direct opposition to Marta, Mamá Toña refuses to deny her racial heritage and affirms, "Me gusta verme como soy: algodón y café" (33) [I like to see myself as I am: cotton and coffee]. Later, she threatens to stay in the living room during Bill's visit by comparing herself to a hearty Puerto Rican tree of great longevity: "(*Señalando el centro de la sala.*) Si me plantara ahí como una ceiba . . ." (49) [(*Pointing to the middle of the living room.*) And if I were to plant myself there like a ceiba tree. . .]. Mama Toña's shift from the back room to the margins of the hallway shows the potential for a rebellious invasion of the center of the house. From her position in the hallway, unseen by both the audience and the inhabitants of the house, Mamá Toña listens in on the events in the living room. When accused by Marta of eavesdropping, she humorously defends herself by saying she obtains her information by the *brujería* [witchcraft] for which her native region is famous. If the house represents the nation, then Mamá Toña's encroachment on the center spatially underlines the pervasiveness of the African roots of Puerto Rican identity and challenges the forces that would conceal them.

Mamá Toña constitutes the emotional center of the play, and she comes to represent a counterpoint to the archetypal, white Puerto Rican *jíbara* mother of Spanish-criollo stock embodied by Doña Gabriela, a character in René Marqués's earlier play *La carreta* [*The oxcart*] (1953). The characterization and casting of the Afro–Puerto Rican mother character, however, present some complications. In his attempt to associate Mamá Toña with what he views as authentic and popular Puerto Rican culture, Arriví relies on a stereotypic gendered identification with the natural and spiritual world. For example, at the same time Arriví criticizes the inhumane gesture of confining Mamá Toña to the back room, his poetic description of her dancing free on the beach also dehumanizes her by depicting her as an (uncivilized and sensual) creature of nature. The physical presence of the black body dancing to the beat of the *bomba y plena* on the national stage reveals the counterdiscursive possibilities of the body in performance, and it tells quite a different story than many of the prize-winning plays staged at the ICP-sponsored theater festivals in the 1950s and 1960s. This body, however, marked by both race and gender, is destined for the male spectatorial gaze, and as much as the play uses the metaphor of sexual conquest to criticize colonialism, it does not problematize the consumption of the female body as the object of the spectacle. To complicate matters further, a white actress in blackface initiated the role of Mamá Toña in the 1958 festival production.[18] One might suspect that these factors compromise the play's subversive potential to give visibility and voice to the subaltern in the very public sphere of the national theater. At the very least, by omission, the absence of the black female body makes a statement on the status of blacks in the performing arts during this period. As the use of blackface suggests, and as will be seen in my analysis of Mamá Toña's mixed-race daughter, in the representation of race, the body works in conjunction with language, makeup, and costume to reveal the constructedness of racial identity.

Although Mamá Toña complains of her physical imprisonment in the back room, she is more psychologically free than her daughter, Marta, who "tuvo la dicha de estudiar y casarse, y vivir en la sala" (117) [had the good fortune to be able to study, get married, and live in the living room]. The play does not detail the circumstances of Marta's romance, but it can be ascertained that she looks white enough for a Spaniard to marry her and that, in turn, she has married the Spaniard in hopes of having even lighter children. If Toña, as Montes Huidobro puts it, represents Puerto Rico "sometido a cópula colonialista" (*Teatro puertorriqueño* 157) [subjected to colonialist copulation], then Marta gives her body in a romance that represents the self-hatred born of a colonialist complex. Marta's space in the nation/house is in the living room. As a teacher and the wife of a Spaniard, she has a public role in Puerto Rican society. She does so under false pretenses, however, and she is the character who struggles the most in defeating the *vejigante*, or mask, that denies her authentic heritage.

In the living room, Marta is literally able to direct the scene and adopt the role of a white woman. She mutes the lighting so as not to betray her mulatto features. Her costume and makeup include a thick layer of white powder, clothes that cover her body completely, and a turban that hides her curly hair. The turban is the most obvious sign of Marta's obsession with being white, for she unconsciously constantly adjusts it with her hand. Marta's costume misidentifies her race, and her self-conscious performance highlights the instability of identities and the ease with which they can be manipulated and reconstructed for certain agendas. But Marta cannot always control the scene as a director would a play, and as a result, she lives in constant fear that her plans for Clarita will not be realized: "Si a Bill se le ocurre pasar al interior de la casa . . ." (39) [If it ever occurred to Bill to enter the house. . .]. If Bill wanders into the back room of the house, he will find Mamá Toña, that is, if he ever examines Puerto Rican society on more than a superficial or business-motivated level, he will have to confront what has been hidden away.

Marta believes she will save Clarita the pain she has suffered by sending her to the United States. She hopes to distance Clarita from both her (national) family's past and the here and now of Puerto Rico, where "se vive con el alma encogida. Unos rencores nos condenan. Se sufre sorda, interminablemente" (37) [people live with diminished souls. We're condemned by all of this bitterness. We suffer in interminable silence]. Marta adopts religious discourse in her mission to transport Clarita to another "world." For example, her goal is to save Clarita from "miedos que desgarran la voluntad. Salvarla de rencores que estrangulan el corazón. Salvarla . . . Salvarla . . . Entregársela libre al reino de los blancos" (63) [fears that tear one's free will. Save her from the bitterness that strangles the heart. Save her . . . Save her . . . Deliver her a free woman to the kingdom of whites]. Later, she suggests that this world of whites is literally a heaven not to be found in "este mundo" (97) [this world], or Puerto Rico. Marta desires to save Clarita from the psychological damage of living inauthentically by removing her from the island, but she fails to understand that Clarita's acceptance of her racial heritage exempts her from the identity crisis she herself suffers.

While Mamá Toña has been hidden in the back room and Marta is most at home in the shadowy living room, Clarita's space is outside of the house. Unlike her mother and grandmother, Clarita is associated with a number of spaces and shows great mobility in moving between them. She works for a North American insurance company as a guide for insurance salesmen who need to acquaint themselves with all social circles of San Juan. Thus she has contact with a wide spectrum of social classes and spaces, including the company office, Luquillo beach, dance clubs in the Condado, and less affluent areas of the city. From her perspective outside the house, she comes to understand the psychological entrapment her family—and by extension, her country—suffers, which is why she insists at the end of the play that the three women together leave the house for the garden. To step outside is to unmask one's true self publicly, and Marta does just this by finally removing her turban.

Clarita's job presents an opportunity for romance that raises identity issues different than those encountered by her grandmother and mother: Puerto Rico's relationship to the United States. Bill's company underscores the economic and cultural influence of the United States on the island during the 1950s. While it could be argued that a positive outcome of North American influence on the island is better job opportunities for women like Clarita, the play's stereotyped portrayal of the southerner Bill paints a mostly negative picture of North American influence. The economic interests of the United States in the island are expressed in terms of conquest, as Bill surveys the beautiful Luquillo beach: "Millones en potencia. Millones. Un poco de inteligencia y los americanos invadirán este paraíso." (67) [Potentially millions. Millions. With a little intelligence Americans would invade this paradise].[19] To facilitate this invasion and to climb the corporate ladder, Bill has sworn to master Spanish completely: "A los clientes les encanta oírme hablar en su idioma" (66) [My clients love to hear me speak in their language]. His ever-present highball complements his characterization as an overzealous businessman and loosens his inhibitions enough to reveal his racism. It troubles Bill to see blacks and whites together in Puerto Rico, and his officemate's nagging question regarding Marta's turban forces him to broach the subject of Clarita's family heritage. Clarita responds by insisting they spend time apart and ends their conversation with the cryptic remark: "Un rompecabezas, Bill, y la conciencia exige resolverlo" (72) [It's a puzzle, Bill, and our conscience demands that it be solved].

Clarita's exposure to various spaces constitutes a major factor in her growing awareness of her cultural identity. She buys Mamá Toña a recording of the same *bomba* she danced to in Loíza and expresses a special interest in her grandmother's cultural heritage. Her explanation—that a surge of interest in all things Puerto Rican has motivated government-sponsored recordings of local music—highlights the promotion of national patrimony (by the PPD and Muñoz Marín) during the 1950s. Clarita's beach outing with Bill, however, leads her to a new level of identity consciousness: "Hay momentos, mamá, en que me doy cuenta que Puerto Rico es un país y Estados Unidos otro" (59) [There are moments, mother, when I realize that Puerto Rico is one country and the United States is another].[20] In contrast to her mother and grandmother, whose cross-cultural romances brought together different sectors of the nation but failed to build a strong national identity, Clarita's romance fails because it never takes place. She rejects Bill and the false promises of harmony that romance might offer. In a scene parallel to Toña's seduction at the beach in Loíza, Clarita refuses Bill's physical advances at Luquillo beach after he reveals his distaste for Puerto Rico's racial makeup. This choice implies the rejection of racism and the affirmation of her Afro-Antillean roots.

In some respects, *Vejigantes* follows a pattern Doris Sommer finds in her study of populist rhetoric in contemporary Dominican literature. For Sommer, populism is a "rhetoric that displaces the relationships of the traditional family in crisis onto a nation in the throes of modernization" (*One Master* xvii). She examines how the country's transition to an industrialized society is articulated in terms of the disruption of a traditional patriarchal family. The land (woman) is defiled by the usurper (oftentimes the imperialist) and "national destiny thus becomes the expulsion of the Usurper to reestablish legitimate ownership by the Husband so that (re)production can proceed naturally" (*One Master* 11). *Vejigantes* does begin with family strife—the three women are at odds due to their conflicting visions of identity—and the play ends in utopian harmony in a paradisiacal garden as they affirm their *puertorriqueñidad*. The play's ideological position, however, seems to be that while there is no denying Puerto Rico's economic romance with the United States (Clarita's job), culturally the island should reject a consequent inauthentic national identity (Clarita's refusal of Bill). This rejection raises an important question that remains unanswered: whom should Clarita embrace to construct a romance of national and cultural identity?

Vejigantes departs from Sommer's model of populism in the striking absence of the traditional patriarchal family. There is no male counterpart to Clarita, and, in fact, the Puerto Rican male virtually does not exist in the play. Puerto Rican men are present only in the first act during the celebration of Santiago, and even then they are dressed in drag as *locas* or as Spanish caballeros.[21] Furthermore, neither the Spaniards nor Bill occupies the stage for very long. Other than Benedicto's brief seduction scene, he and Marta's Spanish husband are reduced to portraits on the wall of Marta's living room. Bill's presence is felt most strongly diegetically, that is, as a verbal construct in the conversations among the women rather than in his two appearances onstage, and his stereotyped characterization as a southern racist further weakens his presence in the play. The play departs from a populist paradigm, for Clarita's rejection of Bill (the foreign imperialist) does not necessarily imply that the patriarchal family will be reestablished. Instead, the play offers a new kind of family, and, having exorcised the *vejigante*, it reconfigures woman as a metaphor for nation.

Arriví's play strongly departs from Pedreira's depiction of Puerto Rico as a defenseless and diminutive feminine island. Woman's body is no longer available for colonization and procreation with the subsequent production of identity complexes. If there is to be romance to forge a national identity, in her future relationships Clarita will seek to preserve her sense of Puerto Rican identity instead of effacing it as her mother did. Because the play does not present such a match for Clarita, it privileges the connections between grandmother, mother, and daughter. This antipatriarchal and nonhierarchal relationship provides an alternative to the traditional Puerto Rican family and a subject position that offers more agency for women. Unlike Marqués, Arriví does not suggest that increased mobility for women constitutes an imposition of a matriarchal foreign model and the loss of Puerto Rican cultural traditions. Rather, the family structure in *Vejigantes* presents new ways to explore a changing national community.

In the vein of Pedreira's *Insularismo*, Arriví finds the components necessary to construct a Puerto Rican identity and proposes that it is a question of having the will to recognize them. These components, however, differ greatly from Pedreira's Hispanocentric, paternalist, and agrarian vision, because Arriví offers the image of an economically independent, urban community of women of Afro-Antillean roots. In this regard, in his treatment of the issues of race and gender in the construction of national identity, Arriví was well ahead of his time. Twenty years after the play's premiere, José Luis González argued that to valorize the African roots of Puerto Rican identity is to recognize the Caribbean rather than the Hispanic or North American nature of the island's cultural identity. This would imply that Puerto Rico's destiny should be the same as that of other Caribbean islands: decolonization and independence (J. L. González 43). Other important dramas of the late 1950s by Marqués and Casas also oppose Puerto Rico's colonial condition. We will see, however, that neither of these two playwrights presents as constructive, or didactic, a vision of national identity as does Francisco Arriví.

The End of the Line: The House of René Marqués

René Marqués (1919–1979) is Puerto Rico's defining dramatist of the 1950s and is one of island's best-known writers of the twentieth century. Marqués was deeply concerned with the problem of Puerto Rican identity, and many of his plays explore the multiple consequences of the island's colonialist relationship with the United States.[22] While he is remembered primarily as a nationalist playwright, his ability to combine the particular issues of his country with more international themes, such as the existential isolation of the modern world, makes many of his plays accessible to broader audiences. Marqués is also noted for his experimentation with dramatic forms and techniques. His plays vary from social and psychological realist to existentialist and absurdist, and his innovative uses of lighting and music influenced playwrights of his generation. Marqués was instrumental, as well, in fomenting theatrical activity on the island through his creation of theatrical groups and participation in national festivals.

Marqués's generation witnessed the island's urbanization and displacement of the dominant rural classes, and consequently, many of their works reflect the Puerto Rican subject's struggle to adapt to this new reality. *Un niño azul para esa sombra* (1960) and *Los soles truncos* (1958) constitute two such examples. Both are symbolic realist plays set in urban San Juan homes, and although the action of the plays takes place in 1958, the characters are highly concerned with another epoch and setting: the lost nineteenth-century agrarian world. In *Los soles truncos*, three unmarried sisters reject contemporary Puerto Rican society and attempt to retain the purity of their European ancestry by secluding themselves in their dilapidated colonial home. When it becomes apparent that they can no longer avoid contact with the outside world, the sisters commit suicide by setting their mansion on fire. *Un niño azul* also ends in self-destruction. In this play, the marriage of Michel and Mercedes LeFranc falls apart under the pressures of competing responses to the island's relationship with the United States. Their son, Michelín, caught between the ideologies of his mother and father, can find no viable ideological position to embrace, and he kills himself.

In contrast to *Vejigantes*, which explores the nation's complex ethnic origins and identities, *Un niño azul* and *Los soles truncos* examine the displacement and identity confusion resulting from the social, political, and economic changes generated by North American influence on the island. In other words, *Vejigantes* addresses identity issues that derive mainly from within the island, whereas these two plays by Marqués consider the cultural conflict that ensued from pressures without. While both playwrights use the theatrical space of the house to construct character subjectivity, Marqués has a special interest in "house" in the sense of the ancestors and descendants that make up a family line. In both plays, failed romances and unfulfilled unions highlight the fading dominance of the criollo landowning classes and Marqués's disillusionment with the changing character of Puerto Rican identity.

My study of failed romance in *Un niño azul* and *Los soles truncos* is framed by recent criticism on how Marqués communicates his vision of Puerto Rican national experience through his works.[23] Efraín Barradas,

Arcadio Díaz-Quiñones, and Juan Gelpí have pointed out the conservative ideology Marqués clings to in the face of North American influence. Barradas, for example, argues that there is one central theme in all of Marqués's works: "La añoranza de un mundo idílico que se ha perdido" ("El Machismo" 69) [The longing for an idyllic world that has been lost]. This is the patriarchal world of the landed criollo classes that ruled before the advent of North American agricultural modernization and industrialization. Barradas and Díaz-Quiñones note that, in lamenting the loss of this lifestyle, Marqués ineffectively diagnoses Puerto Rico's problems because his vision does not evolve to take into account new factors in the makeup of national community and because he never proposes a viable solution to the problem of Puerto Rican docility (Barradas "El Machismo" 71–73; Díaz-Quiñones "El Almuerzo" 153–54). Instead, Marqués repeatedly explores the lasting psychological wounds, or trauma, of colonialism. Kai Erikson writes that "trauma shared can serve as a source of communality in the same way that common languages and common backgrounds can. There is a spiritual kinship there, a sense of identity, even when feelings of affection are deadened and the ability to care numbed" (186). Puerto Rican identity, in the literary world of Marqués, is bound by trauma.[24] In the two plays studied here, memory serves as a way for the characters to combat the trauma of loss and change produced by North American colonialism. But, like Marqués, trapped in an outdated worldview that blinded him to issues of class and race and that provoked controversy by defending machismo, his characters are unable to transcend the past to live in the Puerto Rican present.

Among the works analyzed in this chapter, *Un niño azul* is the most explicit in attributing a failed national romance to the presence of the United States on the island. The play portrays the impact of a marriage ruined by political differences on a little boy. Acts 1 and 3 take place in the present, 1958, in the LeFranc family's luxurious home in the Condado, on Michelín's tenth birthday. Act 2 presents a flashback that provides the details justifying the events of the first and third acts. Through flashbacks, colored lighting, and musical motifs, Marqués evokes spaces beyond the onstage house and terrace to create the ambience of cultural and psychological confusion. Michelín is characterized as a strange and precocious boy trapped between the opposing ideologies of his parents. At present, he lives with his Americanized and materialist mother, Mercedes, and Cecilia, a family friend from his father's side, who serves as a nanny. Michelín's father, Michel, is an idealistic professor-revolutionary who has been imprisoned for eight years because of his participation in a 1950 nationalist uprising. During this period, his mother has had an affair with a North American and has adapted to the new social order of the Estado Libre Asociado (established in 1952). Alienated by his mother's behavior, Michelín seeks comfort from Cecilia and the sheltering branches of the family's backyard *quenepo* tree (which is never seen by the audience because by the play's present it has been cut down and replaced by a six-foot-tall iron trellis). When Michel returns from prison, he realizes that his wife has betrayed him and finds that he no longer has a job. Seeing himself displaced from his public roles as husband and professor, he leaves, ostensibly to join a cause for justice in Chile. In the final act of the play, Mercedes reveals to Michelín the truth about his father's destiny: he has died an alcoholic on the streets of New York City. This ugly fact leads Michelín to commit suicide by poisoning himself, as his friends and family await his appearance at his birthday party.

While Michelín is the play's protagonist and is the character who has received the most critical attention, the relationship between his parents and their family origins is crucial to the play's ideology. Following Doris Sommer's concept of national family romance, one might expect that the romance between Michel and Mercedes would strengthen the nation, as their union appears to consolidate classes and interests. Michel, the grandson of a French revolutionary, comes from a family that immigrated to the island during the first half of the nineteenth century. Papá François, the family patriarch, married in Mayagüez and through his attachment to the land came to consider himself a "buen jíbaro" (166). Mercedes's family, in contrast, represents new money and the commercial world of banking. Michel points out to Mercedes that her affinity to the North Americans is artificial since there are none in her family; rather: "Hubo sí baturros, corsos y africanos" (128) [There were, however, Aragonese, Corsicans, and Africans]. Although there is nothing mentioned about the racial identity of Mercedes's family other than Michel's comment, the vehemence with which she insists that her family did everything it could to fight for its freedom—"la libertad que nos da el dinero y la posición social" (137) [freedom afforded by money and social status]—suggests that, because of race, her family was less privileged than Michel's. The more aristocratic bloodlines of his family permitted the luxury of fighting for ideals and national independence. The marriage between different races (European and mestizo), classes (the new money of an ascending class and the disappearing agrarian world of old money), and ideologies (materialism and idealism) should have strengthened the nation. The play implies, however, that love and politics cannot go hand-in-hand in Puerto Rico because of the nation's political status with respect to the United States. Michel states that "quizás el amor a la libertad y el otro amor sean incompatibles" (123) [perhaps the love for liberty and the other love are incompatible]. In other words, in a colonial context, his love for Mercedes is impossible, and the productive, nation-building union of classes and ideologies is untenable as long as he must fight for independence.

In addition to blaming the United States for creating the scenario for Michel and Mercedes's failed marriage, Marqués subtly criticizes Michel for his poor choice in a marriage partner. If Mercedes represents betrayal on a personal and a national level, then the nanny, Cecilia, embodies the traditional rural world of Michel's past. She sings peasant lullabies, prepares food with traditional *jíbaro* ingredients, and, most important, defends the values of this world. She is deeply committed to Michel and his family, and when he asks her to live with his wife and son while he serves his jail sentence, she states that nothing could stop her from coming to his family's aid. For Cecilia, there is no other "familia mejor, más digna, más recta" (112) [family better, more dignified, or correct] than that of Michel's. While he is away, her task is to instill the traditions of the past in Michelín, but she knows that this is impossible: "le habría dado el mundo de don François. Porque me parece que era un mundo bueno. Pero ni teniendo un poder muy grande hubiese podido hacerlo. Porque aquel mundo está ya muerto. Sólo . . . Sólo he tratado de darle al niño las cosas que no han muerto de aquel mundo. ¡Cosas que no deben morir en ningún mundo! (113) [I'd have given him Don François's world. Because it seems to me that it was a good world. But even with immense power, I wouldn't have been able to do it, because that world is already dead. I just . . . I just wanted to give the child the things that aren't yet gone from that world—things that shouldn't die in any world!]. Cecilia understands the importance of family unity in combating the cultural transmutations suffered by the island in the 1950s, which is why she so readily comes to Michel's aid. She, in turn, urges Michel to save his family: "¡Tienes que luchar! Hay un hogar, una mujer, un niño, ¡tu hijo! ¡Defiéndelos, Michel! Defiéndelos del mundo que intenta destruirlos" (124) [You have to fight!

You have a home, a wife, a child, your child! Defend them, Michel! Defend them from the world that is trying to destroy them]. Nevertheless, as other critics have noted, Michel is the prototypical docile Puerto Rican, and he bows out of the marriage.[25]

One of the questions the play tacitly poses is, if Michel had married Cecilia instead of Mercedes, would they have had the strength to maintain their beliefs and identity? Characters never explicitly suggest that Michel should have married Cecilia, but a good deal of evidence implies that their union would have preserved better the ideals and values of Don François's world. We learn that Michel's family raised Cecilia as his sister. As a widow with a grown son, she is now able to repay his family's kindness by coming to live with Michel's wife and son. Her new role in the family is somewhat undefined, however, which creates tension by underscoring that being a sister to Michel is not her only possible role. She explains that she does not feel comfortable interfering with Mercedes's life decisions because she is not a family member, but Michel insists that she really is. Cecilia responds: "Bueno, ése es otro decir. Somos hermanos de crianza. Pero para ella y para todos los demás no somos hermanos, realmente. Creo que a menudo ha resentido mi presencia en esta casa" (125) [Well, that's a manner of speaking. We were raised as if we were brother and sister, but to her and to everyone else we aren't really siblings. I think that she has often resented my presence in this house]. Mercedes, in fact, resents the ease with which Cecilia serves as a surrogate mother to her own son. Cecilia's mode of dress and servantlike behavior further confuse her role in the family. Her severe black dress and white apron make her look like a servant, and she seems to perform the tasks of one. For example, she does not have to carry the clean laundry from room to room, but she does, and this adds yet another layer of tension. According to Montes Huidobro, the laundry becomes the motif of "the white sheets," constantly bringing to mind the intimacy of the bedroom (414). These character nuances—the widow, mother, servant, and possible lover roles—blur Cecilia's former characterization as a sister figure enough to insinuate the romantic possibilities between her and Michel.

Marqués presents two romantic options in *Un niño azul*, then, that reveal his stance on national identity. From the play's perspective, the marriage between Michel and Mercedes has betrayed the cause for independence and permitted the progressive Americanization of the island. The other alternative—the possible union between Michel and Cecilia—

epitomizes Marqués's problematic yearning for the lost past. For Marqués, recuperating the island's agrarian past entails regaining national control over the political, economic, and social destiny of the island. While this vision might seem to strengthen Puerto Rico's sense of identity, Marqués fails to take into account that the world he privileges includes a lifestyle and value system that many Puerto Ricans of the 1950s had rejected. Marqués's vision seems anachronistic in the urban world of San Juan where, in these years, there is much more social mobility for blacks, women, and the working class than existed during the nineteenth century.

Marqués's nostalgia for the criollo hacendado world traps his characters in an idealized and unrecoverable past epoch and does little to negotiate constructively with the changing composition of Puerto Rican identity. The failed and unrealized romances in *Un niño azul* are underscored spatially to create a sense of entrapment that ultimately results in the destruction of the LeFranc family. As in *Vejigantes*, character subjectivity is constructed by each character's association with various theatrical spaces the play presents diegetically (unseen space communicated verbally and through sounds) and mimetically (perceived space) and by their voiced perceptions of these spaces.[26] Mercedes and, to some extent, Michelín are linked to the play's mimetic spaces of the LeFranc family home's living room and the terrace. Michel also appears in the house, but only in a flashback and in the space of his son's imagination. He is mostly associated with diegetic spaces created through dialogue such as the past, jail, and New York. The various spaces in the play are representative of different worlds and ideologies, but, rather than guiding the characters to consider the diversity of worldviews that would lead them to understand their own stance as unstable and provisional, this plurality serves to isolate and entrap.[27]

Mercedes and Michel are unable to reconcile because they are devoted to mutually exclusive worlds. Mercedes is committed to living her life in the present, and her philosophy is to confront reality, no matter how cruel it may be. When Michel was sent to jail, society rejected Mercedes, and she felt just as imprisoned as her husband. She refused to live in isolation, however, and explains: "Tuve que vivir, buscar nuevas relaciones, nuevas amistades, no en tu mundo ni en el mío, sino en esa zona entre los dos mundos que es la tierra de nadie" (138) [I had to live, look for new relationships and friendships, and not in your world or mine, but rather in that zone between two worlds that is no-man's-land]. The play represents this new zone mimetically through the eclectic French-, Greek-, and North American–style furnishings of the house. As Montes Huidobro has suggested, the decoration of the house is emblematic of Puerto Rico of the 1950s in the sense that the lack of autochthonous markers and the jumble of styles underscore the identity confusion of the period (*Teatro puertorriqueño* 411). A large portrait of Mercedes clearly identifies the luxurious living room as her territory. Telephone conversations with her lover, Phillip, and with her new friends diegetically reveal Mercedes's connection to an Americanized world of clubs and exclusive fashion retail. As we will see, this world has no room for the past, which is exemplified by the destruction of the garden *quenepo* tree to make room for Mercedes's parties with her new acquaintances.

In contrast to Mercedes, none of the spaces with which Michel is associated represent the present reality of Puerto Rico. He is portrayed primarily through the dialogue of other characters in the isolated worlds of jail, his idealistic past, the streets of New York, and the dreamworld of his son. Michel's most extensive physical presence in the play takes place not in the 1958 present but as a flashback that reveals why, upon his return from jail, he has chosen to leave his wife and his country. This flashback, in turn, contains scenes that communicate his alienation from his wife's Americanized social milieu. Through voices and sound effects, these scenes create onstage worlds that characterize Michel. For example, dimmed lights and the competing melodies of patriotic Puerto Rican and French songs, a North American military march, and the sounds of machine guns re-create Michel's participation in a nationalist uprising. The voices of a judge and a jury relay the events of his trial, and a few minor prop changes such as bars placed across a hallway transform the living room into a prison. The focus on Michel's past experiences and his absence from the present depict him as trapped between his wife's new world and an impotent fight for independence. His only option is to leave Puerto Rico. Through the physical displacement of Michel, then, the play shows the increasing marginalization of *independentistas* and the shrinking space for political and cultural dialogue in the 1950s.[28]

The worlds of Michel and Mercedes are so far apart ideologically that there is no possibility for the productive crossing of borders that could create a dialogue that might confront the island's new political status, look toward the future, and esteem traditions of the past. In her study of time and space in *Un niño azul*, Bonnie Hildebrand Reynolds concludes that the competing ideologies of Michel and Mercedes leave no space for their son. She writes: "Caught between the libertarian ideals of his father and the materialistic world of his mother, Michelin's personal conflict involves the suffocation of his own potential. [. . .] Michelin's conflict is that of the Puerto Rican island, caught between a search for individual identity and a materialistic world which gradually destroys the possibility of finding (or developing) that identity" (*Space* 43). Rather than the metaphor of woman as nation posed in *Vejigantes*, in this play the child Michelín embodies Puerto Rico and its infantile relationship to the United States that Marqués describes in "El puertorriqueño dócil."

Michelín—potentially the island's future—exists in the shadows of his parents' ideologies and is unable to create his own space or identity. In relation to his family's home, he is characterized physically as occupying borders. In the first scene of the play, Michelín enters the terrace carrying a caged canary and disappears out of the audience's sight into the garden. He reappears on the terrace and greets his friend Andrés seated on a banister, a border between two spaces. When Andrés asks where he has come from, Michelín replies: "De cualquier parte" (78) [From anywhere]. In other scenes, crossing borders into the adult world of the living room emphasizes his marginality. For example, when his basketball rolls from the terrace into the living room, he follows it and overhears a telephone conversation between his mother and her lover. Later, during his parents' confrontation in the living room, Michelín's hand can be seen on the banister of the staircase leading from the living room to the bedrooms upstairs, indicating that he is a participant in the scene, albeit an unknown one. Upset after witnessing his parents' argument, Michelín frantically tries to leave the house, but he finds himself literally trapped at every turn.

The only place where Michelín feels comfortable is the dreamworld of his games and fantasy conversations with his father. He prefers the *sombra* [shadow] of illusion to the realities of the present, where he literally does not have a place to grow and develop a unique identity.[29] Unlike his friend Andrés, Michelín is not interested in birthday parties, candy, or playing cowboys. His preferred activity, which he convinces Cecilia to participate in as well, is to "jugar al pasado" (85) [play out the past]. Similar to Marta in *Vejigantes*, who was able to "direct" the scene in her own home, Michelín is able to exercise control by replaying scenes from the past. One might expect that memory would help Michelín to overcome the trauma caused by the loss of his *quenepo* tree/father. Like a director, Michelín theatrically re-creates moments from the past and directs the actions of the characters: "Empecemos. Tú estarás cerca de la puerta para anunciarle a *ella* que los hombres ya han terminado su faena" (87) [Let's start. You will be next to the door in order to announce to *her* that the men have ended their task]. In this case, he reenacts the scene in which his mother poisons the backyard *quenepo*.

Michelín also creates alternative worlds to the present by falling into dreamlike states in which he can conjure up conversations with his father. A bluish purple light and the music of a lullaby distinguish these moments from the present reality of the house. Michelín tells his doubtful friend that his father comes to visit "cuando yo lo quiero" (82) [when I want him to], which emphasizes again the sense of control that creating and directing these worlds provides him. Ironically, his father, who chooses not to deal with his problematic marriage and Puerto Rico's new political status, insists: "No es bueno jugar tanto al pasado. Puede ser . . . puede resultar peligroso. Podemos perder conciencia del presente. Y es preciso vivir en el presente. Aunque el presente sea la más dolorosa realidad" (98) [It's not good to act out the past so much. It can be . . . it can be dangerous. It's possible to lose consciousness of the present. And it's necessary to live in the present, although it may be a most painful reality]. Not only does Michelín lose perspective of the present, his flights to the past tend to repeat traumatic scenarios rather than to imagine an alternative plot that would allow him to let go of the pain of his loss.[30] Moreover, Mercedes exposes her son to the painful reality of the present, and he learns that his idolized father has died, not fighting for freedom in Chile but alone on the streets of New York. Without a fantasy world to sustain him, Michelín cannot exist because he literally has no space of his own, in other words, no voice or agency in the present world. He ends his life on his birthday with the blue poison his mother used to kill the *quenepo* tree, and his body is found hanging like a small Christ on the trellis that replaced the uprooted tree.

Although a trellis now stands in its place, the *quenepo* tree becomes a central motif that supports the connection between family and national identity in *Un niño azul*. The *quenepo*, like the *flamboyán* in Arriví's play, constitutes a symbol of *puertorriqueñidad* and evokes a family tree, a record of the relationships that have constructed the nation. How different characters perceive the tree indicates their stance on national identity. For Mercedes, it has no material value (it did not produce fruit), and it has stood in the way of her life in the new social order of the protectorate, so she has it removed. Similarly, Michelín's friend Andrés tells how the two trees in front of his house were cut down: "Mi tío dijo que tenían como cien años y que era una pena. Pero papá dijo que no era pena ninguna, que había que sacrificarlo todo al progreso" (167) [My uncle told me that it was a pity to have to cut it down since it was around a hundred years old. But my father said that it was not a pity and that it had to be sacrificed in order to make progress].

Michel and his son, in contrast, see the tree as a symbol of their roots, of tradition and identity. When Michel was imprisoned, the tree became a companion and substitute father for Michel, as Andrés notes: "En la escuela te pasas hablando del quenepo macho, que es alto y poderoso, como un padre" (83) [At school you spend the whole time talking about how the *quenepo macho* is tall and powerful, like a father]. When Mercedes realizes the significance of the tree for Michelín, she regrets having it removed. These regrets come too late in the play, however, and she is ultimately characterized as a femme fatale who oppresses and destroys her husband. Ripping out the roots of the tree is tantamount to castration, and, together with her infidelity and the destruction of his manuscripts, the act leads Michel to cry, "¡Qué poder tan absoluto el tuyo! ¡Cuán totalmente me has aplastado!" (141) [How absolute your power is! How thoroughly you have crushed me!].[31] As Thomas Feeny has commented, this type of female character derives from Marqués's displeasure at what he sees as the rise of a matriarchy that displaces men and alters traditional Puerto Rican culture (192). The loss of the tree, then, alludes to much more than the destruction of a single nuclear family; it signals the death of a way of life marked by Puerto Rico's patriarchy embodied in the LeFranc family line. Michelín's yearning for his absent father is indicative of Marqués's nostalgia for a world he has witnessed disappear. The boy's death parallels that of his father's, and as they both die poisoned by liquids, a cycle of destruction repeats itself. After the potentially constructive romance between Michel and Mercedes falls apart and the possibility of a union between Michel and Cecilia remains unfulfilled, the play ends with a sense of sterility: without a family tree to sustain the island's roots or identity, there can be no growth in the future. In this sense, the child's death becomes the extreme consequence of a failed romance.

A corresponding nihilistic tone can be found in Marqués's more famous play written the same year, *Los soles truncos* (1958). In this piece, three elderly sisters prefer to die rather than to accept that their way of life has progressively disappeared. Like *Un niño azul*, *Los soles truncos* presents two central romances, one failed and the other unrealized, that serve to examine the island's problem of identity. The two-act play exposes a privileged landowning family's decline during Puerto Rico's transition from a traditional nineteenth-century agrarian society to the twentieth century dominated by North American capitalism and modernization. Although all the action of the play takes place inside their Old San Juan home during one day in the late 1950s, flashbacks signaled by music and a change in stage lighting provide a half a century of family history that poetically illustrates how the Burkhart sisters have come to live a life of seclusion in their decayed colonial house. The death of the eldest sister, Hortensia, and the impossibility of keeping creditors at bay lead Inés and Emilia to commit suicide in a blaze they consider a triumph over the corrosive effects of time.

The marriage between the sisters' parents, Papá Burkhart and Mamá Eugenia, exemplifies Puerto Rico's nineteenth-century romance that failed to bring about a sense of identity that might lead to national independence. Given the couple's European origins (he is German and she is Spanish), it is conceivable that their families came to Puerto Rico after the proclamation of the Real Cédula de Gracias (1815) welcomed Catholic Europeans to the island to maintain white dominance and gain new agricultural technical skills. Most of these foreigners became Liberal Conservatives and were interested in preserving the island's colonial status with Spain. As Tamara Holzapfel has stated, the family's "attachment to everything foreign" is the source of much of its failure (154). The Burkharts surround themselves with German, Spanish, and French furnishings and send their daughters to Strasbourg to be educated. Inés reveals her father's ambivalence toward Puerto Rico when she describes him as a "naturalista alemán metido a hacendado del trópico" (23) [a German naturalist stuck with farming in the tropics (13)].[32] Likewise, it is doubtful that Mamá Burkhart, who died of "el dolor de ver flotar una bandera extranjera donde siempre flotara su pendón rojo y gualda" (33) [the grief of seeing a foreign flag flying where her own pennant had always flown before (22)], ever considered herself Puerto Rican. The Burkhart family grieved the loss of Spanish sovereignty and the invasion of the North Americans, not the lost opportunity for independence.

As characterized by the play, the Burkharts have never identified with Puerto Rican *jíbaros* like the LeFranc family did in *Un niño azul*. Although we learn that Papá Burkhart was committed to the family's land and ordered his daughters never to sell it to the North Americans, as Inés points out: "Tierras que no se trabajan, siempre serán de los bárbaros" (48) [Lands that lie fallow will always revert to the barbarians (33)]. Following her sister Hortensia's lead, Inés has refused to sell the land only to lose it eventually in a public auction. The play suggests that the Burkhart desire to resist the North Americans was deeper than the commitment to making their land productive. Cultivating the land might have benefited Puerto Ricans, but the Burkharts have been more interested in their private battle against the "bárbaros" than in the future of the island. This is because they have never identified themselves as Puerto Rican; they were transplanted Europeans whose family tree never fully took root in Puerto Rican soil. In contrast, in *El país de cuatro pisos*, José Luis González maintains that it was the African slaves imported during Spanish rule who were forced to make a connection to the land and that as a result, this group had more difficulty imagining itself belonging somewhere else (20). Thus, for González, Afro-Antilleans, rather than the white criollos, constitute the first Puerto Ricans of the island. The Burkharts' European heritage is undoubtedly an important component of Puerto Rican national culture, but the play censures the failure of this class to create a productive romance with other groups on the island. Instead, the upper class looked inward and maintained its European identity at the expense of the development of a strong national sentiment. This is relevant to Puerto Rico's evolving relationship to the United States in the 1950s, because, as Ralph McLeod suggests, "The new colonialism has been made possible by the almost inherently colonial attitude of the Puerto Ricans, especially among landowning families that maintained strong ties with Europe to the detriment of their country" (103).

Through the retrospective scenes, we learn that the Burkhart daughters have carried on a tradition of pride and class interests by refusing to "open" the family up by marrying. The play's central unrealized romance is between Hortensia and a Spanish lieutenant. Papá Burkhart accepts the lieutenant as a worthy marriage partner for Hortensia only after studying the Spaniard's family ancestry to assure that he carries no Moorish blood. However, Hortensia never marries the lieutenant; she breaks the engagement when Inés (motivated by jealousy) reveals that he not only has a lover, a black *yerbatera* (herb seller) from Imperial

Street, but also that he has he has fathered a child with this woman. Hortensia's reaction, to never marry or love again and the decision to shut herself off from the world—"¡no saldré jamás!" (26) [I'll never step foot outside of this house again! (16)]—derives from racism and class consciousness. It is unbearable to her that society knows that her fiancé has had a relationship with someone beneath her class and, especially, someone of African heritage. Interestingly, it is never explicitly stated that the woman is black. However, a reference to the child's blue eyes, the mention of the woman's occupation, and Hortensia's extreme reaction to the affair make it clear that she is poor and of African descent. The son produced in the romance between the Spaniard and a poor black woman (whose occupation as a *yerbatera* demands an understanding of native plants and herbs) is an example of the cultural synthesis that Arriví suggests in *Vejigantes* should be recognized as a fundamental part of Puerto Rican identity. Although it provides a seemingly minor subtext in Marqués's play, the Burkhart family's racism explains in great part why they have never identified with the fundamentally racially mixed island.

To connect with this mixture through marriage would have drawn the Burkharts into a national romance of which they wanted no part. When Hortensia says "NO a la vida" (19) ["No" to life (10)], her sisters join her out of their guilt for also loving the Spaniard and ruining their sister's chance for happiness. By sequestering themselves in their home, the sisters become isolated from the contemporary world. Withdrawing from society was originally a way for Hortensia to salvage her pride. Such limited interaction with the world, however, leaves too much time for the sisters to develop silent feelings of bitterness and guilt. Emilia tries to blame any ugliness on the changing world outside of the house, but Hortensia corrects her and says, "No, en nosotras mismas, Emilia. Celos, envidia, soberbia, orgullo. Rencor" (34) [No, no, in ourselves, Emilia. Jealousy, envy, pride, selfishness, anger (22)]. For Inés and Emilia, protecting the house from the outside world becomes a mission of atonement for having ruined Hortensia's aspirations; Emilia says, "La casa debe expiar por nosotros [*sic*]. Es nuestra cómplice. Nadie debe rescatarla de su expiación. Lucharemos por conservarla" (29) [The house should suffer *with* us. It's our accomplice. No one must save it from its suffering. We *will* struggle to keep it, won't we? (19)]. The house and its formerly luxurious furnishings recall the Burkhart family's glorious colonial past, and Emilia and Inés fight to retain the beauty of this world for their sister whose dreams they have destroyed. From the perspective of the audience, however, the dilapidated state of the mansion and the sister's life of misery (both economic and emotional) are signs of the decadence and decline of their social class.

The sisters' attempt to defy the onslaught of time is characterized by a worldview that looks to their European past for answers instead of to the Puerto Rican present that they try to deny even exists. The invasion of the North Americans in 1898 and the death of Papá Burkhart are two events that traumatize the sisters and destroy their sense of security as members of the nineteenth-century's hegemonic class. Upon their father's death, time "se partió en dos: atrás quedóse el mundo de la vida segura. Y el presente tornóse en el comienzo de un futuro preñado de desastres" (48) [divided in two: behind us lay our life of security. The present became the beginning of a future filled with disaster (32–33)]. Just as in *Un niño azul*, the nostalgia for the past is in part a yearning for stability embodied by the lost father. For the Burkharts, the past is a traditional world characterized by paternalist relationships between the upper class and their servants. The image of Papá Burkhart's cadaver carried upon the shoulders of four black servants captures the hierarchy that kept the world secure for the criollo landowners. Gelpí argues that the sisters duplicate the lost paternalist family structure and shows how each character is identified with a certain familial role (124–25). Metaphorically, Inés represents the father, Hortensia stands in for the mother, and Emilia plays the part of the child. I would add that the sisters adopt the roles of the paternalist triad in an attempt to recuperate the security of their former life. In other words, the reproduction of this family composition is a method to cope with the trauma of historical change. By re-creating a paternalist family, the sisters create a sense of structure in their enclosed world that produces an impression of timelessness, as though the family has never changed.

Like Michelín in *Un niño azul*, moreover, to cope with their precarious present state the sisters adopt theatrical techniques, such as a special space in which to play out their drama and props to "play" the past. Emilia, in particular, evokes past scenes to escape the harsh reality of their financial situation. To avoid mopping the floor, she transforms the living room into a party for the governor: "*Hace una impecable reverencia cortesana ante la butaca y se sienta en el sillón de Viena. Se oye lejano el vals de Chopin"* (18) [*She curtsies neatly before the chair and seats herself in the Viennese rocking chair opposite. The Chopin waltz from offstage accompanies her spoken reverie* (8–9)]. In other flashback scenes in which her sister Hortensia appears, a strange musical sound followed by a blue, dreamlike light signal the transition from the present to the past. For the audience, these scenes have a practical purpose: they provide the Burkhart family history and explain how the sisters arrived at their present situation. The flashback scenes also serve to emphasize that the sisters are not only physically cut off from the world but that they have also become psychologically trapped in an anachronistic epoch.

The sisters' rejection of the contemporary world literally constitutes the decision to close off the family from romance. The house in which they sequester themselves, furthermore, provides a complex symbol that comes to have different meanings. On one level, it is the house of *los soles truncos*, which refers not only to the architectural design of three windows over the balconies of the house but also to the three sisters who are "truncated" in the sense that they cut themselves off from the expected heterosexual life cycle that includes marriage and procreation. When Hortensia decides to retreat from the world, she makes a point of asking Inés never to open the three balcony doors below the truncated windows again. The house becomes an extension of their bodies, and its doors, windows, and balconies are points of entry that the sisters consider dangerous. For example, the description of men knocking on the door as a "golpetear estruendoso" (48) [tremendous pounding (33)] and Emilia's fear of direct sunlight as they enter—"Por favor, caballeros, me molesta el sol" (39) [Please, gentlemen, the sun is bothering my eyes (34)]—underscore her panic provoked by contact with the outside world. The shutting of all entrances into the house is emblematic of what Gelpí identifies as the erotic suppression of the sisters (133).

The outside world of the play's present is constructed diegetically through sounds such as honking horns, the pounding on the door, the voices of street vendors, and the dialogue of the inhabitants of the house. For the Burkharts, these sounds evoke a threatening male world of laws and economics in which they refuse to participate. As Ileana Rodríguez observes, moments of transition such as modernization favor the public sector, that is, male-dominated spaces (51). Rodríguez argues that women confront change from the family space, the house, and that they have the most power in the rural world of the hacienda, where they form part of a clearly hegemonic class (55). This world has been lost for the Burkhart sisters; thus, as creditors pound at the front door and attempt to enter the house, they are under the siege of a new (male) urban order that makes their cloistered existence vulnerable. The voice of the male Pregonero [Street Vendor] that penetrates the house at the beginning of each act is ironic on several levels: "¡Malrayo, polvo de amor, besitos de coco, pruébelos, doña! ¡Malraaayo, polvo de amor, besitos de coco para endulzarse el alma, cómprelos, doña!" (16) [Evil beams . . . love powders . . . coconut kisses . . . try them, lady! Love powder, coconut kisses to sweeten the soul, buy them, lady! (7)]. Reynolds, for example, signals the irony of the sisters' financial misery that prohibits the purchase of the treats (24). But there are other ironies as well: the sweetness of the products contrasts with the emotional bitterness raging within the house, these traditional Puerto Rican treats tempt the Europeanized sisters, and the erotic nature of the sweets' names contrasts with the sisters' suppressed sexuality.

The economic realities of the 1950s also threaten to invade the Burkhart family mansion, placing the world within the house and the world outside in constant tension. The contrast between the visible space represented (the house) and the invisible space described (the world outside) creates the play's dramatic tension. As in *Vejigantes*, an interest in the development of tourism is a sign of North American economic influence. Capitalists are literally knocking at the door in *Los soles truncos* because they plan to convert the house into something profitable, a hotel. This possibility is historically accurate, for we should recall that in 1949, Old San Juan was declared a historic zone, and in 1955 the ICP began restoration of this historical district. The sisters are horrified by the prospect of turning their house into a hotel because their microcosm of the past would become contaminated by "la risa de los turistas, la digestión ruidosa de los banqueros, la borrachera sucia de los que gritan" (52–53) [the laughter of the tourists, the loudness of the bankers, the filthy drunkenness of those who shout (37)]. The plot to reconstruct and preserve the house reveals the sisters' folly of trying to maintain an epoch that has already passed into the history of the island. That is, the fact that their home needs restoration implies that their world no longer exists in the Puerto Rican present. The interest in preserving the mansion is economic, but the project is also a matter of national pride, for it attests to the importance of the colonial world in the cultural heritage of the island. Since the Burkhart family never identified with being Puerto Rican, however, it would be difficult for them to consider their house as a part of the national patrimony (Montes Huidobro, *Teatro puertorriqueño* 390). I would add that since they have no interest in the Puerto Rican present, contributing to the Puerto Rican economy and perhaps improving their own financial situation are not valid motivations either.

Marqués's choice of a hotel as the future of their house is particularly apt in supporting the play's theme of family romance. For Gelpí, a hierarchical and exclusive definition of nation characterizes nineteenth-century paternalist discourse (132). A hotel can house many kinds of families that could displace the patriarchal structure of the traditional nineteenth-century family embodied by the Burkharts. To make the family home available to guests is tantamount to an erotic "opening" that would make the Burkharts' Europeanized upper-class world vulnerable to other national constituencies. In other words, the mutation of the family structure would force the sisters to join "la gran familia puertorriqueña" [the great Puerto Rican family] of the 1950s, a primarily mestizo, urban, and middle-class family. They have chosen long ago, however, not to multiply in order to maintain the purity of their European heritage.

The prospect of their home being converted into a hotel forces the Burkhart sisters to act. They save their world from contamination by making the house and themselves vanish in a suicidal fire. Like Michelín in *Un niño azul*, who never finds his own voice or national space, the sisters also end their family line because its role in the nation has all but disappeared, and they have no desire to adapt to a new one. As Angelina Morfi observes, Marqués has to kill the sisters, since once their past disappears, they, too, must disappear (513). However much Marqués may yearn for the values and stability of a bygone world, his plays *Los soles truncos* and *Un niño azul* highlight some of the factors involved in the demise of the criollo hacendado class. While North American influence is much to blame, Marqués also recognizes the flaws in Puerto Rico's family tree. Instead of love relationships that bind the nation together, conflicting ideologies and poor choices in partners tear romances apart. The self-destructive act of suicide literally cuts down the family tree, leaving little hope for future romances to regenerate what Marqués considers traditional Puerto Rican culture.

Myrna Casas: The Family Romance Degraded

Like Francisco Arriví and René Marqués, Myrna Casas (b. 1934) has played an important role in the development of Puerto Rican theater as a dramatist, professor of drama, director, actress, and founder of her own theater company, Producciones Cisne. Casas, Luis Rafael Sánchez, and Gerard Paul Marín are the principal playwrights of a generation of writers who began to approach the social problems of the island in formally and thematically innovative ways in the 1960s.[33] Her first play, *Cristal roto en el tiempo* (1960), nonetheless is very much a part of the Marquesian vein of theater of the 1950s in its themes, psychological poetic realism, and experimentation with time, lighting, and music. Compared to Marqués and even Arriví, Casas has been a much less publicized voice in the debate on national culture, and her works treat national themes with more ambiguity.[34] The characters in *Cristal roto* are not spokespersons for particular stances on the problem of identity, and there are fewer contextual clues to orient the spectator or reader toward conflicting visions of Puerto Rican experience. However, the themes Montes Huidobro finds in the play, such as "los recuerdos, el fracaso, la debilidad y la culpabilidad" (*Teatro puertorriqueño* 512) [memories, failure, weakness and guilt], are unmistakably Puerto Rican. These themes describe the characters' psychological state, the outcome, in great part, of problematic love relationships and the disintegration of the family. Similar to Marqués, Casas mourns the loss of the island's agrarian past, but with respect to the issue of gender, she views Puerto Rico's patriarchal traditions more critically than does Marqués. Through its failed family romance, *Cristal roto* participates in the traditional patriarchy identity stories prevalent in the discourse of the nation at the same time that it subverts this vision of national community.[35]

In a sense, the setting of a colonial mansion-turned-brothel in *Cristal roto* continues the story of *Los soles truncos*. Similar to the prospect of transforming the Burkhart mansion into a hotel, the Salazar family home reveals how the decayed upper class must finally open its doors, as the national family is reconfigured during a period of social and economic transformation. Through the dialogue of the characters onstage and the voices of characters from the past (that reveal the guilt complexes suffered by the living characters), the play reconstructs the conversion of the house into a brothel. Upon the death of the family patriarch, Don

José, the Salazar family begins to fall apart. His demented wife is placed in an asylum, and their son, Pepito, has squandered the family fortune. In an attempt to regain the money, Pepito sets up the business of the brothel but dies in a car accident, leaving his younger sister, Laura, alone with the new family venture.

The action of the play, which takes place *"hace algunos años o quién sabe si ahora"* (266) [*some years ago, or who knows, maybe now*], captures a critical day in the lives of several women who work in the brothel. The business is on the brink of financial ruin, and one of the more profitable prostitutes, Amelia, abandons the house in search of better opportunities in New York. At the same time, Doña Laura fires María, an aging and alcoholic prostitute who has progressively lost touch with reality. The broken glass of the play's title refers to María's fragile mental state and the broken dreams of the brothel inhabitants. It also underscores the play's static quality; there is little action because the dreams have already been destroyed. Instead, the play dramatizes the painful psychological consequences of modern social problems, especially as they affect women. Sudden changes in stage lighting, bursts of violin music, and accusatory voices from the past highlight the atmosphere of anguish and guilt that pervades the house.

As in the other pieces examined here, Casas uses the family space, the house, as a metaphor for the nation. The play's most striking dramatic device is the character agency of the house. As the play opens, the audience sees the skeleton of a colonial mansion and hears a Voice that announces: "Soy la conciencia de una casa. En esta casa encontraréis un mundo lleno de tristeza, angustia, soledad. A través de los años todo ha culminado en una sola palabra, dolor" (267) [I am the conscience of a house. In this house you will find a world filled with sadness, anguish, and solitude. Over the years it has all culminated in one word: pain]. The house adds that the blame for this painful state lies not with the passage of time, but rather, *"Sois vosotros los únicos responsables de la derrota porque la cobardía es el camino más fácil a seguir"* (268) [*You are the only ones responsible for this downfall, because cowardice is the easiest path to follow*]. Critics have suggested that the Voice speaks to the women of the brothel, but I would argue that it addresses audience members as well, for a detail in the stage directions signals that the house has no walls.[36] This opens the house up, merging what Hanna Scolnicov terms the "theatrical space"—the space created by the production, in this case the brothel—with "theatre space"—the physical space in which a performance takes place, the theater itself ("Theatre Space" 11). If the Voice were speaking exclusively to the brothel inhabitants, it would use the feminine pronoun *vosotras*, for this is a house entirely of women. The play suggests, then, that cowardice and defeat are something the audience and the characters share, which widens the interpretation from the specific issues of the characters to a collective problem that includes the spectators. The women who sell their bodies as prostitutes are not the only ones who have "sold out." The house itself—that is, the nation—has taken the "easiest path": selling out to the United States by settling for Commonwealth status. Montes Huidobro points out that without walls, the nation's identity seems to dissolve, leaving the island exposed and vulnerable to North American imperialism (*Teatro puertorriqueño* 216).

Casas further develops the identification between house and nation through the characters' reactions to the uncertain (financial) state of the brothel. The Voice of the house is the first to signal the dead-end situation of the brothel/nation: "Una casa se derrumba lentamente día tras día" (268) [A house collapses slowly day by day]. Not surprisingly, one way for characters to escape the collapsing house is to emigrate to New York. When Manuela, the brothel's housekeeper, warns Amelia about going to New York, house and nation become one: "Si crees que te van a tratar como en esta casa, te equivocas. Aquello es grande y a nadie le importa lo que le pase a uno" (276) [If you think they're going to treat you the same way they do in this house, you're mistaken. That city is huge and no one cares what happens to you]. In contrast, the voice of Amelia's sister in New York persuades her to leave the island, "En esa casa no tienes futuro" (269) [You don't have a future in that house]. For Amelia, to leave the house is to abandon the nation. Casas presents only the options of staying or leaving entirely; there is no intermediate alternative of leaving prostitution to seek another kind of employment in Puerto Rico. Thus the house has come to embody the entire island in a state of prostitution. There is no space outside of the brothel to offer Amelia better opportunities.

The other option for the lower class is to stay and try to maintain some of the nation's dignity. The privileged classes—the Salazar family—have irresponsibly "sold out," leaving the island's working class to pick up the pieces. This is the case for Manuela, the family servant who has long ago made a promise to Don José not to abandon the family. A "pobre jibarita"

(288) when she joined the Salazar household, like Cecilia in *Un niño azul*, she is the character most closely associated with the traditional agrarian world. The stage directions describe her as the backbone of the house, and Amelia comments, "Manuela está dentro de esta casa como si fuera otra pared. Ésa se va el día que la entierren" (318) [It's as if Manuela were one of the walls of the house. She'll only leave the day they bury her]. In other words, Manuela and the popular class she represents provide the foundation of the island. Throughout the entire play, Manuela constantly cleans the brothel, underscoring her task as national housekeeper. Especially important to Doña Laura is the cleanliness of the grand colonial-style door, the only structure visible in the house's frame of empty walls. Manuela is aware of the falseness complicit in trying to maintain appearances: "La puerta limpia. Limpia y blanquita para que de la calle parezca todavía una casa elegante. Todo el mundo tiene su puerta blanca, pero los cuartos sucios y revolcados" (286) [A clean door; clean and white so that from the street the house stills appears elegant. Everyone has a white door, but inside the rooms are dirty and in disarray]. She cannot clean away Doña Laura's guilt, just as the Burkhart sisters in *Los soles truncos* could not cleanse their guilt by preserving the beauty of the colonial world for Hortensia. However, as the structural base of the nation, Manuela continues to support the very class that betrayed the world she values.

As in Marqués's plays, in *Cristal roto* there is nostalgia for the stability of the past when fatherly male figures guided the nation. The death of the Salazar family patriarch sets off a chain of events that are disastrous for Doña Laura's future. Her sharp words and physical abuse of the prostitutes indicate her struggle to assert control over a situation that is spinning financially out of control. Like Inés in *Los soles truncos*, in her attempt to regain the security of the past, Doña Laura adopts the behavior of the master of the house. Nature images, similar to the *quenepo* tree in *Un niño azul*, emphasize a happier and more stable past. The play's initial stage directions describing the interior of the house, for example, mention a "palma moribunda" (267) [moribund palm tree] that stands out in contrast to the well-kept furniture. The dead tree is an obvious sign of the decadent state the elegant mansion has come to occupy. Later, when Doña Laura insists on throwing it out, Manuela replies that she would like to take the plant out to the garden to replant it: "Estoy segura que así revive. Lo que necesita es aire y sol" (313) [I'm sure that this way it will be revived. What it needs is air and sunlight]. Manuela, more than Doña Laura, understands the connection between the strength of the family and its relationship to the land. Replanting the (family) tree expresses a desire for a more rooted future.

The tree motif reappears when Pepito as a child identifies himself as Laura's protective tree: "Te protegeré siempre con mis ramas fuertes. Sí, soy tu árbol protector" (270) [I'll protect you always with my strong branches. Yes, I'm your protective tree]. In contrast, María describes her present situation as "esta realidad desierta como tierra sin árboles ni viento" (321) [this barren reality like earth without trees and wind], and similarly, the Voice of the house tells the characters and the audience that they live a "sueño amargo, sin árboles ni viento, un sueño roto por el sendero largo y seco, el sueño eterno hacia la nada" (349) [bitter dream, without trees or wind; a broken dream along a long and dry path, the eternal dream toward nothingness]. In an interview, Casas has explained that in her plays, trees represent identity, or lack thereof, on a personal level (she had a peripatetic youth) and on a national level (Pánico 414–15). Through the tree motif, Casas expresses her characters' rootlessness, an implicit comment on Puerto Rican identity during the late 1950s.

Cristal roto, nevertheless, constructs a less idyllic picture of Puerto Rico's past than do *Los soles truncos* and *Un niño azul*. While here the figure of the patriarch may also evoke security and a stronger sense of identity, decadence and sordidness surface as well. Casas also subtly subverts Marqués's idealistic vision by including fragments of the past that, when combined as a whole, portray male domination and sexual abuse as products of mechanisms for sustaining patriarchal social order. The play exposes the patriarchy as it really is, a system of social structures and practices in which men exercise control over women. For example, through the voice of Manuela's husband, Casas reveals that Manuela has had sexual relations with Don José: "Al infierno con los Salazar. Le has rendido bastante servicio. (*Ríe burlón.*) Sí, y qué servicio . . . más del que debías dar" (285) [To hell with the Salazar family. You've served them enough. (*Cynical laughter.*) And what service, indeed . . . more than you should have provided]. In contrast, Manuela—the character most closely tied to the agrarian past—describes Don José as "un hombre de verdad, noble y bueno" (288) [a real man, noble and good]. Oblivious to Don José's abusive behavior, Manuela ironically explains his wife's dementia: "La pobrecita no hizo más que sufrir con la muerte de don José. No en balde perdió la razón, lo quería demasiado" (287) [Don José's death caused nothing but suffering for the poor thing. It wasn't for nothing that she lost her mind. It's that she loved him too much]. Because the play does not fill in the details, the spectator is left to speculate that perhaps Don José's wife's dementia stemmed from her husband's infidelity. The contrasting characterization of Don José is perhaps explained best by noting that Manuela is so effectively interpellated by the patriarchy that she herself perpetuates it.

In the traditional patriarchal family evoked by the play, the unequal power relations between men and women permit males to behave irresponsibly with no censure. Thus, according to María, a longtime prostitute in the brothel, Pepito, the young patriarch of the Salazar family, has become "un monstruo sin conciencia" (297) [a monster without a conscience]. Pepito is characterized as greedy, vain, and reckless (he dies in a car accident because he drives too fast). He wastes his (and his sister's) inheritance and refuses to work to regain it: "No, no puedo trabajar. No soporto esa palabra. Todo saldrá bien, verás. Tengo muchos amigos" (291) [No, no, I can't work. I can't stand that word. Everything will work out, you'll see. I've got lots of friends]. By mentioning Pepito's friends, willing participants in the brothel business, Casas widens the critique of male behavior to a whole class of young people capable of sacrificing dignity for economic success. Unlike Laura, who has a real attachment to her home and whose conscience is tormented by her father's condemning voice, Pepito explains that it is the family business that interests him, not the house. To open the house to prostitution degrades women as housekeepers of the nation and sacrifices family pride and tradition.

The Voice of the house repeatedly tells the characters and the audience that cowardice is to blame for its present state of anguish and isolation. One has to ask if the cowardice refers in part to Laura's compliance with Pepito's plans. An incestuous relationship between the siblings could explain her excessive loyalty to her unlikable brother, and it supports the generally sordid account of the past as embodied by the Salazar family.[37] Opposed to his plans, Laura nevertheless acquiesces because "Pepito siempre fue el mas fuerte. Nunca tuve valor para oponerme a él" (291) [Pepito was always the stronger one. I never had the courage to confront him]. It is my sense that the audience can assume that she may not have been able to oppose or stop him in other respects as well. Pepito's voice recalls a scene from their childhood that underscores Laura's fragility and his power over her: "Ven, Laurilla ven. No te escondas . . . , ven conmigo

..., nadie te hará daño ..., jugarás conmigo y nada más ... Vente conmigo. ... Así, juntos los dos ... siempre" (293) [Come on Laura, come on. Don't hide ..., come with me ..., no one will hurt you ..., you'll play with me and that's all ... Come with me ..., that's it, the two of us together ... forever]. Even more telling is Laura's reaction to the memory described in the stage directions that follow: "*La música ensordecedora ahoga la voz del niño. Doña Laura vuelve la cabeza hacia la izquierda en un grito contenido de protesta. Su mirada es de intenso disgusto*" (293) [*The deafening music drowns out the boy's voice. Doña Laura turns her head to the left in a stifled scream of protest. Her expression is one of intense displeasure*]. Laura's intense reaction suggests that going to the garden to play with her brother is something that causes her great pain and guilt. An incestuous relationship with her brother also would help explain why Laura has never married. When a prospective suitor materializes, Pepito rejects him and forces her to stay at the brothel: "Te quedas y me ayudas. Yo te enseñaré. Además, ¿qué vas a hacer? ¿Casarte con el tonto del español? (*Ríe sarcástico.*) ¡Claro que no! Una Salazar casada con un triste comerciante" (291–92) [You're staying to help me. I'll teach you. Anyway, what are you going to do? Get married to that foolish Spaniard? (*Sarcastic laugh.*) Of course not! A Salazar married to a pathetic businessman]. His commentary on the Spaniard's class perhaps masks his real motives of not wanting to lose control over his sister. Like Don José's relationship with Manuela, Pepito, through sexual domination, coerces his sister into complying and supporting the patriarchy.

Incest, in the context of nationalist discourse, represents a failed romance because it is not productive in constructing the nation. It is an "inward"-looking relationship that does not cross barriers of race or class to join together different groups to build a stronger community, nor is it associated with procreation, which is so important for the nation's future. By not marrying the Spanish merchant, Laura has lost any opportunity for her family's financial success. On a national level, a marriage between the elite and the merchant class could have strengthened Puerto Rico and made it less vulnerable to the United States. Like the sisters in *Los soles truncos*, however, Laura says "no" to life and becomes trapped in a sterile environment. Her brother now dead, Laura expresses her anguish at her failure to make connections with others: "Nunca pude conservar una amistad, nunca pude retener nada a nadie" (289) [I could never conserve a friendship, I could never retain anything or anyone].

In addition to the incestuous romance between brother and sister, the brothel, while it may bring together groups that otherwise would have little interaction, also exemplifies a nonproductive romance. María, for example, yearns for a loving and life-affirming union to the point of madness. Blue stage lighting signals the moments in which she loses contact with reality. María drinks rum and hears sounds and voices that help to create a fantasy world in which she plays out scenes with her ex-lover. He had promised that they would have a baby, and her only personal possession is a music box (a gift from him) that plays a lullaby. María's desire for a baby is further underscored when she speaks to Manuela's grandson, Paquito, and invents a son just his age. As in the other plays discussed in this chapter, María's fantasies provide a metatheatrical mode of coping with reality, in this instance, her terribly degrading profession. Due to María's delicate mental state, Manuela sends her few clients. When she does send María a young man, the incident that ensues forces Doña Laura to fire her. Ernesto, characterized as a sensitive outsider, reluctantly visits the brothel as a part of the initiation process of his college fraternity. During the course of their conversation, María begins to confuse him with the son she wished she could have had and becomes hysterical when he attempts to kiss her. The play reintroduces the theme of incest (this time between mother and son) to emphasize María's particular failed romance: her profession that brings people together in a sexual union without the express purpose of creating a family.

As Montes Huidobro has pointed out, the Voice of the house that announces the play's themes of cowardice and guilt establishes the didactic framework of a parable (*Teatro puertorriqueño* 512). In my reading, the brothel allegorically represents the degraded state of the family/nation and is the result of the combination of the passage of time (historical process) and the decisions made by its owners (the upper class). The play suggests that while the women are left to pick up the pieces of the title's broken crystal (Puerto Rican identity), the nation's popular base (represented by the *jíbara* servant, Manuela) shares in the upper class's cowardice and guilt for its excessive loyalty. Manuela's loyalty serves to expose some of the means by which the patriarchy coerces women into supporting it. Compared to Arriví's play, the didactic element here is less explicit, and unlike *Vejigantes*, at the end of the parable Casas does not provide a positive solution for her female characters.

While specific references to Puerto Rico's political status are absent from the piece, the play's romances make clear its dialogue with Marqués's

vision of national identity. Instead of idealizing the bygone days of financial stability and paternalism, the play reveals the gendered and class-
based cracks in the aristocratic facade of the national house. The disintegration of the Salazar family has been in part its own doing, and rather
than focusing on the losses of the family's privileged world, the play
highlights instead how the economic and social transformations of the
first part of the twentieth century have affected women and the lower
classes. By incorporating gender and class issues in her examination of
the Puerto Rican family and nation, Casas adds an alternative view to the
debate on national community of her time.

Family scenarios dominated by failed romances and disappearing
houses (both ancestral and architectural) reappear with striking similarity in Puerto Rican drama of the mid-twentieth century. By examining
the national family tree in a moment of intense self-reflection and historical change, Puerto Rican playwrights such as Francisco Arriví, René
Marqués, and Myrna Casas seem to echo the Cuban José Martí's call for
unity in the face of North American imperialism in his famous essay
"Nuestra América" [Our America] (1891):

> Ya no podemos ser el pueblo de hojas, que vive en el aire, con
> la copa cargada de flor, restallando o zumbando, según la acaricie el
> capricho de la luz, o la tundan y talen las tempestades; ¡los árboles
> se han de poner en fila, para que no pase el gigante de las siete leguas!
> Es la hora del recuento, y de la marcha unida, y hemos de andar en
> cuadro apretado, como la plata en las raíces de los Andes. (157)

> [We can no longer be a people of leaves, living in the air, our
> treetop crowned with blooms, crackling or humming at the whim of
> the sun's caress, or thrashed and felled by storms. The trees must
> form ranks to block the seven-league giant! It is the time of reckon-
> ing, of marching together, and we must go forward in closed ranks,
> like the veins of silver that lie at the roots of the Andes.]

The familial disunity in their plays makes manifest a failure to create
consensus on the future course of the Puerto Rican people. Romances
that might wed disparate groups and strengthen the nation fail in part
because U.S. cultural and economic imperialism blocked the creation of a
nation-state (which would be embodied by a national hegemonic family).
Their plays also show, however, that the complexity of Puerto Rico's
collective identity also has its roots in the Spanish colonial period. In each

piece, moreover, the construction of the theatrical space of the house and the perceptions of the characters of this space are instrumental in communicating contrasting images of national community. For Arriví, to leave the family home constitutes a liberating and identity-affirming act, whereas for Marqués and Casas the isolation and atemporality of the space inside the house signify a traumatic retreat from the experience of historical change. When read together in the context of other narratives of the nation, their dramas show the theater to be a powerful player in Puerto Rican identity debates of the 1950s.

Scene 2

•◆•

Tearing Down the House
The End of an Epoch in Cuba

The institution of theater is embedded in the cultural milieu of a particular historical moment, and as a product of and commentary on society, it participates in a cultural dialogue that shapes certain visions of the nation. Through the recurrent motif of generational conflict, Cuban family plays from the mid-twentieth century enact a nation in search of rupture. Throughout the Republican era (1902–58), historical circumstances such as North American interventionism, economic dependency, political authoritarianism, and corruption kept the issue of national and cultural identity at the center of Cuban intellectual discourse. In plays by Rolando Ferrer, Virgilio Piñera, Abelardo Estorino, and José Triana, the discord between parents and their children represents the desire for *cubanía,* or the affirmation of a national identity in an oppressive, neocolonial context. These playwrights employ the conflictive and stifling atmosphere of the family home as a sign of the disintegrating Cuban Republic and the need for national redirection. In each play, the younger generation attempts to differentiate itself from its parents, to do, in playwright José Triana's words, "what our parents have not done" (Doggart 83). That is, the children seek to create a politically and economically autonomous nation able to chart its own destiny, a task their parents' generation failed to complete. Two works written before the Cuban Revolution (1959), *Lila, la mariposa* [Lila, the butterfly] by Rolando Ferrer and *Aire frío* [Cold air] by Virgilio Piñera, portray sons and daughters struggling to break free from their parents' modes of behavior, whereas the children in two plays written after the Revolution, *El robo del cochino* [The theft of the pig] by Abelardo Estorino and *La noche de los asesinos* [Night of the Assassins] by José Triana, openly rebel against their families.

In all four plays, tearing down the house, or the project of rebelling against parental authority, implies a restructuring of the institution of the family along with the rest of society. Consequently, a common thread in these plays is the omnipresent house in the mise-en-scène and its status as a metaphor for the nation. Spatial metaphors, as I have suggested earlier, facilitate thinking about the relationship between the theatrical space of the play (the family home) and the theater space (the audience or wider collectivity). Theater is potentially efficacious, for as Baz Kershaw explains, the "'possible worlds' encountered in the performance are carried back by the audience into the 'real' sociopolitical world in ways which may influence subsequent action" (139). Or as Ngugi wa Thiong'o creatively puts it, the "self-contained field of internal relations" of the performance becomes "a magnetic field of tensions and conflicts" that can potentially ignite other spaces in society (39, 40). "The real politics of the performance space," writes Ngugi, "may well lie in the field of its external relations; in its actual or potential conflictual engagement with all other shrines of power" (40). In Cuba, these other fields of power referenced by plays I will analyze include political dictatorship (Republican and revolutionary) and the institution of the family. This chapter will demonstrate that in the mid-1950s, the Cuban theater movement, immobile for much of the Republican period, articulates a desire for change that plays out historically in the Cuban Revolution and that portends the powerful potential of theater in revolutionary culture.

Scholarship on the debate over Cuban national identity frequently overlooks Cuban dramaturgy.[1] A brief review of the cultural and historical contexts of the first half of the twentieth century will show that the theater's use of generational conflict forms part of a discourse on national community that highlights the mutable quality of Cuban identity identified by Gustavo Pérez Firmat in *The Cuban Condition: Translation and Identity in Modern Cuban Literature* (1989). In one of his many meditations on Cuban culture, ethnologist Fernando Ortiz reflects on the adequate word to describe Cubanness. For Ortiz, the term *"cubanía"* contrasts with *"cubanidad,"* which one achieves by virtue of being Cuban. That is, *cubanidad* denotes passive national identification or a civil status while *cubanía* comprises a spiritual condition: "cubanidad plena, sentida, consciente y deseada" ("Cubanidad" 95) [full Cubanness, felt, conscious, and desired]. I would argue that the process of negotiation between literary models Pérez Firmat calls translation manifests this conscious will to create a Cuban identity. From Jorge Mañach's essay *El estilo en Cuba y su sentido histórico* [Cuban style and its historical meaning] (1944), Pérez Firmat borrows the notion that Cuba lacks a sense of national selfhood because, as an island, its vulnerability to the outside world made it unable to form an insular, or cultural, separateness necessary for a strong national consciousness. Pérez Firmat argues that "one important result of Cuba's lack of *insularismo* is what I have called a 'translation sensibility.' Because of the island's peculiar history, the Cuban writer or artist is especially sensitive to opportunities for translation, in both the geographical and linguistic senses of the word. Not having a native store of cultural goods and conditioned by history to the ways of the transient rather than the settler, the Cuban writer has the habit of looking outward, of being on the lookout for opportunities for displacement, graphic and topographic" (4).[2] Pérez Firmat chooses works of various genres from writers belonging to the first and second generations of the Republican period to show how a distinctive Cuban voice emerges from the translation of foreign models. Texts by writers such as Fernando Ortiz, Carlos Loveira, Nicolás Guillén, and Alejo Carpentier constitute examples of what Pérez Firmat calls "critical criollism" in that they consciously manipulate and recast or "translate" European literary traditions as they create their uniquely Cuban expression (9).

The essays from which Pérez Firmat draws his theory of translation and the works he examines from this perspective belong to Cuba's period of cultural nationalism of the 1920s-1930s. The first twenty years of the Cuban Republic established a pattern of institutionalized political corruption and economic dependency on the United States, which resulted in interventions to protect American interests in the Cuban sugar industry. Like other areas in Latin America, Cuban nationalism reawakened by the 1920s, and students at the University of Havana began demanding political and administrative reforms. Their discontent spread, and soon other areas of society, such as labor unions and newly formed political parties, joined in the call for change. Intellectuals including Jorge Mañach, Juan Marinello, Rubén Martínez Villena, and Alejo Carpentier formed associations such as the Grupo Minorista and published manifestos, first against the Alfredo Zayas government (1921–25) and later against dictator Gerardo Machado's regime (1925–33).[3] In arts publications such as *Revista de Avance* (1927–30), editors combined explorations of vanguardist currents with a deep concern for the nation. In order to regenerate the Republic, writers sought to understand Cuba's idiosyncrasies. Consequently, many well-known essays of the period examine Cuban identity, including Jorge Mañach's *Indagación del choteo* [Examination of *choteo*] (1928), Juan Marinello's *Americanismo y cubanismo literarios* [Literary Americanism and Cubanism] (1932), and Fernando Ortiz's *Contrapunteo cubano del tabaco y el azúcar* [Cuban counterpoint: Tobacco and sugar] (1940). Summarizing the subject matter of these diverse writings, Pérez Firmat finds four central areas of study: "the 'Cuban character,' the meaning of national culture, the tension between Cuba's Iberian and African heritage, and the effects of U.S. imperialism" (6). In particular, the rise of Afro-Cubanism in the 1920s constitutes an important component in the expression of *cubanía* during this period of cultural nationalism. In her study of race and the erotics of Cuban nationalism, Vera Kutzinski points out that artists such as Alejo Carpentier "perceived Afro-Cuban secular and religious culture as a cultural alternative to North-Americanization and as a political vehicle for national integrity and survival" (142). The investigation of Cuban identity from a variety of perspectives, in short, formed part of a movement for cultural revivification that intellectuals hoped would have political repercussions.

Pérez Firmat constructs his theory of Cuba's translation sensibility in part on *Americanismo y cubanismo literarios* (1932) by poet and literary critic Juan Marinello. In this essay, Marinello considers the issue of language in the formation of national identity. For Marinello, all Latin American writers are caught in the paradox of writing about the New World in the language of the Old World: "*Somos* a través de un idioma que es nuestro siendo extranjero" (97) [We *are* in a language that is both ours and foreign]. To escape this idiomatic imperialism, criollo writers must find their original voice in the tension between the two worlds. Pérez Firmat argues that criollist literature "emerges from a reading, a repossession—call it also a 'translation'—of the master texts of the European tradition" (12). That is, criollo writers must make Spanish their own language by transforming "la entraña idiomática con golpe americano, haciendo cosa propia lo que hasta aquí fue préstamo" (Marinello 99) [the idiomatic core with an American stroke, claiming ownership to something that until this point has been a loan]. What I would like to highlight in Pérez Firmat's notion of Cuban translation is the idea of process. If the Cuban inclination is to translate from models, then a fundamental factor in Cuban identity is its mutability and constructed character. *Cubanía* is an activity rather than a state. To possess it one must want it and make it, a notion akin to Pérez Firmat's theory of Cuban translation.

The idea of Cuba as a culture-in-the-making is best exemplified by Ortiz's concept of transculturation. In his short essay "Del fenómeno social de la 'transculturación' y de su importancia en Cuba" [The social phenomenon of "transculturation" and its importance in Cuba], Ortiz considers the island's history as a record of continuous cultural exchanges. The term "transculturation" expresses:

> los variadísimos fenómenos que se originan en Cuba por las complejísimas transmutaciones de culturas que aquí se verifican, sin conocer las cuales es imposible la evolución del pueblo cubano, así en lo económico como en lo institucional, jurídico, étnico, religioso, artístico, lingüístico, psicológico, sexual y los demás aspectos de la vida. ("Del fenómeno" 129)

> [the highly varied phenomena produced in Cuba as a result of the extremely complex transmutations of cultures that have taken place here, and without a knowledge of which it is impossible to understand the evolution of the Cuban people, either in the economic or in the institutional, legal, ethnic, religious, artistic, linguistic, psychological, sexual or other aspects of its life.]

Throughout the history of Cuba, the contact between the indigenous peoples of the island, white immigrants from a variety of nations, African slaves, and, to a lesser extent, peoples of Asian descent has forged a uniquely Cuban culture. Ortiz prefers the notion of transculturation to acculturation, the traditional term used for the exchange between cultures, because it captures the complexity of the process of constructing a syncretic culture like Cuba more fully. Transculturation includes deculturation, the destruction or loss of certain elements of a culture as it enters into contact with another, and acculturation, a period of readjustment and ultimately the creation of a new culture, a neoculturation (Ortiz, "Del fenómeno" 134–35). Pérez Firmat points out that the neologism "transculturation" is "critically criollo" as it recasts or translates "acculturation," a term used in North American sociology (20). More important for my purposes, the concept of transculturation underscores the transitional and "unfinished" character of Cuban identity that we will see enacted as generational conflict in Cuban drama.

Although Pérez Firmat does not discuss Jorge Mañach's essay *Indagación del choteo* (1928) in conjunction with his theory of Cuba's translational aesthetic, what Mañach describes as the national tendency to mock authority also underscores the mutational qualities of the Cuban character. Mañach examines Cuban *choteo* from a variety of perspectives. By looking at etymologies of the word *choteo*, the geographically determinist and psychological causes of the phenomenon, and at its social consequences, Mañach arrives at the following definition: "El choteo es un prurito de independencia que se exterioriza en una burla de toda forma no imperativa de autoridad" (41) [The *choteo* is an itch for independence that emerges as a mockery of all nonimperative forms of authority]. The desire to buck authority and to abolish hierarchy relates to Pérez Firmat's concept of translation that implies the mediation between two systems by the translator who can transform or, at times, make fun of a model through imitation. In a similar way, the *choteador* mocks an authority figure (or a situation that traditionally commands respect) and thus undermines any sense of hierarchy. Although *choteo* is ostensibly humorous, it also involves a conflict between two forces and the impulse to assert one's identity over another's. Similarly, in the generational conflicts in Cuban plays from the mid-1950s and the mid-1960s, the children's rejection of the model of their parents' generation expresses their *cubanía*, their wish for an economically and politically self-governing Cuba.

Mañach's ultimate objective is to show that *choteo* manifests a national spiritual and moral crisis. As Gabriela Ibieta notes, if *choteo* is an individual reaction to authority, "es precisamente porque al nivel público, y por extensión, nacional, no existía tal independencia, o, mejor dicho, existía solamente en forma, en apariencias" (75) [it is precisely because at the national level, such independence did not exist; or rather, it existed, but only in form and appearance]. Throughout the first three decades of the Republic, the debasement of national ideals (primarily in the arena of politics) resulted in a nationwide attitude of irreverence and mockery. For Mañach, *choteo* loses its humorous and beneficial qualities "cuando no es una reacción esporádica, sino un hábito, una actitud hecha ante la vida" (70) [when it is no longer a sporadic reaction, but a habit, an attitude toward life]. *Choteo* had become a defense mechanism, a mask adopted to escape from unpleasant national realities. Mañach blames many of the island's problems on the impromptu quality of the young Republic's political and cultural infrastructure: "La improvisación tuvo que regir por mucho tiempo en todos los sectores de la vida cubana" (63) [Improvisation ruled for a considerable time in all sectors of Cuban life]. For Mañach, improvisation signifies unpreparedness and incoherence rather than inventiveness or ingenuity. Much like the concepts of transculturation and translation, however, improvisation denotes impermanence and change. From Mañach's perspective, the nascent Republic was in the process of inventing itself and was yet to be completed. Consequently, Mañach ends the essay on a positive note, for he believes that, as a systematically skeptical attitude toward Cuban public life, *choteo* belongs to a historical period that will end as Cuba's new institutions mature.

History has shown that Mañach's optimistic perspective in his 1928 essay was premature. The problems that plagued the early years of the Republic never disappeared, and the island continued to struggle to define *cubanía*, a sense of national selfhood. In several essays on national identity, we have seen the translational process in the colony's effort to separate culturally from the *madre patria* [mother country]. From a historical perspective, the transformational quality that characterizes *cubanía* should not be surprising. In fact, Louis Pérez argues that Cuban national culture is distinguished by an inclination toward revolt: "Whether in the name of liberty, or equality, or justice, Cubans of diverse origins [. . .] on one occasion or another, often in concert but just as often in conflict, mobilized to challenge the premise and practice of iniquitous authority. These themes dominate Cuban history, and recur with remarkable regularity" (vii–viii). The struggle for independence from Spain, for example, spanned three decades (1868–98) and involved two generations of Cubans. When North Americans intervened, however, the war for national liberation became the Spanish-American War, and the emergence of a politically and economically autonomous nation was thwarted. Instead, under U.S. occupation, Cuba produced its first constitution in 1901 in which the Platt Amendment made the island a de facto U.S. protectorate.[4] In sum, the Cuban independence movement had "achieved self-government without self-determination and independence without sovereignty" (Pérez 192). The long war of independence, however, had instilled a strong sense of *cubanía*, and the impulse to determine collectively the nation's identity and destiny had become part of the Cuban experience.

The economic domination of the United States in Cuba, particularly of the sugar industry, created problems that prevailed until the 1959 Revolution: the dependence on a mono-export economy vulnerable to boom-bust cycles, institutionalized political corruption, and the erosion of Cuban culture. The structural weakness of the nation's economy and the instability and corruption of its political system produced cycles of rebellion and authoritarianism. The first strongman to rise to power in the Cuban Republic was General Gerardo Machado. The demand for national regeneration during the 1920s' period of cultural nationalism ended in Machado's election in 1925, and for the first few years of his term he ran an honest government that acted in the best national interests. Nevertheless, by ensuring his reelection in 1928 by outlawing his opponent's party, Machado took an unmistakable step toward dictatorship. However, the 1929 Wall Street crash deeply affected his second term because Cuba's economy was entirely dependent on the American market. As the economic crisis grew, so did political unrest, and in the 1930s Machado answered with increasingly violent measures. Finally, in 1933, amid a general strike in Havana, the United States withdrew its support of the regime, and Machado resigned and went into exile.

In the ensuing months, an uneasy coalition of military men and radical students proclaimed a revolution under the banner of "Cuba for Cubans." The brief revolution failed, however, for the government reforms did not go far enough for the leftists and had gone much too far for the Cuban elite.[5] Former army sergeant Fulgencio Batista emerged as Cuba's new leader thanks to the machinations of U.S. politicians. As the backing behind puppet presidents, as elected president, or as dictator, Batista dominated Cuban politics from 1934 until the 1959 Revolution. Under Batista, the acquisition of personal power and wealth soon took precedent over resolving the nation's problems. In the 1940s, unprecedented corruption including embezzlement, graft, and malfeasance of public office was pervasive in all levels of government, and a new word was invented to describe the violence of Cuban politics: *gangsterismo* (Pérez 284). The attitude of cynicism and resignation that followed the failed revolution of 1933 colored the public's reaction to Machado in the 1920s and Batista in the 1930s–50s differently. Nevertheless, neither dictators nor North American imperialism could obliterate *cubanía*, and as long as there were forces that impeded self-determination, Cubans would continue to buck authority in an attempt to gain control of their nation's destiny. Years of disillusionment following the failed 1933 revolution finally gave way to a renewed surge of nationalism, as a new generation of revolutionaries led by Fidel Castro, disgruntled students, and exiled politicians organized throughout the 1950s to overthrow Batista.

The dramatic action of all four of the plays examined in this chapter takes place during the final years of the *batistato*, 1952–59. The society portrayed in these plays was weak and divided. Economically, by the 1950s the sugar industry was stagnant and had ceased to be a source of economic growth. The upper class maintained its privileged position, and the lower class, especially the rural sector, remained poverty stricken. The middle class was very insecure; by economic standards it was small, and in terms of self-identification it barely existed (Ruiz 146). Politically, Cuba had reached the end of an era. Political dishonesty had discredited all traditional political parties, and most Cubans looked at politics with skeptical dispassion. Traditionally strong Latin American institutions, the Catholic Church and the military, did not serve as cohesive forces. The army was "a personalist military force lacking close links with either the wealthy or the poor" (Ruiz 159), and the Catholic Church failed to attract a mass following because it marginalized rural (especially Afro-Cuban) followers. The family constituted the dominant social institution because other groups such as the church, school, and community were weak (MacGaffey and Barnett 62). In other words, the traditional family appeared strong only by default. Thus the familial disintegration we will see in the plays of this period exemplifies another manifestation of Cuba's splintered society.

The twilight of the Batista regime provided playwrights with bountiful material with which to examine Cuban society. Matías Montes Huidobro considers the family a basic thematic component of the nation's theater: "La familia parece ser el punto de vista preferencial de la dramática cubana. Todos los dramaturgos insisten en ella" (*Persona, vida y máscara en el teatro cubano* 25; hereafter referred to as *Teatro cubano*) [The family appears to be the preferential point of departure of Cuban drama. All dramatists insist on this]. He argues that in Cuba there is a tendency to idealize the family and to equate it with "la gran familia cubana" [the great Cuban family] or the nation. Playwrights oftentimes contradict this vision of the united family, however, by staging a dark and often violent image of a household engaged in fraternal and paternal conflicts (Montes Huidobro, *Teatro cubano* 25–26). The family home, then, serves as a space from which dramatists can scrutinize the national body politic. Both Montes Huidobro and Rine Leal cite José Antonio Ramos's *Tembladera* [Tremor] (1917), a realist play that deals with a family divided over the sale of their sugar mill, as the first play to use the private family conflict to signal a larger, collective problem (Montes Huidobro, *Teatro cubano* 80; Leal 105). Many critics consider this play the best that Cuba had to offer until 1947, when Virgilio Piñera wrote *Electra Garrigó*, another play featuring the family that is best known for its Cubanization, or in Pérez Firmat's terms, its Cuban translation of the Greek myth.

Like the Cuban nation's struggle to direct its destiny, the efforts to create an autochthonous theater movement dominate the history of theater during the Republic. Cuba's strong nineteenth-century theater tradition regressed during the context of the political frustration of the Republican years. Magaly Murguercia finds five general factors that impeded the development of a strong national theater: the rapid proliferation and subsequent disappearance of small theatrical groups, the lack of state support, a colonized mentality that oriented theater practitioners toward foreign works, the resulting dearth and poor quality of native authors, and an atmosphere of skepticism that discouraged sociopolitical theater (77). Two landmark moments, however, helped build the foundation for a national theater. The first took place in 1936, when Luis Baralt's theatrical group La Cueva [Cave Theater] initiated a *"teatro de arte"* [artistic theater] movement. This movement produced a decade of theatrical education in which more than fifteen new private theater institutions trained theater technicians, directors, and actors.[6] During this period, in their quest to modernize Cuban theater, most of the theatrical groups performed works by foreign authors. In the late 1940s, however, playwrights Carlos Felipe, Virgilio Piñera, and Rolando Ferrer, who combined modern techniques with national themes, signaled the future of Cuban drama.

The brief *"teatro de salitas"* [little theater] movement between 1954 and 1958 constitutes the second significant moment in Cuban Republican theater. Las Máscaras [Masks], a group with roots in the earlier *"teatro de arte"* period, initiated the new trend with the four-month run of their 1954 production of Jean Paul Sartre's *The Respectable Prostitute* (1946). Until then, the plays produced by groups lasted only one or two nights. Following the Las Máscaras success, a variety of small theaters that offered consecutive performances opened in Havana. This little theater movement created a larger spectatorship, allowed the artists and technicians to fine-tune their performances, and provided a somewhat more stable financial situation for the groups. Again, given the culturally paralyzing climate under the Batista dictatorship in the 1950s, the plays performed were primarily foreign.

The theatrical activity during the Republic failed to create a strong national theater movement because it catered to a small urban public and did not produce a body of national dramatists.[7] It did produce, however, theater practitioners schooled in the latest international theater currents. Consequently, there were many well-prepared artists ready to participate in the institutionalization of Cuban theater that came with the 1959 Revolution. The Revolution's Marxist ideology dramatically altered the sociopolitical and cultural structures of the island. Government subsidies and the decommercialization of the arts immediately produced a new generation of theater schools, groups, and dramatists. For example, the government created the Teatro Nacional de Cuba [Cuban National Theater] as early as 1959 and the Escuela Nacional de Arte [National School of Art] in 1962. For the first time in Cuba, politicized groups such as Teatro Estudio [Studio Theater] emerged and produced plays by Bertolt Brecht. In addition, the Festival of Latin American Theater (1961) and *Conjunto*, a theater journal founded by Manuel Galich in 1964, made productive connections between Cuban drama and other Latin American theater movements. As an indication of how much the prospects for Cuban theater had changed, in one year, 1960, forty-nine Cuban works were performed (Leal 131), compared to the total of twenty-seven during the four years preceding the Revolution (Muguercia, *El teatro cubano* 171). With the Revolution, Leal writes, "el teatro cubano conquista su identidad" (129) [Cuban theater conquers its identity].

The dramatic text, destined for performance, represents the literary genre most subject to contextual factors, and the formation of a distinctively Cuban voice in the theater was a lengthy process. Therefore, in contrast to Perez Firmat's study of Cuban identity based on literary works from the formative years of the Republic, I consider playwrights who, at the very end of the Republican period, were just beginning to assert their *cubanía*. In *Lila, la mariposa, Aire frío, El robo del cochino*, and *La noche de los asesinos*, a young generation voices its desire for a different Cuba by struggling against parental authority. The confining family and the stifling space of the house become metaphors for the need to knock down the house and rebuild the family and, by extension, a new society. The outcome of this generational conflict varies depending upon when the play was written and the author's position concerning the Revolution. Rolando Ferrer and Virgilio Piñera are transitional dramatists in the sense that, although they continued to work after the Revolution, much of their significant work in the theater was done before 1959. Leal notes that these writers treat common themes: "Su mundo teatral pertenece a la pequeña burguesía, a sus conflictos familiares y psicologistas, a un universo cerrado, asfixiante y sin posible salvación, que se contempla a sí mismo con angustia, frustración y escape onírico" (141) [Their theatrical world belongs to the psychological and familial conflicts of the petite bourgeoisie, to a closed and stifled universe with no possible salvation that contemplates itself with anxiety, frustration, and oneiric escapism]. After the Revolution, in works by a new generation of playwrights, including José Triana and Abelardo Estorino, the family theme persists with a slightly different focus: "ahora se muestra su desintegración, sus falsos valores, y su resquebrajamiento ante el impacto revolucionario" (Leal 149) [now it reveals its disintegration, its false values and its rupture under the impact of the Revolution].

The Hovering Butterfly: Sentimental Dictatorship in *Lila, la mariposa*

Rolando Ferrer (1925–1976) participated in the formative years of Cuban theater in the 1940s and 1950s in a variety of roles: as a stagehand, actor, assistant director, and budding dramatist. After the Revolution, he joined the National Theater in the Amateur Department, taught theater courses, adapted many classical texts, and continued to write his own plays. *Lila, la mariposa* (1954), Ferrer's most important prerevolutionary play, portrays a sentimental dictatorship imposed by a mother (Lila) upon her son (Marino). The play depicts a deformed Cuban society because, as in the case of Marino, its natural development has been held back by authoritarian figures and North American neocolonialism. Thus the family conflict, the mother's sentimental dictatorship, points to the larger problem of a nation's struggle for autonomy. Lila's death at the end of the play liberates Marino and situates the Cuban family, like the nation, in a moment of transition. As Eberto García Abreu notes, the play suggests that "La familia como patentizadora de modelos de conducta ahistóricos está en extinción" (289) [The family as illustrator of ahistoric models of conduct has become extinct]. *Lila, la mariposa* leaves the audience with questions regarding what kind of family Marino will form to replace his formerly incarcerating one.

Lila, la mariposa premiered in 1954 at Teatro de las Máscaras under the dictatorship of Batista, a period during which artists made very little overt commentary on contemporary national realities. The play's family thematic, however, foregrounds issues such as racism and imperialism that Ferrer frequently writes about after the Revolution.[8] *Lila, la mariposa* stands out in the 1950s' *salitas* theater movement for its cultural specificity in a moment when foreign texts dominated. The play embodies what Pérez Firmat would call Cuba's translational aesthetic because Ferrer employs structures and figures from Greek tragedy and myth, as well as poetic language reminiscent of Federico García Lorca, to write a distinctly Cuban play. Like Marino, who wishes to distance himself from his mother, on a textual level the play constitutes an example of Cuban dramaturgy striving for an independent voice.[9]

As the title of the piece indicates, Lila, like a butterfly, hovers around her son, Marino, in a desperate attempt to bind him to her. Marino is her only reason for being, and when it becomes apparent that he desires his independence, she commits suicide. The family unit in *Lila, la mariposa* also includes Lila's sister-in-law, Hortensia. The play's mimetic space—the space perceived by the audience and the characters onstage—consists of the bottom floor of their home, which doubles as a dressmaking shop. The house/shop is located on Havana's seaside avenue, the Malecón. This torments Lila, because the sea constantly reminds her of the womanizing husband who left her and of what she considers the inevitable loss of her son. The shop is named La Mariposa, after a book of poems written in honor of Lila by a poet who fell in love with her twenty-five years earlier. Prefiguring her relationship with her son, the poet had envisioned Lila as a creature who fluttered around the object of her desire, never able to touch it without destroying herself. In the shop, three *costureras* [seamstresses], Lola, Clara, and Meche, and a maid, Marina, work for Lila and Hortensia. The combination house and shop mixes the private family space with the public work space, highlighting the connection between family and nation. As much as Lila would like to shield her son from the outside world, the business creates an atmosphere in which the larger society constantly permeates the home.

Ferrer satirizes the parade of characters who pass through Lila's house to create an almost grotesque vision of society. The most memorable character outside the family with a significant role in the plot is Señora Estévez, called La Cotorrona for her gossipy chatter. Ferrer includes this ludicrous character, along with her monstrous daughter, El Energúmeno, to criticize the materialism and self-absorption of the upper class. He adds a note of anti-imperialism by emphasizing the fact that the woman's husband works for a foreign company, the All Sea Company. Fully aware of Lila's debilitating fear of losing her son to the sea, La Cotorrona selfishly offers Marino a job with her husband's company only because she wishes to make amends for her daughter's inappropriate behavior during an earlier visit. Other characters that round out the play's construction of Cuban society include Cabalita, a drunk who speaks in nonsensical riddles; Pregonero, a street vendor, who insists he is not black in hopes of making more sales; and other neighborhood members who, during Lila's wake, tell jokes, gossip, and contemplate whether the casket might fall.

The play's dramatic action moves inexorably toward tragedy. The *costureras*, who serve as a chorus in the style of Greek tragedy, frame each act with a riddle about a tree: "Adivina, adivinador . . . , ¿cuál es el árbol que no echa flor?" (295) [Who can guess the riddle . . . , which is the tree that does not blossom?]. At the end of the first act, the following answer clearly refers to the play's main conflict, Lila's stifling influence on Marino:

Clara. El que no se riega.
Meche. El que no le abonan la tierra.
Clara. El que le cortan las ramas. (312–13)
[Meche. The one that isn't watered.
Clara. The one that isn't fertilized.
Meche. The one whose branches are cut off.]

As in Puerto Rican plays from the same period, the tree embodies family and regeneration. Lila is literally killing her family by not allowing her son to grow up. If we recall the anti-imperialist message expressed in José Martí's use of the arboreal metaphor in "Nuestra América" [Our America] we can see more clearly the allegorical implications of the mother/son relationship (157). In Ferrer's play, Marino's mother (dictatorship) hampers development. To escape, Marino is tempted to go out to sea, which could mean working for the All Sea Company (imperialism) or simply leaving the island (exile). As we will see, the play's ending favors the nationalist stance of remaining rooted in one's home country as the best means to counter neocolonialism and to effect change.

The second act uncovers a secret that leads to the play's climax. Hortensia reveals to Marino his true age and her opinion of his mother: "Tú no tienes trece años, tienes quince, tu madre te engaña, tu madre es una egoísta, pero es también una mujer enferma, y los enfermos son débiles y fuertes, abusadores, tiranos" (320) [You aren't thirteen, you're fifteen, your mother is deceiving you, she is selfish, but she is also sick, and the sick are weak but also strong, abusive, and tyrannical]. At some point during the second act, one of the *costureras* places a pair of sharp scissors in Lila's bedroom, preparing the scene for her suicide. The third act begins with Lila's wake and ends with Marino contemplating his future with his aunt Hortensia and girlfriend, Adelfa. The answer to the concluding tree riddle, "¿Qué hace el árbol?" [What does the tree do?], suggests a hopeful future for Marino:

> Clara. Crece.
> Lola. ¿Qué tiene dentro?
> Meche. Otro árbol. (345)
> [Clara. It grows.
> Lola. What does it have inside?
> Meche. Another tree.]

The play's most intriguing dramatic device is the chorus of *costureras* because it is fundamental both to the plot and to the play's examination of the Cuban family. The women resolve the conflict between mother and son by arranging Lila's death. Thus the mythical dimension of the *costureras* affects the historical realities of the household, for Lila's death allows Marino the liberty to determine his own destiny.

The presence of Lola, Meche, and Clara in the house, along with their status as seen but unseen characters, implicitly comments on "la gran familia cubana," or the nation. Marina, a servant, is the only character to see the *costureras* in their magical guise beyond their roles as workers. The play's initial stage directions describe them as a part of Lila's home: "*Llegaron con los muebles, con la boda, o sabe Dios cuándo. Negra, mulata y blanca, son, en el religioso mundo de la criada, mágicas encar-*

naciones de fuerzas naturales desencadenantes de la tragedia" (295) [*They arrived with the furniture, with the wedding, or God knows when. Black, mulatto, and white, they are, in the religious world of the servant, magical incarnations of natural forces unleashed by tragedy*]. The women literally form part of the structure of the house, but in many respects they have not been seen and understood. The women's speech, full of verbal play in the form of riddles and *refranes* [proverbs], identifies them with Cuban *choteo* and the popular classes. Their mysterious origins, their occupation, and their role in Lila's death make them an obvious Cuban version of the three Greek Fates.[10] However, the racial diversity of the *costureras* embodies the Cuban people. In addition, their garments are adorned with aquatic images, such as shells and coral, and each woman is identified with a natural element. Although it is impossible to identify each character with a particular *orishá*, a goddess in the syncretic Afro-Cuban *santería* pantheon, these details and the women's seemingly magical powers suggest their association with the religious-magical realm of black culture.

When Marina points out Lola's, Meche's, and Clara's supernatural capabilities, Hortensia dismisses her fears. For Lilian Cleamons Franklin, this expresses an implicit view on class and race: "In literature it is the members of the lower economic strata, both black and white, who exhibit evidence of superstition and belief and 'black magic.' In contrast, Hortensia, as a representative of the hardworking white middle class, has little time or interest in the folly of superstition" (179). Hortensia sees the *costureras* in their capacity as workers but is unable to see their influence in the house or the possibility that they have a critical vision of her class or her family. The *costureras* are instigators of change, and their destructive act has as its goal to rebuild the family. They counter Marina's accusations of their destructive powers, insisting that they serve "para adelantar" [to move ahead] and "para construir" (312) [to build]. These women form a part of the Cuban family, or nation, that has been made invisible or powerless by its class and/or race. The play implies that this very group can serve as an agent for change and that space must be made for them in the national family. In this sense, *Lila, la mariposa* anticipates the events of the Cuban Revolution.

The conflicts between parents and children provide the most pervasive evidence of the need to renovate the family and, by extension, a troubled society. The play offers several authoritarian parent-child relationships.

Two relationships have produced uncontrollable children. La Cotorrona, trapped in a vicious cycle of authoritarianism and permissiveness, cannot control her daughter. She labels her child alternately a monster, a savage, and an imbecile and laments there is no school on weekends: "Deberían tener clases las veinticuatro horas del día, y los sábados, y los domingos, y los días festivos. (*El Energúmeno hace una seña fea con el dedo mayor.*) Me va a enfermar" (303) [They should have class twenty-four hours a day, including Saturdays, Sundays, and holidays. (*The Diabolical Girl makes an ugly gesture with her thumb.*) I'm going to be sick]. As the gesture indicates, the daughter counters her mother's insults with inappropriate bodily behavior. Similarly, in an offstage scene, El Energúmeno challenges her mother by blowing her nose on a lace tablecloth. Marina's relationship with her daughter is also tense. She calls her daughter La Boba, not as an affectionate nickname but to signal her mental disabilities. La Boba acts out verbally, and her repeated exclamation (probably in reference to the casket) at Lila's wake—"Sapiti pon, que no tiene tapón" (333) [*Sapiti pit*, it doesn't have a lid]—embarrasses Marina.

The relationship between Marino's friends Adelfa and Capitán and their parents is strained as well, but neither of these siblings displays such abnormal behavior. Capitán argues with his father, and as Adelfa notes, both react to parental control physically: "Yo corro y mi hermano corre. (*Suspira.*) Algún día seré bailarina: la cintura bien apretada y baile y baile y baile" (315) [I run and my brother runs. (*Sighs.*) Someday I'll be a ballerina with a very narrow waist and I'll dance and dance and dance]. Capitán plans to leave home to work on a ship, and Adelfa says one day she, too, will abandon her family to achieve her dream of becoming a dancer. Here dance, like El Energúmeno's bodily transgressions, expresses the independence that colonialism suppresses.[11] The parental dictatorships all of the children suffer in the play evoke a colonialist situation. Comparing colonialism with motherhood, Franz Fanon writes that, on the unconscious level, the colonized do not view colonialism as "a gentle loving mother who protects her child from a hostile environment, but rather as a mother who unceasingly restrains her fundamentally perverse offspring from managing to commit suicide and from giving free rein to its evil instincts" (*The Wretched* 211). In Fanon's view, colonialism impedes societies from developing on their own terms and often produces deformed relationships and psychological complexes. Consequently, in Ferrer's play, the children either seek to escape from their families or they stay, accept their supposed inherent inferiority, and behave accordingly. As we will see, Lila's colonialist tyranny is hardly motivated by her belief that she must save her child from his own destructive behavior.

Lila's sentimental dictatorship creates a stifling atmosphere in the house much like that of Cuba under a military dictatorship. The characters' perceptions of the family home create a sense of heaviness and entrapment. The mood inside the house contrasts with that on the streets outside. The house is surrounded by activity, on one side the constant motion of the sea, and on the other the bustle of cafés and traffic on the Malecón. Inside the house, however, the stage directions note that nothing has been altered since Lila first moved there twenty years earlier. Hortensia, among others, complains about the house's stifling heat, but Lila limits the opening and shutting of doors and windows because she cannot bear to look at the sea. The sea, a sign of freedom for Marino and Capitán, has an asphyxiating effect on Lila. After recounting a nightmare she had about the sea, Lila demands a fan, but at the same time, she also asks Hortensia to close the window. Unlike the house in René Marqués's *Los soles truncos*, however, here there can be no attempt to convert the house into an impenetrable, timeless space, for it also serves as a shop.

Since Lila cannot keep the world from entering her home, she tries to keep her son from leaving the house. That is, what Lila says and does is more imprisoning than the space of the house itself. When Marino is out of her sight, she constantly calls out for him. In the mornings she awakens him by calling to tell him his breakfast is ready, but unlike most mothers, her voice is *"miedosa, obsesiva, demasiado dependiente del hijo"* (301) [*fearful, obsessive, and overly attentive to her son*], and his slow response provokes a fit of tears. Lila is jealous of Marino's sleeping hours because she cannot know what he is thinking. Likewise, Hortensia adds: "No le guste que juegue, porque no sabe qué está pensando, ni que estudie, porque no sabe lo que está aprendiendo" (303–4) [She doesn't like it when he plays because she doesn't know what he's thinking; nor does she like it when he studies, because she doesn't know what he's learning]. Lila also tries to control her son physically. When Marino finally does come down for breakfast, she circles him until she traps him for a kiss; when she senses his desire to distance himself, she physically clings to him. She also keeps her son inside by telling his friends he is not home when they come to visit. But the most significant way Lila manipulates her son is by lying about his age and treating him as though he were a helpless little boy. She has convinced herself that he is thirteen when he is really fifteen and has asked his teachers to hold him back in school even though he has passed his exams.

Lila's falsehoods contradict her public image as an ideal mother and expose her weaknesses. As Montes Huidobro has noted, "La madre es uno de los elementos más tradicionalmente reverenciados e idealizados por la tradición sentimental del pueblo cubano" (*Teatro cubano* 26) [Traditionally, the mother has been one of the most revered and idealized elements in the sentimental tradition of the Cuban people]. From the perspective of those who are not close to her, Lila appears to be the traditional self-sacrificing mother. She presents herself this way to her clients: "Se sofoca con tanto trajín. Levantarme, ocuparme del hijo, volverme a ocupar del hijo. Luego el ajetreo del taller" (301) [One is suffocated by the hustle and bustle of life. I get up, get my child ready for school, take care of him again when he returns. Then there is the busy activity of the shop]. Furthermore, at Lila's wake, mourners describe her as happy and lighthearted, as an extraordinary woman, a magnificent wife, and an exemplary mother. In reality, Lila is hardly a powerful matriarch or a lighthearted, doting mother. Although the shop is named for Lila, Hortensia and the *costureras* do all the work, as Lila's obsessive fear of losing her son makes her mentally fragile and prone to nervous attacks. When Hortensia tells Marino that La Cotorrona has offered him a job, Lila's reaction reveals an important motive for holding her son back. She complains that Hortensia wants her son to grow up and to live: "Y ¿qué es la vida? Los hombres dejan a sus mujeres por sus queridas, o se mueren" (329) [And, what is life? Men either leave their wives for their mistresses, or they die]. Her fear of losing her son as she did her husband selfishly outweighs her apparent desire to protect Marino from a harsh world. The play thus demythologizes an idealistic view of the Cuban matriarchy and in fact points to some of its negative effects.

Although Lila restricts Marino's movements and thoughts, like so many dictators, her need to dominate ultimately destroys her. This leaves Marino the opportunity to develop his own identity. Because of Lila's domineering behavior, Marino exhibits a weak stage presence; he has few lines and appears indecisive. Stage directions throughout the play, however, suggest Marino's need to assert himself, as in his first entrance: "*Bajo una apariencia moderada, una gran fuerza interior pugna por manifestarse"* (307) [*Beneath a seemingly measured disposition lurks a great interior force pushing to manifest itself*]. When he tearfully complains that he feels "amarrado" [tied down], his girlfriend, Adelfa, encourages him to leave his family because: "Te vas volviendo chiquito como una hormiguita, y alguien te podría aplastar" (318) [You're becoming tiny, like a little ant, and someone could crush you]. He begins to counter his mother's attempt to control him by physically shrugging her away and by telling her that he will not listen to her: "(*Tapándose los oídos.*) No te voy a oír, no te voy a oír" (329) [(*Covering his ears.*) I will not listen to you, I will not]. Nevertheless, upon Lila's death, Marino clings to her coffin, crying uncontrollably, and appears to be paralyzed without her.

Marino takes his first step toward independence after his mother's death when a visit from his friend Capitán provokes him to ask: "¿Qué es un hombre?... ¿Qué es hacerme un hombre?" (341) [What is a man?... What does it mean to become a man?]. Suddenly Marino no longer feels the lure of the sea or the desire to leave his home. The stagnant atmosphere of the house ceases to weigh upon him, and he comments: "Esta casa es fresca" (341) [This house is refreshingly cool]. Marino chooses not to go to sea with Capitán, and he tells Hortensia he will not work for the All Sea Company either. This implies a commitment to Cuba; he will not personally sell out by working for a foreign company, and he does not have to abandon the island to become his own person. He notices the material condition of his home and makes plans either to paint it or to move because, as he remarks, "Está muy vieja" (342) [It's very old]. Whether Marino moves or renovates his present house, he will remain on the island to build a new family and home.[12]

Lila's death catapults Marino into a period of flux and uncertainty, but the hope is that his generation will be able to distinguish itself from that of his mother's. As Randy Martin states, "Generational differences are convenient symbols for divergent historical moments that may introduce a new voicing that carries a distinct perspective" (171). In revamping the house, or Cuban society, in the mid-1950s, Ferrer's play makes clear that a different sort of family must accompany these changes. The Cuban national family must be more inclusive with respect to race and class and less authoritarian to effect any real transformation. Through a mother's sentimental dictatorship, *Lila, la mariposa* implicitly suggests that free from repressive regimes, the nation can move forward and regain control over its future.

The Disintegration of *La Sagrada Familia*

Similar to *Lila, la mariposa,* Virgilio Piñera's *Aire frío* (written in 1958 and first performed in 1962) exposes family authority figures in a state of decline to paint a less than idyllic portrait of the Cuban family and nation. Piñera (1912–1979) represents one of the predominant voices in twentieth-century Cuban literature. Before the Revolution he was involved in important literary groups and their publications, such as *Orígenes* (1944–56) and *Ciclón* (1955–57), and he wrote poetry and fiction in addition to drama. In the field of Latin American literature, Piñera is credited with experimenting with absurdist techniques (in both fiction and drama) before they became fashionable in European avant-garde literature.[13] Although Piñera won the Premio Casa de las Américas in 1968 for his absurdist play *Dos viejos pánicos* [Two old panics], his work came under criticism because its stance toward the Revolution was unclear. He became increasingly uncomfortable with the artistic limitations imposed by the revolutionary government in the late 1960s, and as a result, for many years his works remained unpublished and unstaged.[14]

Most critics consider *Aire frío* Piñera's masterpiece. This long, three-act drama captures in minute realist detail eighteen years (1940–58) of the absurdly precarious existence of a middle-class Cuban family. In the introduction to his 1960 *Teatro completo,* Piñera describes the play as autobiographical and explains its peculiar blend of realism and absurdism: "al disponerme a relatar la historia de mi familia, me encontré ante una situación tan absurda que sólo presentándola de modo realista cobraría vida ese absurdo" (29) [as I prepared myself to tell the story of my family, I found myself before a situation so absurd that only by presenting it through a realistic mode could its very absurdity be expressed].[15] The plot's absurdist lack of direction reflects well the stagnant state of the family and the nation, but Piñera's play does indeed have a theme typical of realism, which he describes at a later date as "la inseguridad de la familia" ("Dos viejos" 69) [the family's insecurity]. In *Aire frío,* Piñera not only uses the family as a lens through which to examine critically Cuba's socioeconomic and political panorama during the 1940s and 1950s, but he also portrays the commonly revered family unit as an institution that has contributed to the Republic's general malaise. The play provides a complete picture of the stifling socioeconomic and political atmosphere of the period but focuses most sharply on the family unit's role in a system that so desperately needed to change.[16] Piñera demythologizes the strength of

the family institution, particularly the roles of the matriarch and patriarch. The children in the play strive to differentiate themselves from
their parents' values and behaviors, and although they display rebellious
attitudes, they are as trapped as their parents are in a stagnant system. In
1958, the year in which the play was written, cold air, the work's metaphor for change, had yet to arrive.

There is no simple way to sum up the plot of *Aire frío* because, other
than the slow decline of the Romaguera family over the course of two
decades, there is no central action that drives it. Angel and Ana head the
family, he as an unemployed failure at fifty-five and she as a retired
schoolteacher and classic self-sacrificing mother. Their oldest son, Enrique,
is married and is the only financially stable member of the family. The
play's protagonist is his younger sister, Luz Marina, who is thirty and
unmarried at the start of the play's action. She supports the family as a
seamstress and is closest to her younger brother, Oscar, a poet who
chooses not to work. Another son, Luis, lives in New York, where he
hopes to make a better living than is possible in Havana. Other than the
day-to-day struggle to survive financially and emotionally—Luz Marina's
obsession with combating the heat by purchasing a fan, Angel's hare-
brained schemes to strike it rich, and Oscar's dreams of publishing his
poetry—very little happens in the play. Two life-altering events, Oscar's
four-year exile in Buenos Aires and Luz Marina's marriage at the age of
forty-four, ultimately leave the siblings with the sense that nothing ever
changes. The action ends in 1958 with the whole family gathered in the
house awaiting Ana's imminent death.

Unlike in *Lila, la mariposa,* in this play a wealth of very specific contextual details serve to link the family's story to national history.
Through the Romagueras, Piñera sketches the Cuban middle-class odyssey during the first half of the twentieth century, from the security of
land ownership and life in a small town to the economic uncertainty of
urban unemployment in the capital, from hope and hard work to the
skepticism and apathy of the 1950s. The family's conversations and everyday experiences bring to light all of the problems of political corruption (including *gangsterismo*), North American imperialism, and inflation. The multitude of contextual details adds up to a picture of social
frustration, economic loss, and political anger that highlight the lack of
viability of the Cuban Republic.

My interest here, however, is in how the Romaguera family fails alongside the decline of the Republic. Martin argues that the play "merges corrupt state power with decrepit patriarchy and a malformed bourgeoisie, and paints these forces into the stilted spaces of the Romaguera home and patriarch" (154). Many moments in the play identify the family with nation and vice versa. In the first act, Luz Marina, painfully aware of what is wrong with both, bitterly remarks: "Cuba, paraíso tropical ... (*Pausa.*) Visite a los Romaguera, en Animas 112, familia respetable que está encantada de la vida" (305) [Cuba, tropical paradise . . . (*Pause.*) Visit the Romaguera family at Animas 112, a respectable family charmed by life]. To visit the family is to expose in microcosm a national crisis. Luz Marina sums up her nation's and her family's loss of dignity by alluding to the oppressive hot weather and a plague of corrupt politicians and cockroaches. When Angel denies that their home is infested with cockroaches, Luz Marina exclaims, "¿Nada más que la cocina? ¡La casa entera! Norte, Sur, Este y Oeste. Aquí no vive la familia Romaguera; aquí vive la familia Cucaracha" (373) [Only in the kitchen? Don't you mean in the whole house! North, south, east and west. The Romaguera family doesn't live here; the Cockroach family does]. In one of the play's sadly ironic moments, as Oscar departs for Argentina, Angel remarks: "Si la literatura es tu meta, la familia ha sido la mía" [If your goal is literature, family has been mine], to which Luz Marina adds: "¡Viva la familia Romaguera!" (336) [Long live the Romaguera family!]. She apologizes for her sarcasm but comments, "la verdad verdadera es que somos unos fracasados" (336) [the real truth is that we are a bunch of failures]. Unlike her father, Luz Marina recognizes that not only have individual members of the family fallen short of their goals, the family as a unit has come apart as well.

The disintegration of the family is played out primarily between Luz Marina and Oscar and their parents. To be sure, Enrique's visits cause familial strife because his self-satisfied attitude and reluctance to support the family infuriate Luz Marina. There is also friction between Enrique (the materialist) and his poet brother, whose ideals he cannot admire. However, the overwhelming conflict is generational, between parents and children who often comment "vives en la luna" [you live on the moon] to express their incomprehension of one another.[17] The two outstanding living-room decorations, a copy of Whistler's famous painting of his mother and a bust of Beethoven, suggest the nature of their conflict: Luz Marina hardly appreciates the image of motherhood projected in the painting, and Oscar is the typically misunderstood and undervalued artist. It is Luz Marina, however, who most struggles to understand her parents' values and who rejects the patriarchal family structure.

Angel is a patriarch in decline. Throughout the play, he repeats with variations a phrase that sounds eerily like a dictator losing control of his or her country: "Esta casa es un relajo. Hasta el día que me decida a empuñar el látigo" (374) [This house is in chaos. Until the day I decide to take up my whip]. His threat to crack the whip is empty, however, because he is in a state of physical and mental decay. In the first act, he is dominated by a toothache and lust for his fifteen-year-old niece, and as the play progresses he begins to lose his eyesight. He spends his days playing dominoes and plotting with dubious characters unrealistic schemes to make money. Luz Marina is the only member of the family to criticize his behavior: "¡Me tienes llena! [. . .] Yo trabajo mañana, tarde y noche. Y tú, ¿qué haces todo el día? Fumar y tomar café. Y por la noche, lo otro" (287) [I've had it up to here! [. . .] I work day in and day out. And you? What do you do all day? Smoke and have coffee. And at night that other thing]. Her constant, vociferous disapproval of his infidelities unnerves him:

> Angel. (*Dando un puñetazo contra la mesa.*) Eres una descastada. Maldita sea la hora en que te hicimos. (*A Ana.*) Desde el día primero volveré a tomar la dirección de esta casa. El dueño de esta casa soy yo, Angel Romaguera. Y sé lo que tengo que hacer. (301)

> [Angel. (*Pounding his fist on the table.*) You're a cold-hearted girl. I curse the day we made you. (*To Ana.*) Starting on the first I'll take charge of this house again. I, Angel Romaguera, am the master of this house. And I know what I have to do.]

Nevertheless, Luz Marina's quick wit always matches Angel's attempt to assert his authority. For example, when Oscar asks her if she would like to accompany him to Jacinto Benavente's play *La malquerida* [The Passion Flower], she takes the opportunity to embarrass her father by pointedly mentioning some of the details of the plot, such as the incestuous relationship between the stepfather and his much younger stepdaughter.[18] For all of Angel's verbal threats of abuse, Luz Marina's intelligence and economic contribution to the household render him powerless.

Luz Marina also distinguishes herself from her father by her realist outlook on life. While she may occasionally be swept up in lottery fever, she keeps her dreams small. The fact that Luz Marina's hope of owning a fan is a far-flung fantasy highlights the absurdity of her middle-class family's poverty. Her father, on the other hand, has grandiose plans for recuperating lost property and striking it rich in the business of selling toilets that vary according to the size of their owners. He tells his family that they will soon be swimming in gold, but Luz Marina writes to her brother in Argentina that "Yo creo que vamos a nadar en otra cosa" (341) [I think we're going to end up swimming in something else]. Angel defends his dreams but notes that his children always criticize his quixotic plans. From his perspective, the younger generation "es demasiado realista" (323) [is too realistic]. Consequently, it has settled for a cynically apathetic outlook with little faith in justice and the government. For instance, when Angel insists that the family's land will be restituted because "La Justicia es una sola, y está de parte nuestra" (343) [There's only one Justice and it's on our side], Luz Marina bursts into laughter. She rebels by distrusting all institutions, particularly the government, the family, and the church.

Luz Marina laughingly refers to her troubled family as "La Sagrada Familia" (378) [The Sacred Family]. Luz Marina's and Oscar's irreverent *choteo*-like attitude, which serves as an escape or strategy to cope with unpleasant realities, clashes with their parents' religious faith. For example, responding to a letter from Oscar, Luz Marina commiserates: "¿Así que en tercera viajaban ochenta monjas y veinte curas? ¿Y más de cien niños? Viejo, eso es peor que el infierno" (341) [So, there were eighty nuns, twenty priests, and more than one hundred children riding in third class? Brother, that sounds worse than hell]. While this probably will provoke a laugh from her brother, their mother automatically reprimands her: "Luz Marina, déjate de faltas de respeto con la religión" (341) [Luz Marina, don't disrespect religion]. On a more serious note, the lack of faith of the children's generation reveals their fatalism. Angel and Ana's religious beliefs have helped them to endure difficult times, but now the children have no hope and have become numb to misfortune. As Luz Marina tells her father: "Dios aprieta y Dios ahoga, papá. [. . .] Antes me desesperaba, ponía el grito en el cielo. Ahora: a otra cosa mariposa" (348) [God tightens his grip and suffocates us, Dad. [. . .] This used to cause me great despair, and I would blame God. But now I think: let's move on]. Luz Marina's rejection of religion also relates to her desire to distinguish herself from Ana, a model of the long-suffering mother who finds refuge in religion.

Neither her father nor her mother provides the kind of family model Luz Marina wishes to emulate. She resents her father for his mistreatment of her mother, but she also blames Ana for her passivity. Admissions such as "Seguiré sufriendo en silencio" (295) [I will continue to suffer in silence] and "Yo estoy resignada; que sea lo que Dios quiera" (303) [I am resigned; I accept God's will] define Ana as the martyred mother par excellence. Ana is the family peacemaker who smoothes over any unpleasantness to maintain the facade of a harmonious household. She rarely complains in front of the men of the house, but she does confide in Luz Marina. Her daughter, nevertheless, vocally opposes her mother's capacity for self-abnegation and flatly rejects her mother's loyalty: "eres tan boba que lo sigues adorando: que a Angel no le falten los cigarros, que no salga sin la peseta en el bolsillo. [...] No hablemos más de este asunto. Ya tengo parado el desayuno en la boca del estómago" (296) [you are foolish enough to keep adoring him: you make sure Angel has his cigarettes, you don't let him leave without some money in his pocket. [...] Let's not talk about this anymore. I already feel sick to my stomach]. Luz Marina is the family's voice of dissent. She challenges her father verbally, rejects her mother's defeatist disposition, and is the most expressive critic of her family's economic crisis.

Luz Marina's defiance is not all just talk, though, for she also acts rebelliously. She, not the patriarch, supports the family economically by sewing and tutoring. In addition, unlike her father and her brother Enrique, Luz Marina appreciates and supports Oscar's artistic goals. Most notably, she departs from the typical patterns set for young women with her attitude toward marriage. When her mother chides her for rejecting suitors, Luz Marina retorts that she would rather join a convent than endure the kind of relationship her parents have. Eventually she becomes fed up with the burden of supporting the family and with her lack of liberty, and in a sudden defiant gesture, she marries at the age of forty-four. Montes Huidobro suggests that Luz Marina hesitates to marry for so long because she is in love with Oscar (*Teatro cubano* 181). This would help to explain why she finally marries while he is in Argentina. A more plausible explanation, however, is that Luz Marina hesitates to marry simply because she does not want to become her mother. Moreover, it is widely known that Piñera was gay and that the play is on one level autobiographical. Oscar's exile to Argentina probably has more to do with his repressed homosexuality than an incestuous relationship with his sister. By marrying, Luz Marina does not escape financial woes, but she does manage to shock the family. It is probable that the *guagüero* [bus driver] with whom she chooses to spend the rest of her life is black, and most certainly from her family's perspective, the liaison represents a step down in class. With her husband, however, she enjoys the freedom of riding along in his bus and accompanying him to baseball games. Luz Marina knows this upsets her mother, but she tells Oscar: "¡Qué le vamos a hacer! Ella hizo su vida; yo tenía que hacer el pedazo de vida que me queda" (365) [What can we do? She made her own life and I had to make mine out of what little was left].

Yet as much as Luz Marina sets herself apart from her parents, her rebellion does not move beyond the confines of the family. As she tells her mother, "Nos pasamos la vida hablando del calor, pero no nos atrevemos a poner los puntos sobre las íes. Y entretanto, nos vamos muriendo poco a poco" (304) [We spend our lives talking about the heat, but we never dare to dot the i's. And in the meantime we're dying bit by bit]. The play implies that for Cuba to break out of a cycle of social, economic, and political crises, the family must also change. The Romagueras, however, are trapped in a downward spiral, and their sense of entrapment exemplifies society's stagnation. Rosa Ileana Boudet affirms that one of the technical achievements of the play is the realization of a static, timeless time that helps communicate the oppressive atmosphere of the Romaguera family home ("Concreción" 15). In my view, this effect is achieved through the irregular passage of time between acts; ten years may have passed or just one. The same holds true within the acts; seven days or two years may have passed between scenes. This has a disorienting effect on the spectator and creates the sensation that historical progress has been suspended. The repetitive nature of the dialogue also contributes to a sense of timelessness. As Enrique points out, and as the spectator soon notices, his conversations with Luz Marina concerning his financial contribution to the family are virtually identical over the course of almost two decades: "Luz Marina, por favor . . . Eres inmutable como las pirámides. No veo el momento de verte poner otro tema sobre el tapete" (379) [Luz Marina, please . . . you're as immutable as the pyramids. I can't see you ever bringing up another topic]. In addition, nothing in the home's decor alters in eighteen years other than the lightbulbs, visually reminding the audience that nothing significant has changed for the family. As Oscar sums it up: "Siempre vuelvo al punto de donde partí" (366) [I always come back to the point where I started].

Although the entire play takes place in the *sala-comedor* (the central room of the house), family members and visitors enter and exit freely. As in *Lila, la mariposa,* this limitation of space does not literally trap the family; rather, how the characters express their perceptions of their world creates climate of oppression. The motif of the heat provides the most evident example. The first line of the play, Luz Marina's exclamation, "¡Qué calor! (*Pausa.*) ¡Qué caloor!" (277) [It's hot! (*Pause.*) It's sooo hot!], sets a paralyzing mood for the whole play. The heat helps create the play's static quality by being a perennial source of conversation for the family and neighbors. The immobilizing heat also contributes to the absurdity of the Romagueras' circumstances, that is, the fact that they have sweltered in growing poverty for eighteen years with no real change. In moments of great frustration, the characters express outright that they feel trapped by their situation. Angel feels "acorralado" (345) [cornered], Ana says she is "encerrada" (316) [confined], and Luz Marina swears she will not have her family see her "sepultada entre estas cuatro paredes" (360) [buried inside these four walls].

The heat signifies a particularly asphyxiating moment in Cuban history, and on a more general level it serves as a metaphor of Cuba's insular, tropical identity. In the following dialogue, Luz Marina's complaint about the heat reveals a consciousness of Cuba's place in the world and a sense of national identity:

> Pero no estoy en París, estoy en La Habana, donde todo quema. El otro día por poco sí me cocino en la guagua. Me tocó el asiento de atrás. Aire caliente por debajo, por arriba. Y cuando llego a esta cochina casa, arroz con frijoles bien caliente. (*Pausa.*) ¿Que me queda a estas alturas? Morirme cocinada. (280)

> [But I'm not in Paris, I'm in Havana, where everything burns. The other day I was almost cooked alive on the bus. I got stuck with the backseat. Hot air coming out from below and above. And when I got home to this dirty house, rice and beans, nice and hot. What's left for me at this point? To die, cooked.]

Heat does indeed kill, and Angel's announcement that three hundred people in India have died from it provokes a typically irreverent Cuban response from Luz Marina: "Me parece perfecto. Calores que matan de verdad y de golpe. Esos indios hacen las cosas en grande. (*Pausa.*) Pero aquí, el calor no te mata (lo que sería una solución) pero tampoco te deja vivir" (281) [I think that's perfect. Heat that really kills with a bang.

Those Indians go all out. (*Pause.*) But here, the heat doesn't kill you (which would be a solution) but it doesn't let you live either]. The heat metaphor supports the play's point that for characters like Luz Marina and Oscar, who challenge traditional constructions of gender and sexuality, Cuban culture is oppressive.

The misery of the heat binds the Romagueras and the nation together, but the family photograph taken near the end of the play in honor of Angel and Ana's fiftieth wedding anniversary is an empty representation of a united family on a supposedly celebratory day. Behind the static photograph of the happy family lies another story of the chaos of arranging the blind family patriarch, the sickly matriarch, and their deaf son, Luis (visiting from New York), along with the rest of the siblings and spouses, to pose for the photographer. The family is even uncomfortable being together in close physical proximity, and the photographer repeatedly has to tell them to gather closer to one another for the photograph. This brief moment of false unity cracks as Ana agonizes on her deathbed seven days later and the children argue over their father's future and the details of their mother's wake. Oscar ends the argument, and the play, on a noncooperative note: "Parecemos salvajes. ¿Es que olvidan que la pobre mamá está allí agonizando? (*Pausa.*) Bueno, hagan lo que quieran" (398) [We're like savages. Have you forgotten that our poor mother is agonizing over there? (*Pause.*) Oh well, do whatever you want]. In contrast to the family photograph, *Aire frío* concludes with the silent visual image of the siblings moving in opposite directions toward different rooms.

In the end, Luz Marina does get the cold air she so desperately yearns for in the form of a fan (provided by Enrique) to comfort Ana during her last days. But as Montes Huidobro eloquently points out: "el aire del ventilador no será ciertamente vivificante y llegará demasiado tarde, para confundirse con el aire frío de la muerte" (*Teatro cubano* 177) [the air produced by the fan certainly won't revive and will arrive too late, only to be mistaken for the cold air of death]. I would argue that the cold air of death still signifies relief, in the sense that with Ana's death the household will crumble and perhaps make way for the birth of a new sort of family. On another level, her death, which takes place in the summer of 1958, represents the demise of the Cuban Republic. As I have suggested, the patriarchal family is just one more component in a landscape of faltering institutions. In Luz Marina, and to some extent in all of her siblings, however, we witness an impulse to live their lives differently than their parents, a change that bodes well for the country's future. Luz Marina, especially, works to form an identity that departs from the traditional definition of woman. In this sense, she seeks a different way to be Cuban. Indeed, as we will see in Abelardo Estorino's play *El robo del cochino*, her rebellion against parental authority augurs the massive transformation of the Cuban family/nation that will come with the Revolution.

To Rob the Pig: A Cuban Housecleaning

Abelardo Estorino (b. 1925) left a career in dental surgery to become a professional writer after the 1959 Revolution. Many consider Estorino Cuba's most important contemporary playwright because for over twenty years he has continued to write and produce plays within the revolutionary context. Estorino began his career in the 1960s writing a series of realist plays that focus on machismo in the provincial Cuban family. As in *Aire frío*, the treatment of gender roles in Estorino's *El robo del cochino* (1961) suggests that change in relations between the sexes constitutes one of the major renovations needed in the Cuban family. In the 1980s, Estorino broke with his illusionist style by employing intertexts and metatheater in plays such as *Ni un sí ni un no* [No arguments] (1980) and *Morir del cuento* [To die from the story] (1983). George Woodyard points out, however, that Estorino's works have retained common thematic concerns: "family units and marital issues, the need for openness, fairness and above all, equality in human relationships" (62).

In *El robo del cochino*, Estorino's most popular play, the tensions within a provincial family reach a crisis point when the supposed theft of a pig links the household to a national conflict: the incipient Cuban Revolution. *El robo* plays out the generational conflict primarily between Cristóbal, a landowner who has scaled the socioeconomic ladder, and his twenty-year-old son, Juanelo. Cristóbal refuses to intervene on behalf of a *guajiro* (a Cuban peasant) who works on his land and is falsely accused of stealing a pig, thus causing an irreparable rift between father and son. By the end of the dramatic action, Cristóbal and his wife, Rosa, have come to embody everything Juanelo rejects in favor of the Revolution. While the youth of the nation moves toward the future, Cristóbal and Rosa represent a generation trapped by the retroactive social conventions of provincial society and the fear of losing their status. By rejecting the models of behavior and ideologies of his parents, Juanelo distinguishes himself from them and implicitly asserts his desire for a more just and egalitarian society.

Unlike Ferrer and Piñera, who made an impact on Cuban drama during the Republican period, Estorino's dramaturgy is a product of the Cuban Revolution. *El robo* thus reflects the revolutionary optimism of the period. *Lila, la mariposa* and *Aire frío,* in contrast, given the frustrated and skeptical climate of the Batista regime in which they were written, contain more ambiguous generational conflicts than plays written during the Revolution's euphoric first years. The desire for change in Cuba highlighted in Ferrer's and Piñera's plays does not necessarily translate into revolution. The dramatic action of *El robo,* in contrast, takes place during the summer of 1958, the very moment the Cuban Revolution began to move toward victory. The problems of Cuban society depicted in the earlier plays reappear in *El robo,* but here the younger generation breaks free of the stifling parental influence because the Revolution provides them with support and direction.

The action of *El robo* transpires in a small town in the province of Matanzas during one day. Rodríguez, who has worked for Cristóbal for years, arrives with the news that his son, Tavito, has been taken away by the Rural Police for stealing a pig. The fact that Juanelo is home because the university in Havana has been closed due to political unrest and that Cristóbal refuses to help free Tavito reveals the tense climate of the summer of 1958.[19] In the second act, underlying family conflicts come to a head as the crisis with Tavito intensifies. Juanelo witnesses an argument between his parents in which he learns unpleasant details about their relationship. Rodríguez interrupts the quarrel when he bursts in to report that the Rural Police plans to take Tavito to the provincial capital. Although everyone understands that this signifies Tavito's torture and possible death, Cristóbal again refuses to help, especially when the real motive for Tavito's persecution becomes apparent. Tavito's family has aided a wounded university student obviously implicated in revolutionary activities. Rodríguez pleads for Cristóbal's help, hoping the landowner's high-level connections in the community will free Tavito. The act ends with Juanelo's defiant decision to accompany Rodríguez to the jail.

In the meantime, Juanelo's relationship with a woman involved in the revolutionary movement has prompted him to examine his family's beliefs and, by extension, the ideology of his social class. Throughout the play, he becomes increasingly contentious with how his father handles the situation with Tavito, and in the third act father and son finally confront each other. In the middle of their discussion, Lola, the family's servant, arrives and announces that the Rural Police has killed Tavito. No longer able to tolerate his family's policy of nonintervention, Juanelo abandons the house to join the revolutionaries. As Emilio Bejel argues, the play's open ending makes the audience the object of its revolutionary agenda, inviting it to participate in the revolutionary process (69). By involving the audience, Estorino underscores the inseparability of family and nation in *El robo*. Just as Juanelo rejects his father, the play calls for the audience to reject Cuba's Republican past and to join in the Revolution.

One of the play's weak points, however, is the separation of the private family space of the house, where the entire play takes place, from the public spaces of the town. Critics have noted that dialogue dominates scenic action and that rather than showing what happens, the characters recount action (Montes Huidobro, *Teatro cubano* 268; Castagnino 241). I would argue that this is due to an unbalanced use of theatrical space. According to Hanna Scolnicov, in realist theater characters typically "congregate in the family drawing-room coming from far-off places, thereby complicating the plot that is developing in the perceived space" (*Woman's Theatrical Space* 91).[20] In Estorino's play, the opposite is true. The plot that develops in the conceived space—what the audience does not see—instigates the family conflict in the perceived space, which the audience sees onstage. The family conflict and the national conflict become intertwined, but the audience never sees what happens outside of the living room. Key events that occur outside of the home lose dramatic effect because the characters' dialogue fails to construct this space vividly. Given the effect Tavito's crisis has on the family, the play could have been more powerful by making visible onstage some of the events involved in the arrest. This would have provided more spatial balance to reflect the connections between the private and public conflicts that the plot elaborates.

Nevertheless, the play's spatial disunity creates the sense that while the nation outside is on the verge of major upheaval, nothing inside the house changes. Circumspect references to "la cosa"—the shortages of meat, electricity outages, and the closing of the university—indicate a growing national chaos that contrasts with the static atmosphere of the house. The house comes to be identified with traditional paternalist agrarian Cuba, a world that the Revolution is about to transform. This world belonged to Don Gregorio, Rosa's father, who had lost his fortune by the time she married. As Cristóbal puts it, "Mucho título, mucho respeto, mucha servilleta en la mesa, pero cuando se murió, ésta no cogió ni un kilo" (61) [He had a nice title, a lot of respect, a lot of class, but when he died, she didn't get a thing]. The large house and its contents, particularly the furniture and Don Gregorio's silver-topped walking canes, however, constitute signs that communicate to the audience power and tradition. Cristóbal provided the family with more capital but resented having to live in a home he never felt was really his, with a father-in-law who made him feel inferior. Yet as a self-made man, Cristóbal is trapped by his desire for the prestige that the house and all its contents bring him. From Rosa's perspective, Cristóbal should not feel burdened by her family's lineage; after all, he spends most of his time outside of the house, whereas she is always "aquí, con estas paredes y estos muebles, que son los mismos de siempre" (82) [here, with the same walls and furniture as always]. Rosa's reply to Cristóbal's suggestion that she change the furniture underscores how important her home is to her sense of identity: "No, son los muebles de mi casa, donde se sentó mi padre. ¿Qué me queda entonces?" (82) [No, this is the furniture that belongs in my house, the house where my father established himself. What else do I have?]. Rosa, then, is equally caught up in her need to maintain family heritage.

The house and the values it embodies are precisely what the play suggests the Revolution would like to make obsolete. Any kind of change, from the way women and men relate to each other to a new class structure, threatens Cristóbal's position in society. Cristóbal is an authoritarian figure who tries to instill fear in his employees and is impatient and demanding with his wife. Cristóbal tells his own son that he is not suited to work on their land: "tratas a la gente con una confianza desde el primer día ¡que te pierden el respeto!" (57) [you treat people from the first day on with such familiarity that they lose their respect for you!]. Moreover, by refusing to help Rodríguez, Cristóbal breaks the typical paternalist relationship that characterizes the agrarian sector. Puzzled, Rodríguez remarks that he has worked for him for many years, but Cristóbal's response shows he feels no protective bond with the *guajiro:* "Está bien. Hemos hecho negocio. Tú trabajas y yo te pago" (87) [All right. We've done business together. You work and I pay you]. Although Cristóbal aspires to have the prestige of a Don Gregorio, he embodies a shift from the landowning patriarchs of the past, who saw themselves as fatherly caretakers of the nation, to a self-serving upper-middle class.

Cristóbal never establishes a paternalist relationship with his workers because he suffers from a complex from having earned his authority by illegitimate means. Unlike Don Gregorio, who was born into the upper class, Cristóbal had to work his way up to gain respect and social standing. His constant explanations as to how he arrived at this point in his life reveal his insecurities. Even though he now occupies Don Gregorio's powerful position, he feels like an impostor, and when he confesses to his son that he climbed the social ladder in part by stealing—"Pues robé, ¡coño!, tuve que robar o me aplastaban. Si no, no había forma de salir de aquella mierda" (99) [So I stole, damn it! It was either that or be crushed. If I hadn't done it there would have been no way to get out of that shit]—he all but admits that his claim to power is illicit. Consequently, he has a defensive philosophy of life: "Hay que pelear todos los días. Cuando te levantas por la mañana tienes que pensar, ¿contra quién estoy hoy?" (101) [You have to fight everyday. When you get up in the morning you have to ask yourself, who am I up against today?]. In Cristóbal's opinion, the best way to defend his land and home is absolute independence: "Cada cual a lo suyo, a su trabajo, a su familia, deja el mundo correr" (74) [Everyone should attend to his own business: his own work, his own family and just let the rest of the world go by]. While he is not a supporter of the Batista regime, Cristóbal believes if Tavito is in trouble, he brought it upon himself by becoming involved in the opposition movement. The play's message, however, is that one must take sides, as Juanelo does by rejecting his parents' ideologies.

Juanelo begins as an unformed character whose own personality takes shape as he begins to distance himself from his father. In the beginning of the play, there is considerable emphasis on the similarities between father and son. As Rosa's friend comments, they look alike: "¡Es igualito a su padre ese muchacho! De ti no sacó nada" (66) [That boy is identical to his father! He didn't get anything from you]. Juanelo flatters Cristóbal's vanity by pointing out that they seem like brothers and that he attracts female attention on the streets (58–59). Although Juanelo is different from his father in that he is not destined to become a *patrón*, he seems to have adopted some of his father's mannerisms and *machista* behavior.

Lola complains: "¡Eres igual que tu padre, pone los pies donde quiera y después tiene uno que estar pasando la bayeta, no se acaba nunca!" (75) [You're just like your father, he puts his feet up wherever he wants, and then one has to clean up after him, it never ends!]. Reminiscing about the past, Cristóbal defensively labels one of Rosa's potential suitors "la mariquita" [the fairy], partly because he played the piano but mostly because he felt threatened by the other man's social status. When Rosa shows Juanelo a picture of herself and "la mariquita," father and son laugh hysterically, driving Rosa to tear up the photograph. In a later scene, Rosa reveals the hurt she feels from her complete exclusion from the pair: "Qué bien se llevan, qué bien se llevan. Todo el mundo venía a decirlo, ¡qué bien se llevan! Parecen hermanos, no parecen padre e hijo (84) [They get along so, so well. Everybody ends up saying it. How great they get along! They seem more like brothers than father and son].

As Bejel and Bravo Elizondo have stated, the affirmation of Juanelo's identity is contingent upon the symbolic death of his father (Bejel 67; Bravo Elizondo 91). The disagreement over how to handle the incident with Tavito is the most obvious catalyst for Juanelo's transformation, but his changing relationship with women is another influential factor in this process, which highlights Juanelo's growing social consciousness as well as the development of more active roles for women in Cuban society. Throughout the play, he has contact with women representative of different backgrounds. Rosa, for example, has been greatly influenced by the Catholic Church's role model for women, the Virgin Mary. Like Ana in *Aire frío*, abnegation, spirituality, and asexuality characterize motherhood for Rosa.[21] She is completely alienated from her husband and son's close relationship and finds solace only in the memory of her daughter who died eighteen years earlier. Rosa's domain is the house, where she spends so much time that her servant, Lola, comments that before she started to work there: "Cuando pasaba, yo decía, esta mujer debe estar enferma. Yo jamás la he visto a usted en la calle" (53) [When I walked by, I always said, that woman must be sick because I never saw you in the street]. When Rosa does leave the house, it is only to attend mass and to visit her daughter's grave. Standing by the window, Rosa admits that she has spent her life as a spectator, waiting for a change that would make her life more fulfilling. As the play develops, Juanelo becomes increasingly aware of how such narrowly defined roles for wives and mothers might change with the Revolution.

El robo offers other models of womanhood that prophesy a more flexible vision of gender roles that the Revolution could provide. Although Lola is poor and may suffer from racial prejudice, on many levels she has far more freedom than Rosa. Unlike Rosa, who stands at the window listening to the music of a party outside, Lola stays out all night dancing. She enjoys the independence of living alone and refers to her latest relationship as "flor de un día" (75) [a short-lived affair]. Rather than denying the seriousness of Tavito's situation, Lola stands up to Cristóbal's frequent commands to "cállate" [shut up] by repeatedly condemning the Rural Police for its actions against the young man. She understands the implications of the changes taking place and tells Rosa that women have an important role in them: "En Santiago se reunieron un montón de mujeres y salieron. Vestidas de negro. ¡Y la policía no pudo con ellas!" (93) [In Santiago a bunch of women got together and went out on the street dressed in black. They police didn't know what to do with them!].

As a middle-class intellectual, Juanelo's girlfriend, Adela, also represents an alternative role for woman. Their relationship has scandalized the community because she is divorced, an older woman, and a professor who has had to leave Havana for political reasons. Adela is a major influence on Juanelo's growing awareness of the workings of race, class, and gender in his country. He tells Lola that with Adela he has learned to express himself and to examine the world in which he lives: "Ahora estoy mirándolo todo como si lo acabara de comprar. Como cuando el viejo trajo la maquina, que levanté el capó y lo miré todo hasta aprenderme cada tornillito" (77) [Now I'm looking at everything as if I had just bought it. Like when my old man brought the car and I lifted the hood and stared at everything until I memorized every last screw]. Not only has Juanelo begun to think about the relationships in his family, his new insights on life also have allowed him to make connections between people he would not ordinarily think have much in common. For example, he tells Lola that her self-confidence and independence remind him of Adela. In other words, the play communicates the idea that people like Lola (a black servant) and Adela (a white middle-class intellectual) must work together in joining the Revolution that will transform both of their lives for the better.

Juanelo's relationships with women other than his mother expand his view of gender roles in Cuban society. Thus the discovery that his mother has suffered in silence over Cristóbal's longtime *querida* [lover] helps him to define himself as different from his father. Juanelo has known about Cristóbal's infidelities, but he did not realize that his mother knew, nor did he understand the extent to which this other woman has been a part of Cristóbal's life until Rosa reveals that, as their baby daughter lay dying, she had to drag Cristóbal away from this woman. Cristóbal tries to explain his double life by blaming Rosa's piety: "Rosa estaba siempre en la iglesia. Y era muy bueno irme allá, a la otra casa y tirarme en camiseta y hacer cuentos y reírme" (86) [Rosa was always at church. So it was good for me to go there, to the other house, to sit back and relax in a T-shirt, tell stories, and laugh]. Given Juanelo's more enlightened understanding of gender roles, Cristóbal's explanation, based on the *machista* assumption that men can give free rein to their sexual instincts while their wives remain chaste, must seem dubious. Juanelo questions the supposed closeness of their relationship and reflects, "Si estamos . . . si andamos siempre juntos, ¿a qué viene eso ahora?" (86) [If we are . . . if we always hang out together, why are you bringing this up now?].

Juanelo's dismay at his father's treatment of Tavito finally provokes a confrontation during which he asserts his independence and *cubanía*, his will to be a different sort of Cuban than this father. Unlike Cristóbal, Juanelo no longer wishes to be a passive witness to the events going on around him. Cristóbal makes explicit his motives for refusing to help one of his laborers by asking: "¿Crees que voy a exponer todo lo que tengo por ese guajiro?" (96) [Do you think I'm going to risk everything I have for this peasant?]. At this point, Juanelo's disagreement with his father has gone far beyond the specific incident to include a fundamentally different outlook on life. He realizes that he has followed his father's footsteps much too closely: "¡Yo estaba detrás de ti! ¡Siempre detrás de ti! [. . .] Yo estaba mirando siempre con los ojos tuyos, con los ojos de ellos. Y muchas veces no me gustaba lo que estaba mirando. [. . .] Yo creo que nunca he dicho lo que pienso" (100–101) [I was always in your shadow, always! [. . .] I always saw with your eyes, with their eyes. And oftentimes I didn't like what I was seeing. [. . .] I don't think I've ever said what I think]. Juanelo, for the first time, criticizes Cristóbal's Machiavellian attitude and attachment to a vicious cycle of materialism: "Trabajas para tener, tener más, tener, siempre tener y tener. Lola disfruta más que tú, cualquiera disfruta más que tú" (96) [You work to have more and more, always to have, have, have. Lola enjoys life more than you do, everyone does]. In the end, Juanelo sides with the *guajiros* and Lola (the working class) and with his girlfriend (the middle class), choosing the Revolution over his father and his family's class interests.

Similar to *Lila, la mariposa*, in *El robo* a comment about the material condition of the family home points to the future course of action of the characters and the nation. Like Marino, who contemplates moving or at least painting the dirty walls of his home, Rosa exclaims several times throughout the play that the house is in need of a good cleaning, and the play ends with her remark: "Esta casa está que da asco" (103) [This house is in a disgusting state]. At this moment, unbeknownst to Rosa, her son is abandoning the house for that very reason—he finds the values that the house embodies "disgusting." Ironically, Rosa's suggestion takes place in the form of a revolution. Rather than interpreting the title *El robo del cochino* simply as a direct reference to Tavito's alleged crime, the act of robbery and the presence of pigs evoke other meanings as well. The title could just as easily refer to Cristóbal, the "pig" (materially greedy), and the "theft" to the Revolution that would seek to distribute the nation's wealth. He who robbed to climb the socioeconomic ladder is about to be robbed by the Revolution.[22] In this reading, Juanelo's separation from his family, especially from his father, becomes the play's central dramatic movement. After all, from Cristóbal's viewpoint, he has lost his son to the Revolution. The play's position, however, is that the benefits from a Cuban housecleaning outweigh the subsequent ruptured family relations. Juanelo's rejection of his father implies that a new society will demand a new family, one with more egalitarian relationships between men and women and with Cubans of different classes and racial backgrounds. The process of finding his own identity plays out a struggle between emergent and residual Cuban values that leads Juanelo (and the audience) to discover a revolutionary way to be Cuban.

"Hay que tumbar la casa": Collapsing the Generational Conflict

Four years after the successful rebellion against parental authority portrayed in *El robo del cochino*, José Triana's *La noche de los asesinos* (1966) presents children who repeatedly perform the societal roles they wish to destroy. Triana's play underscores the similarities between the parents' and the children's generations, suggesting that the Cuban family and nation after the Revolution is not so different after all. Triana's own experience as an artist during the postrevolutionary period also puts into question whether the Revolution ever freed Cubans from a cycle of authoritarian governments.

José Triana (b. 1933) began to write his first plays and some poetry while studying in Europe in the mid-1950s. Upon the defeat of the Batista regime in 1959, he returned to join the Revolution. He served as a literary adviser to the Consejo Nacional de Cultura and the publishing house Letras Cubanas and began immediately to produce his plays. Triana's drama combines traditional Cuban forms with elements related to the theater of cruelty, ritual theater, and the theater of the absurd. *La noche de los asesinos* made him Cuba's best-known playwright internationally, and although the play won the 1965 Casa de las Américas prize, its ambiguous message led critics to question Triana's ideological stance. Along with playwrights Virgilio Piñera and Antón Arrufat, Triana was accused of privileging individual artistic commitment over political responsibility to the Revolution. Consequently, despite Triana's stature as one of Latin America's major playwrights, much of his work after 1966 remains unperformed in his home country.[23]

La noche is a metatheatrical two-act play in which three adult siblings, Lalo, Cuca, and Beba, repeatedly rehearse the murder of their parents in a squalid attic or basement.[24] The enigmatic nature of the play has created a critical debate over the meaning of the work, mainly over its position with regard to the Cuban Revolution. Because the dramatic action takes place in the 1950s, it can be interpreted as denouncing Batista's dictatorial regime and other institutions of power. Some, however, consider the play as a criticism of the revolutionary process itself, which imposed a new system of oppression.[25] *La noche* completes the cycle of plays discussed in this chapter in which the tension between parents and children manifests first prerevolutionary frustration, then revolutionary optimism, and finally the questioning of just what kind of new family the Revolution has actually created. *Cubanía* is present in all of the works, and the fact that Triana envisions *La noche* as "un estudio de nuestro carácter, de la personalidad, de la conducta" (Estorino, "Destruir" 6) [a study of our character, personality, and conduct] suggests that for some Cubans, the search for identity did not end with the Revolution. That is, although the Revolution ostensibly freed Cuba on a national (political and economic) level, some individuals struggled with the new definitions of what it was to be Cuban in a Marxist society. In *La noche*, through role-playing, Lalo, Cuca, and Beba parody the authoritarian constructs of the family and the judicial system. However, the children are unable to translate their parents' behavior into an identity that would distinguish them and in effect are trapped in the very roles and structures (embodied by the house) that they try to destroy. In this respect, the opposition between parents and children falls apart because the children's game indicates that they simply replace their parents and repeat their authoritarian behavior. Triana's play poses interesting questions about the possibilities of Cuba ever breaking away from a cycle of oppression and highlights the contradictions of revolution.

Beyond the collapse of generational conflict, the play blurs other types of dichotomies as well. Triana's text exemplifies *cubanía* and Cuba's translational aesthetic, for it constantly negotiates between models to fashion its own unique vision. The genesis of the play can explain in part the diversity of interpretations it has provoked. First, Triana began to write *La noche* as early as 1958, but he did not finish it until 1964.[26] In my view, this erases the opposition between the play's supposed pro- or counterrevolutionary stance. The richness of the play is precisely that it embodies both positions. From the perspective of 1958, *La noche* serves as a criticism of the oppressive Batista regime, and the children's quest to kill their parents is a necessary evil to achieve freedom. By 1964, however, Triana had witnessed the progressive institutionalization of the Revolution and was troubled by its authoritarianism; the children had begun to repeat the errors of their parents. In an interview, Triana explains that while no one in his generation wanted the return of the Republic, there was "un deseo de limpieza, de cambio real, verdadero, más profundo, pero con más tacto, con menos histeria, con menos represión" (Escarpanter 2–3) [a desire to cleanse, to effect real, profound change, but with more tact, less hysteria and less repression]. That is, if the play criticizes anything, it is the abuse of power, and this existed in both the pre- and postrevolutionary periods.[27]

What had started out as a simple "boceto en una forma muy naturalista de las relaciones familiares: la madre, el padre, los hijos, es decir, en un ambiente lo más real posible" (Estorino, "Destruir" 7) [naturalist sketch depicting familial relationships among a mother, father and children—that is—in the most real atmosphere imaginable], moreover, became a highly experimental piece in the style of Artaud's theater of cruelty. In the final product, the central theme of generational conflict remains the same, but the style for communicating the theme drastically changes. Again, due to the play's evolution, it is difficult to sustain one reading to the exclusion of another. The play does contain the seeds of a domestic drama, but in terms of structure and character development one could hardly interpret the play from a realist perspective. The theater of the period, however, was used as an instrument of the Revolution and as such demanded that the plays portray a recognizable social reality. In comparison to plays by Abelardo Estorino, Héctor Quintero, and José R. Brene from the early 1960s, Triana's work stands out for its lack of realism. Thus Triana expresses his concerns with the Revolution's use of power on both a thematic and aesthetic level. Not only is he in dialogue with the artistic tenets of the Revolution, he also underscores his relationship to the European avant-garde and "converts First World artistic products into vehicles for the expression of his own specific cultural and historical concerns" (Taylor, *Theatre* 66). In other words, *La noche* is a translational text that manipulates literary styles to express a singularly Cuban voice. Translation, the negotiation between two systems or models, necessarily implies the collapsing of dichotomies, both thematic (the play's stance on the Revolution) and stylistic. In the same vein, furthermore, the opposition between parents and children also disappears because in their attempt to reject the models of their parents, the children imitate them.

In *La noche,* therefore, Triana removes the family from the realist haven of the middle-class living room and places it in a marginal space of the attic or basement. The play's cyclical structure makes it impossible to sum up the dramatic action sequentially as one could a typical well-made play. In the first act, Lalo both directs and stars in the performance of the murder of his tyrannical parents. We never witness the crime because it never takes place; indeed, the children repeatedly rehearse the violent act as a ritual that they hope one day to translate into real action. The balance of power among the three siblings appears to be weighted in Lalo's favor as he forces his unwilling sisters to participate in the bloody game, but references to both past and future performances indicate that they alternate occupying the dominant position. Although only three actors appear onstage, with little warning, Lalo, Cuca, and Beba step into the roles of a variety of characters to create a more complete scenario of the murder that includes its motives and consequences. As a result, before the first act ends when Lalo symbolically stabs a table, the siblings enact the crime by rapidly assuming and then dropping the roles of their tyrannical parents, gossipy neighbors, police, and a newspaper vendor.

In the second act, Cuca takes control of the game. She and Beba play the part of the police and prosecutors who interrogate Lalo to force him to confess his crime. Although they are supposedly dead, the parents reappear to defend their treatment of the children. This time the siblings portray them as weak and petty, no longer the cruel oppressors depicted earlier. Similarly, the formerly defiant Lalo breaks down under his sisters' emotional taunting and pleads for love: "si el amor pudiera . . . Sólo el amor . . . Porque a pesar de todo, yo los quiero" (201) [if only love could do it . . . If only love. Because in spite of everything, I love them (81)]. The final line of the play—Beba's "Ahora me toca a mí" (201) [Now it's my turn (81)]—leaves the children's future open. Not knowing what Beba will do with her "turn" allows the audience some degree of hope; perhaps she will break free from the pitfalls of the victimizer/victim paradigm in which she and her brother and sister are trapped.

As Diana Taylor observes, *La noche* "gives us nothing to hold on to" in terms of orienting the audience in time and space (*Theatre* 68). The stage directions do indicate that the play takes place during the 1950s, but as for the play's internal action, it is impossible to determine a beginning and an end or even how long the characters have sequestered themselves in this peripheral space of the house. In this room, the audience sees an assortment of objects that could belong anywhere: a table and chairs, a vase, a dust rag, and a knife. No one enters or exits the rather mysterious space, and there is no verbal construction of an outside world that would help situate the house. Therefore, some critics do not associate the play with a specific sociohistorical context.[28] Despite the lack of contextual clues, however, the connection between family and nation becomes evident, particularly when we consider *La noche* in relation to the other plays discussed in this section. In *La noche*, we see the same expression of *cubanía* in the children's desire to assert their identity as well as the identification between the theatrical space of the house and the nation.

Priscilla Meléndez notes in her study of dramatic space in *La noche* that the oppressive space of the house has its parallel in the asphyxiating social, economic, and political order of Cuba of the 1950s ("El espacio" 29). I would add that the play extends the metaphor of the incarcerating house into the 1960s as well. If one considers the construction of theatrical space, *La noche* seems to undertake a dialogue with the 1961 revolutionary optimism of *El robo* and in fact picks up where Estorino's play left off. *El robo* ends with Rosa's comment about the filthiness of her home, and in Triana's play, the first reference to the house highlights its lack of cleanliness:

> Cuca. Deberías ayudarme. Hay que arreglar esta casa.
> Este cuarto es un asco. Cucarachas, ratones, polillas, ciempiés . . . el copón divino.
> Lalo. ¿Y tú crees que sacudiendo con un plumero vas a lograr mucho?
> Cuca. Algo es algo. (140)
> [Cuca. I want you to help me. We have to tidy up this house. The room is a pit. Cockroaches, rats, moths, caterpillars . . . the whole bloody lot.
> Lalo. How far do you think you're going to get with that duster?
> Cuca. It's a start. (32–33)]

If in *El robo* Juanelo abandoned his "casa asquerosa" [disgusting house] (the embodiment of so much that was wrong with Republican society) to join the Revolution, why does Triana, in 1966, imply that the house/nation still needs "cleaning"? *La noche* insinuates that either the Revolution did not do away with Republican "filth" or that it replaced it with a different set of problems: a new infestation of cockroaches, as Luz Marina from *Aire frío* would suggest.

The characters' management of the room's objects reflects different approaches to the nation's problems. Despite Cuca's insistence on maintaining order, Lalo takes command in the beginning of the play by demanding that certain household objects be moved. As Frank Dauster maintains, the desire to move the furniture represents "their need to make their own world, without prefabricated regulations" ("The Game" 182). The arrangement of the house represents the established order that Lalo desperately wants to destroy:

> Lalo. Tú no te das cuenta que lo que yo propongo es simplemente la única solución que tenemos. (*Coge la silla y la mueve en el aire.*) Esta silla, yo quiero que esté aquí. (*De golpe pone la silla en un sitio determinado.*) Y no aquí. (*De golpe coloca la misma silla en otro lugar determinado.*) [. . .] Papá y mamá no consienten estas cosas. Creen que lo que yo pienso y quiero hacer es algo que está fuera de toda lógica. Quieren que todo permanezca inmóvil, que nada se mueva de su sitio . . . (149)

[Lalo. You don't realise that what I am proposing is simply the only solution we have. (*Takes the chair and moves it about in the air.*) I want this chair to be here. (*He suddenly puts the chair down in a particular place.*) And not there. (*He suddenly moves the same chair to another particular place.*) [. . .] Dad and mum don't allow such things. They think that what I think and what I do are completely illogical. They want everything to stay where it is. Nothing must move from its proper place . . . (41)]

During his trial, Lalo explains that he had become obsessed with arranging the house his way and that voices (the house) demanded that he rebel: "La sala no es la sala, me decía. La sala es la cocina. El cuarto no es el cuarto" (190) [The living room is not the living room, I said to myself. The living room is the kitchen. The bedroom is not the bedroom (73)]. To impose his order on the house would not be enough, however, because he would continue to be haunted by his parents' image: "Si me sentaba en una silla, la silla no era la silla, sino el cadáver de mi padre. Si cogía un vaso de agua, sentía que lo que tenía entre las manos era el cuello húmedo de mi madre muerta" (191) [If I sat down in a chair, the chair wasn't the chair but my father's corpse. If I picked up a glass of water, I felt that what I had in my hands was my dead mother's damp neck (73)].

In the end, Beba, playing Lalo, calls for complete destruction of the house: "Hay que quitar las alfombras. Vengan abajo las cortinas. La sala no es la sala. [. . .] ¡Hay que tumbar esta casa!" (200) [Pull down the curtains. The living room is not the living room. [. . .] Tear this house down! (80)]. The other options, to continue to clean the house or to rearrange its furniture, signify working within the same problematic structures the Revolution has sought to destroy. The play also rejects the alternative of exile. To abandon the house is to go into exile, and, as Lalo mentions, he has tried to leave but feels too lost outside of the house. Ultimately, the house must be entirely dismantled; otherwise, there will always be discontent brewing in its basement and attic. In this respect, Taylor sees the play as a criticism of the Revolution: "The violent usurpation of political power did not guarantee social renovation. The challenge of the Revolution was to create a new system of power that would not reproduce the oppression and dependency of the ones before" (*Theatre* 79).

Beyond being trapped on a national level in a cycle of authoritarianism, it also seems doubtful that the children will reinvent themselves individually because they are not able to distinguish themselves from their parents.[29] Like the initial characterization of Marino in *Lila, la mariposa* and Juanelo in *El robo,* the siblings in *La noche* lack a strong sense of selfhood and a will to act. Unlike the children in the other plays, however, Lalo, Cuca, and Beba are undeveloped characters without unique psychologies, and they slip in and out of different identities (including each other's) with ease. In Lalo's opinion, they are like interchangeable objects: "¿Qué importa esta casa, qué importan estos muebles si nosotros no somos nada, si nosotros simplemente vamos y venimos por ella y entre ellos igual que un cenicero, un florero o un cuchillo flotante?" (150) [Who cares about this house, who cares about this furniture if we ourselves are nothing, if we simply pass through the house and between the furniture, just like an ashtray, a vase, or a floating knife? (41)]. If the siblings ever bring their game to completion, they will secure at least one identity: as assassins. But, as Beba points out, they keep going in circles, caught in their own game: "Vine aquí a ayudarlos o a divertirme. Porque no sé qué hacer. . . . Vueltas y más vueltas . . . Uno parece un trompo" (155) [I came here to help you and to have fun. Because I don't know what else to do. . . . Spinning round and round . . . one seems like a top]. The murder ritual traps them in a cyclical pattern that provokes frustration and an even stronger sense of oppression than what they claim to suffer at the hands of their parents. At times they become so wound up they snap and break away from the game: "Quiero explotar. Quiero irme. Pero no soporto este encierro. Me ahogo" (164) [I want to explode. I want to go. I can't stand being shut in. I'm suffocating].

Parricide is an extreme measure for Lalo, Cuca, and Beba to free themselves from their parents. The characterization of the parents is contradictory, and because they only appear through the eyes of the children, it is not very reliable. On the one hand, the play portrays the parents as tyrants who physically and verbally abuse their children. Lalo, as his father, barks: "Lava los platos, lava los manteles, lava las camisas. Limpia el florero, limpia el orinal, limpia los pisos. No duermas, no sueñas, no leas" (187) [Wash the dishes, wash the tablecloths, wash the shirts. Clean the vase, clean the bathroom, clean the floors. Don't sleep, don't dream, don't read (70)]. Later, as himself, Lalo details to the judge how his parents psychologically and physically abused him. On the other hand, the mother defends herself as one who sacrificed everything for her family: "Señor juez, si usted supiera las lágrimas que he derramado, las humillaciones que he recibido, las horas de angustia, los sacrificios. . ." (193) [Your Honour, if you knew the tears I have shed, the humiliation I have suffered, the hours of anguish, the sacrifices. . . (75)]. All in all, the parents come off more as hypocrites, disillusioned with each other and their bourgeois aspirations, than as tyrannical monsters. There is enough evidence to explain why their progeny do not want to see themselves in their image but even more to suggest that they are doomed to do so.

In their search for self-definition and in the course of the murderous game, Lalo, Cuca, and Beba try on a variety of roles, none of them very original. As Román de la Campa observes, the children play these parts "para parodiarlos y caracterizar sus valores de clase. De este modo, las figuras autoritarias que se imponen en sus vidas [. . .] simbolizan caricaturas de la sociedad" (27) [to parody them and to characterize their class values. In this way, the imposing authoritarian figures in their lives [. . .] symbolize caricatures of society]. For example, the children parody the conventions of a neighborly social visit by making small talk about typically unmentionable health problems. Lalo, for instance, asks: "(*Con sonrisa hipócrita.*) Usted, Margarita, se ve de lo mejor. ¿Le sigue creciendo el fibroma?" (146) [(*With a hypocritical smile.*) Margaret, you're looking *terrific*. Is that cancerous growth of yours still growing? (38)]. Equally humorous is the sibling's portrayal of the police who investigate their crime. Alternately bumbling and abusive, the police, who seem to relish imagining the bloody details of the murder, triumphantly pronounce hackneyed lines from a by-the-numbers police pursuit. In a similar way, the children parody judicial discourse by exaggerating it. Cuca's theatrical opening argument as a *fiscal* is a barrage of rhetorical questions: "¿Puede y debe burlarse a la justicia? ¿La justicia no es la justicia? Si podemos burlarnos de la justicia, ¿la justicia no deja de ser la justicia?" (182) [is he permitted to make fun of the Law? Should he make fun of the Law? Is not the Law the Law? If we are *permitted* to make fun of the Law, does the Law stop being the Law? (66)]. Finally, the children also mock the institution of marriage. They parody their parents' marriage by representing the bride (played by Lalo) and groom's hypocritical prenuptial conversation: "Sonríete. Ahí están el canchanchán del doctor Núñez, y su mujer . . . ¿Tú crees que la gente lleve la cuenta de los meses que tengo? Si se enteran, me moriría de vergüenza. Mira, te están sonriendo las hijas de Espinosa . . . esas pu . . ." (165) [Smile. There's that creep Dr. Nuñez and his wife . . . Do you think people are counting the months? If they find out, I'll die of embarrassment. Look, Espinosa's daughters are smiling at you, those sluts . . . (53)]. These scenes, which seem to be parodic bits of the realist drama Triana began to write inserted into the disorienting world of the ritual game, construct a picture of the society the children reject. Making fun of existing social roles, however, does not guarantee their subversion or the subsequent creation of more viable ones.

The process of creating their own voice is thwarted because the children are trapped in the very roles they despise. In her theory of parody, Linda Hutcheon points out that the prefix "para" from the Greek noun *parodia* can have two opposite meanings, "counter" or "beside" (*A Theory* 32). There is always a model involved in parody that usually is repeated with critical distance to mark difference rather than similarity (Hutcheon, *A Theory* 6). In *La noche*, rather than "countering"—that is, deconstructing—the social roles, parody traps the children "beside" or "in" those very roles. Furthermore, Richard Hornby writes that in drama, when a character takes on another role, ironically, the role is often "closer to the character's true self than his everyday, 'real' personality" (67). Lalo, Cuca, and Beba's "real" personalities are but fragments, and they lose themselves in other identities rather easily. While their intent is to reject their parents, the neighbors, and the justice system through caricature, we never see them act outside of these models of behavior. We see Lalo, Cuca, and Beba either as siblings in a power struggle over their murder ritual or as members of a society they detest. Parodic role-playing in this work functions conservatively in that rather than providing models that the children "translate"—that is, recast to develop their own identities— it retains the children within certain patterns.

Parody and its limitations can also be related to the culturally specific Cuban phenomenon of *choteo*. *Choteo*, similar to parody, seeks a target to ridicule.[30] The *choteo*-like characteristics of the children's game troubled Vicente Revuelta, the director of the original 1966 production of *La noche*. He cites the scenes in which the mother complains about her pregnancy as the *choteo* of Lalo's very birth and life (Estorino, "Destruir" 12). For Revuelta, the mockery of a very serious occasion such as Lalo's birth is but one form of *choteo* that "entre nosotros en toda una época ha sido una cosa terrible, porque en definitiva anulaba—como se ve en la obra— la acción]" (Estorino, "Destruir" 13) [for us has been a terrible thing during an entire period, because it definitively annulled action, as can be seen in the play]. He also recognizes that in revolutionary Cuba, *choteo* was likely to evolve and that its destructive instinct might have more positive results if aimed at objects worthy of scorn (Estorino, "Destruir" 13). In the end, the play itself represents a *choteo* of the very concept of revolution. The Cuban Revolution attempted an abrupt, radical change on social, political, and economic levels, but the play foregrounds the concept in terms of revolving, or completing a cycle. Revolutions both require and cultivate a sharp contrast between past and present, and in Triana's play the children, like the spinning tops with which Beba identifies, endlessly repeat the victimizer/victim relationship they share with their parents.

In *La noche,* Triana constructs a complex representation of the Cuban family and nation by employing "translational" techniques that demand multiple readings from the reader/spectator. Consequently, Triana's investigation of the Cuban character was decidedly unpopular from the viewpoint of the Revolution because it blurred the dichotomies revolutionary ideologies require to sustain themselves. *La noche* breaks down the oppositions between Cuba's Republican past (the parents' generation) and revolutionary Cuba's present (the children). On an aesthetic level, the play mixes realism and experimentalism, making its meanings difficult to ascertain and perhaps less vulnerable to censorship. From the play's perspective, the conflict between generations collapses because the rebellious children have become the oppressive parents of a new generation.[31] As Martin indicates, this position was not popular with the Revolution: "The metaphor of an incarcerating family could be appropriate for those disaffected by the Revolution or its development, but this insular focus did not seem in keeping with the orientation of those who now constituted the theatrical (and political) public in Cuba" (156). The conflict between generations, from a prerevolutionary standpoint, became increasingly irrelevant in the new revolutionary society. After all, the past supposedly had been destroyed by the Revolution. *La noche,* in contrast, suggests that the children were unable to create a revolutionary family free from the oppression that characterized Cuba's Republican family.

With Triana's *La noche de los asesinos,* the family play in Cuba has come full circle. In the mid-1950s, in works such as *Lila, la mariposa* by Ferrer and *Aire frío* by Piñera, family dynamics between parents and children serve as a tool to discuss national problems, specifically, the struggle for Cubans to break free from a stifling neocolonial society. With Estorino's 1961 *El robo del cochino,* the generational conflict clearly becomes an allegory of the Revolution. In all three plays, escaping parental authority and the oppressive space of the family home imply the restructuring of what constitutes a family and how roles for men and women are defined. By 1966, *La noche de los asesinos* raised doubts as to whether the Cuban Revolution effectively reconfigured the family/ nation. Viewed jointly, these plays make manifest how Cuban theater from the mid-1950s to the mid-1960s exerted pressure toward social change by providing a special site for national self-reflection. By means of performing familial disharmony, Cuban drama contests any nationalist rhetoric that might construe the population as an essential or united "gran familia cubana." Moreover, the *cubanía* manifested in drama as generational conflicts adds another layer to the transcultural character of Cuban identity as conceptualized by Ortiz and Pérez Firmat. As Triana states, it is Cuba's transformational qualities that create its unique identity: "Nuestro pueblo sigue como caminado por su propio paso, casi aéreo, que va y se transforma, vuela, entra en otras naciones, parece que se deshace y vuelve y se reincorpora" (Escarpanter 10) [Our nation travels on at its own pace, almost aerial; it goes and transforms itself, it sails, explores other nations, seems to disintegrate and then returns and reincorporates itself].

Act II

1980s and 1990s

Scene 1

•◆•

Reimagining National Community
Performance and Nostalgia in Recent Puerto Rican Drama

In 1984, Edgardo Rodríguez Juliá wrote a series of essays based on family photographs from the turn of the century to the present for the San Juan newspaper *El Reportero*. He later collected more photographs and added narrative texts to compile *Puertorriqueños (Álbum de la sagrada familia puertorriqueña a partir de 1898)* [Puerto Ricans (Album of the sacred Puerto Rican family since 1898)] (1988). Rodríguez Juliá's album pieces together a history of the Puerto Rican family, which, in turn, captures the socioeconomic, political, and cultural evolution of the island. The persistence of the family as a metaphor for nation attests to the desire of the only colony in the Western Hemisphere to imagine itself as a national community. The family album, in short, exemplifies the themes of history and national self-image prevalent in Puerto Rican cultural discourse of the 1980s and 1990s. My discussion of plays by Francisco Arriví, René Marqués, and Myrna Casas from the 1950s demonstrated that while Puerto Ricans never agreed on what kind of family should embody the nation, writers nevertheless attempted to define *a* Puerto Rican collective experience. In the 1960s and 1970s, however, Puerto Rico underwent social, economic, and political changes that motivated a shift in how intellectual discourses address the problem of identity. This is true of many parts of the world where emerging social movements and increasing globalization, facilitated by mass media and transnational capitalism, have led cultural theorists to rethink nation and national identity as historically contingent and socially constructed categories of knowledge and bodily experience.[1] In Puerto Rico, the master discourses that have framed investigations of Puerto Rican identity, nationalism, and colonialism, have given way to the interplay of practices and discourses of class, race, gender, sexual orientation, and migrant experience as organizers of Puerto Rican identities. Rodríguez Juliá's *Puertorriqueños* illustrates this new perspective, for the photo album offers multiple lenses through which to view the history of the island, underlining the many subjectivities that make up *puertorriqueñidad.*

Moreover, playwright Roberto Ramos-Perea contends that Puerto Rican writers no longer endeavor to pin down the character of the nation or engage in an existential examination of the national psyche because "Ya sabemos lo que somos" ("De Cómo" 56) [We already know what we are]. Thus to defend and affirm whatever this identity may be constitute the new challenges for contemporary artists. In plays from the mid-1980s to the mid-1990s, rather than staging a family that embodies a limited vision of national culture, playwrights portray families that dramatize the processes that form various Puerto Rican communities and what is at stake by maintaining or contesting these images of collective identity. Plays by Antonio García del Toro, Roberto Ramos-Perea, Luis Rafael Sánchez, and Myrna Casas expose identities in a constant process of creation and negotiation. Like the tension created in Rodríguez Juliá's family album by displaying the task of piecing together a past that was never intact, these plays follow two seemingly contradictory directions. *Hotel Melancolía (Nostalgia en dos tiempos)* [Melancholy Hotel (Nostalgia in two movements)] by García del Toro and *Callando amores* [Silencing loves] by Ramos-Perea exhibit a sense of nostalgia and an interest in preserving cultural and national traditions. Through the use of intertexts, however, these works critique identity stories from the 1950s and imply the need for alternative strategies and spaces from which to imagine a Puerto Rican community. In Sánchez's *Quíntuples* [Quintuplets] and Casas's *El gran circo eukraniano* [The Great USkranian Circus], on the other hand, the presence of traveling acting troupes highlights the performative and the mobile character of Puerto Rico's national community. Despite the self-conscious performance of an unstable identity, *Quíntuples* and *El gran circo eukraniano* also betray some yearning for origins and a more rooted identity. The use of metatheater and the emphasis on identity as performance in works from the 1980s and 1990s, however, suggest that there is no essential model of the nation or the family to which to return.

While dissension over cultural and political identity marked Puerto Rican society in the 1950s and 1960s, historian Fernando Picó also describes this period as a tranquil decade (260). Between 1955 and 1965, under the leadership of Luis Muñoz Marín and the pro-Commonwealth party Partido Popular Democrático [Popular Democratic Party] (PPD), the island experienced a period of relative social peace as crime rates and emigration decreased, the middle and working classes grew, the standard of living improved, access to health care and education increased, and cultural activities flourished. Nevertheless, a 1967 plebiscite on political status revealed that, in spite of its many successes, the PPD never achieved consensus on this issue, for 39 percent of the vote went to the supporters of statehood.[2] In 1968, Luis Ferré, leader of the Partido Nuevo Progresista [Pro-Statehood Party] (PNP), narrowly defeated the PPD candidate for governor, breaking the twenty-year political hegemony of the PPD. The growing popularity of the statehood party has evolved in great part because of economic factors. Although initially beneficial for many Puerto Ricans, in the long run the industrialization program developed by the PPD created a dependent economy and massive unemployment.[3] Phasing out the agricultural economy, however, did create a new social sector involved in services, in government, and in industrial occupations. Economically linked to the United States, this group became ideologically inclined toward statehood. At the same time, those marginalized by the industrial transformation of the island migrated to urban centers and grew dependent upon federal aid to survive. These groups, displaced by the reorganized economy, became equally interested in strengthening ties with the United States through statehood while the elite, economically successful *estadistas* [statehood supporters] championed their cause (A. G. Ramos 267–68).

The PPD and the PNP shared leadership throughout the 1970s, but neither party could resolve the economic problems brought on by a recession and the world oil crisis (1973–74). Between 1970 and 1977, unemployment intensified, and more formerly self-sufficient families began to depend on federal funds for their income. Inflation and a drop in the quality of life translated into wider social problems: an increase in emigration, violent crimes, drug abuse, environmental pollution, and poor public services (Morales Carrión, "A Postscriptum" 313). At the same time, the youth of Puerto Rico, radicalized by international events such as the Cuban Revolution (1959), the military coup in Chile (1973), and the war in Vietnam, protested a wide range of social injustices. On the home front, students clashed with police while protesting obligatory military service and the presence of the Reserve Officers Training Corps (ROTC) on the University of Puerto Rico campus. The suspicious deaths of two young, proindependence militants in 1978 revealed the depth of tensions on the island and sparked public concern about political repression beyond the protests of a confrontational young generation. The incident, which came to be called the Caso Maravilla, breached the people's trust in their local government and police force because in 1983, questioning on live television exposed a government cover-up by disclosing that Puerto Rican police agents had executed the militants.[4] In this tumultuous decade, only the experiences of outrage provoked by the events of the Caso Maravilla and the sorrow over the 1980 death of Puerto Rico's great twentieth-century political leader, Luis Muñoz Marín, seemed briefly to unite the nation.

The increasing ideological force of the PNP politically polarized the cultural sphere in the 1980s.[5] Through new legislation and the appointment of a new director of the traditionally pro-Commonwealth Instituto de Cultura Puertorriqueña (ICP), back-to-back PNP administrations (1976–84) launched an initiative to discredit what they viewed as the elitist, folkloric, and Hispanocentric approach to Puerto Rican culture embodied by the ICP and the PPD. In contrast, the PNP's cultural discourse promoted an inclusive "universal" culture not limited by autochthonous components (making a cultural identity that would be less of an obstacle to annexation to the United States). Ironically, the PPD responded with a movement to promote Puerto Rican culture that emphasized its traditionalist and classist ideology and culminated in the institution of Spanish as the sole official language in 1991. The PNP countered in 1993 by making both English and Spanish official languages. The PNP must support official bilingualism, presupposing that the United States would never admit a Spanish-speaking territory to the Union; for cultural nationalists, this position always leaves open the question of whether Puerto Rico's unique cultural identity can be preserved under statehood. Thus, while elections, plebiscites, and referenda show that the Commonwealth party has lost political ground since the late 1960s, the prostatehood party cannot seem to resolve the autonomist impulse of the island.[6] The debate on political status persists, but its terms are changing, for new circumstances and historical experiences demand redefinitions of what is understood as colony, as well as nation, especially with regard to language and geographical borders.

As we have seen, throughout the second half of the twentieth century competing interests and ideologies stretched to the breaking point the colonialist/nationalist paradigm that limited many Puerto Rican intellectuals during the periods of cultural nationalism in the 1930s-50s. In the 1960s and 1970s, voices excluded from a class-based, paternalist, and European construction of the nation made themselves heard, problematizing hegemonic discourses of collective identity. As the working class and other marginalized groups gained new visibility, they appeared as the subject of literary works, such as Luis Rafael Sánchez's *En cuerpo de camisa* [In shirtsleeves] (1966). This collection of short stories introduced many themes popularized in Puerto Rican literature in the 1970s. During this decade, José Luis González and Isabelo Zenón Cruz, through their stories and essays, highlighted Puerto Rico's African heritage, while the Nuyorican poetry by Tato Laviera added the significant migrant perspective to the Puerto Rican national community.[7] Rosario Ferré and Manuel Ramos Otero, also attentive to issues of race and class, investigated the themes of gender and sexual orientation as well.[8] Josefina Rivera de Álvarez calls the literature of the times "testimonial y desacralizadora" (659) [testimonial and desacralizing] because it captured the sociopolitical activism of the period in formally and thematically innovative ways. By incorporating the voices of socially marginalized groups such as blacks, homosexuals, immigrants, drug addicts, and prostitutes, these writers used a language that challenged the linguistic norms of the dominant classes and forged a space for new perspectives.

The national house—or the theater—that the ICP and playwrights like René Marqués, Francisco Arriví, and Emilio Belaval had built during the 1940s and 1950s loomed large over the dramatists of new generations. By the late 1960s, young playwrights felt stifled by the state-sponsored national theater festival because, as Rosalina Perales observes,

siempre representaban los mismos autores—ya consagrados— obras que versaban sobre los mismos temas: la nostalgia por el jíbaro, el conflicto de nuestra identidad, la evocación del pasado perdido, el eclecticismo social etc. Las técnicas y estructuras eran tradicionales y las puestas en escena satisfacían a un público ya oficializado. ("Teatro" 74)

[they always presented works by the same authors—already can-
onized—whose plays rehearsed the same themes: nostalgia for the
jíbaro, our identity conflict, reminiscences of our lost past, social
eclecticism, etc. The techniques and structures were traditional and
the stagings satisfied an already mainstream audience.]

As we have seen, the 1968 elections that broke the political hegemony of
the PPD ushered in an era of generational rupture, deep ideological divisions, and a sense of instability. Roberto Ramos-Perea labels the theater
that evolved in this context "La Nueva Dramaturgia Puertorriqueña"
[New Puerto Rican Dramaturgy] (NDP). Perales, in contrast, uses the
phrase "teatro de fricción" [frictional theater] because it captures the
confrontational nature of the performances of the period and the context
in which they took place ("Teatro" 73).[9] For Ramos-Perea, the foundation of the performance group El Tajo del Alacrán (1968) marks the beginning of the NDP movement. The group's name refers to a street
weapon, and the names of subsequent groups such as Anamú (1969) and
Morivoví (1972) (named after persistent weeds) and Teatro de Guerrillas
[Guerrilla Theater] (1969) suggest their combative stance (Reynolds, "La
nueva dramaturgia" 148).

Popular theater and collective creation define the first cycle (1968–75)
of the NDP movement. Directors, actors, and playwrights such as Lydia
Milagros González, Jaime Carrero, Pedro Santaliz, Walter Rodríguez, and
Rosa Luisa Márquez worked together to create performance pieces using
an antipoetic, streetwise language new to the Puerto Rican stage. Like
writers of all genres during this period, these theater practitioners dramatized politicized topics and socially marginalized groups to raise consciousness about specific Puerto Rican problems. Unable to stage their
works in traditional venues, they performed on the streets, in public
parks, and in other unconventional performance spaces. By abandoning
formal theater stages, they freed themselves of cumbersome sets and
technical equipment and created a closer, more active relationship between the work and the public. This new audience/actor connection and
the collaborative nature of the texts emphasize the potential of performance to raise collective consciousness.

With its new themes, modes of expression, ideological base, and didactic intent, the new movement undoubtedly renovated Puerto Rican theater. For Ramos-Perea, the treatment of the problem of identity differentiates the new playwrights from former generations. He concedes that

earlier playwrights who examined Puerto Rican culture, such as Francisco Arriví and René Marqués, were writers concerned with the conflicts of their times, but he argues that new dramatists who denounce injustices and who question social, economic, and political problems produce more committed works ("Teatro" 90). The NDP movement worked under the assumption that, first, there was no need to search for an identity that Puerto Rico already possessed. Consequently, the artists asked: "¿Qué vamos a hacer para defender nuestra puertorriqueñidad? ¿Qué armas, argumentos o decisiones tanto en el teatro como en la realidad, vamos a esgrimir en la defensa de nuestro acervo particular y nuestra idiosincrasia?" ("Teatro" 91) [What are we going to do to defend our *puertorriqueñidad*? Which weapons, arguments and decisions not only in the theater but also in reality are we going to wield in defense of our particular cultural heritage and identity?]. They also recognized Puerto Rican subjectivity as a composite of various socially and culturally constructed roles and positions; thus, unlike in the 1930s and 1950s, nationalism did not constitute the basis for discussing collective identity. The newly recognized heterogeneity of *puertorriqueñidad* led writers to articulate the question of national community through discourses other than that of the nation and the family. Consequently, although family was certainly an implicit theme in the youthful rebellion against authority, the family scenario was not a major image in the theater of the 1960s and 1970s.

By the mid-1970s, the NDP movement moved into a second phase that continued well into the 1980s. In this period, playwrights such as Zora Moreno, Ramón Conde, and Pedro Santaliz, whose roots were in popular theater, and new dramatists like Ramos-Perea, Teresa Marichal, Víctor Abniel Morales, José Luis Ramos Escobar, who emerged from the university theater scene, maintained a socially conscious focus, but the performance activity turned to more traditional theater spaces and modes of writing (Ramos-Perea, "Perspectivas" 22).[10] In addition, for the new dramatists to gain recognition and support, they knew that they had to interact more productively with the influential cultural organizations that until then had not supported their work. Sociedad Nacional de Autores Dramáticos [The National Society of Dramatists] (SONAD) was founded in 1984 to seek better conditions for producing plays in Puerto Rico and to provide a forum for more dialogue among playwrights of different generations. Thanks to this organization, in 1986 the annual ICP-sponsored theater programming included the Primer Festival de Nuevos Dramaturgos [First Festival of New Dramatists], and in 1987 the

Centro de Bellas Artes celebrated its first festival of contemporary Puerto Rican theater. The participation in government-funded festivals and the task of inscribing the efforts of the NDP movement in Puerto Rican theater history marked a new phase for Puerto Rican theater.[11] After years of finding material for their plays in the immediate social, political, and economic crises of the island, in the mid-1980s dramatists turned to the past and once again to the family to shed light on the problem of identity. As we will see in plays from the 1980s and 1990s, the representation of the family itself shares many similarities with how families are portrayed in works from the 1950s. That is, family quarrels, failed romances, and an interest in the past reappear in the contemporary pieces. How the playwrights employ the family to examine collective identity, however, reveals historical changes in the modes of representing families as a metaphor for national community and, as a result, important changes in long-standing debates about national self-image.

The use of history in Puerto Rican artistic works of the 1980s and 1990s is one area that illustrates a shift in how writers approached the subject of national identity. In the 1970s, historians such as Ángel G. Quintero Rivera, Juan Ángel Silén, and Fernando Picó switched the focus of Puerto Rican historical studies from celebrated political leaders and their stance on the status of the island to the development of class conflicts and the recuperation of historical voices and experiences left out of traditional trajectories of the nation (Quintero Rivera 213).[12] This interest in reexamining the national past has influenced the artistic projects of the 1980s and 1990s of contemporary writers such as Edgardo Rodríguez Juliá, Rosario Ferré, Ana Lydia Vega, Magali García Ramis, and Luis López Nieves and graphic and performance artist Antonio Martorell.[13] Nostalgia, "the expression of yearning for an earlier time or place or person from one's past history," as Roberta Rubenstein explains, contributes to a sense of identity in the present (13). Similarly, García Ramis notes that the persistence of history in Puerto Rican literature constitutes, in part, an anticolonial gesture and argues, as have other critics, that the desire to reconstruct the past aims to form an identity and history obscured by the island's colonial situation ("Para narrar" 63). However, recent writers exhibit an awareness that nostalgia leads to the fantasy of an idyllic past, which contrasts with the uncritical cultural nationalism and class-based longing for the land of former generations.

In their treatments of history, contemporary authors deflate former essentialist anticolonial narratives by using parody and multiple points of view. In her essay "La manteca que nos une" [The lard that joins us], for example, García Ramis pokes fun at solemn and prescriptive visions of national identity by proposing that Puerto Ricans are bound together by a diet laden with fat: "un tun tún de grasa y fritanguería recorre las venas borincanas, nos une, nos aúna, nos hermana por encima de la política y los políticos, los cultos y las religiones, la salsa y el rock, el matriarcado y el patriarcado" (83) [a hodgepodge of grease and refried foods runs through our Puerto Rican veins and joins us together, making us one; it creates our fraternity above politics and politicians, above cults and religions, above salsa and rock music, and above matriarchy and patriarchy]. Her humorous catalog of greasy Puerto Rican foods and suggestion that the country's slogan be "Por mi grasa hablará mi espiritu" (89) [Through my grease my spirit will speak] contrasts with the taxonomic and paternalist tones of national identity essays.[14] Other works, such as Ferré's *Maldito amor* [Cursed love] (1986) and Rodríguez Juliá's *El entierro de Cortijo* [Cortijo's burial] (1983), focus on recuperating the histories of marginalized groups neglected in bourgeois versions of Puerto Rican history. Many of these narratives also blend fact and fiction, problematizing the category of truth and highlighting both history and fiction as human-made narratives. These techniques manifest a postmodern environment in which master narratives have become suspect. As César A. Salgado explains,

> Tras los desencuentros del telos dialéctico en la posmodernidad (y la potente impresión que dejó en el país el encubrimiento y la desinformación oficial llevada a cabo en torno a los asesinatos en el Cerro Maravilla), la presunción de un Archivo transparente, no-intervenido, se vuelve insostenible para el imaginario ochentista. Para tal imaginario tal Archivo adolece de sospechosas manipulaciones y ocultamientos patriarcales, de supresiones imperiales conspirativas, y resulta ser sólo un emisor de ficciones ideológicas. La verdad histórica deja de ser un propósito narrativo. (436)

> [After the divergences of postmodernity's dialectic telos (and the powerful impression left on the country by the official cover-up and misinformation carried out in relation to the Cerro Maravilla murders), the assumption of a transparent, unmediated Archive becomes untenable for the 1980s imaginary. For such an imaginary,

this Archive suffers from suspicious manipulations and patriarchal cover-ups, from conspiring imperial suppressions, and becomes
only a producer of ideological fictions. The historical truth stops
being a narrative objective.]

In the works I will briefly mention here, the postmodern move away
from locating historical "truth" is also seen in subjective testimonies of
the island's *intrahistoria*, the practices of everyday life that make up the
idiosyncrasies of Puerto Rican culture. This approach to recording collective identity implicitly evokes the family because the household is the
ideal site for remembering the customs of daily life. Consequently, the
family figures prominently as a space for exploring national history in
cultural production from the 1980s. This trend is in line with Antonio Martorell's idea that the intimate and subjective point of view of the *crónica*
[chronicle], as opposed to traditional narrative or journalism, best illustrates the history and personality of a people (García Ramis, "Quiero"
60). Martorell puts into practice his view on chronicling Puerto Rican
culture through his plastic art. His 1972 portfolio of woodcuts, *Catálogo
de objetos* [Catalog of objects], for example, records commonplace household objects used before the 1950s and indirectly comments on the cultural changes that North American industrialization had forced upon
Puerto Rican culture (Rivera 69). Martorell's 1978 exhibit *Álbum de familia* [Family album], which consisted of a series of drawings based on
photographs taken from family albums, also served to restore cultural
memory. In 1992, Martorell's collection of environmental installations,
La casa de todos nosotros [The house of all of us], displayed at New York
City's Museo del Barrio, again turned to the family as a locus of national
history. The exhibit brought together individual houses that Martorell
presented in different locations on the island throughout 1992. The mul-
timedia show consisted of a series of inventive houses built of various
materials. Fittingly, "Kamikaze," a house/bed that recalls family origins,
opened the exposition. Other structures included a house made entirely
of dollar bills, "La casa verde" [The green house], which brings to mind
Puerto Rico's economic dependency, and a house in the form of a plane,
"La casa en el aire" [The house in the air], a reference to the circulating
Puerto Rican population. The exhibit reminded viewers of the common
bonds of *puertorriqueñidad* while the separate houses allowed for individual imagination and nostalgia. Martorell's mode of representing the
family embodies a changing view of family as nation, for as his exhibit

suggested, there is no longer one single house that can hold the heterogeneous "gran familia puertorriqueña," but there is a house for everyone.[15]

Rodríguez Juliá's national family album *Puertorriqueños* also represents the *crónica* style of recording collective experience. Like Martorell, Rodríguez Juliá uses the family to examine the nation's past with humor, yearning, and a critical eye. Through photographs, postcards, and verbal recollections, Rodríguez Juliá re-creates the history of Puerto Rico via images of the family colored by "la burla y la compasión" (11) [mockery and compassion]. On the one hand, the ironic tone created by the textual commentary juxtaposed with the photographs makes many middle-class traditions captured in the photographs seem suspect; on the other hand, the album tries to resurrect positive cultural values besieged by contemporary social problems: "pretendemos rescatar la compasión, pretendemos rescatar el vecindario, la familia y la comunidad a pesar de haberle hipotecado el alma a la Mastercard y los cupones" (172) [we want to recuperate compassion, we want to recuperate the neighborhood, the family, and the community even though we've mortgaged our soul to Mastercard and food stamps]. A potentially nostalgic essay by Ana Lydia Vega, which recounts her visit to the parking lot where her childhood house used to stand, shares this ironic tone:

¡Pero y qué un párking! ¡Qué cafre destino el de mi madre casa! ¡Ay, San René Marqués, patrono de añoranzas hacendadas! [. . .]

¿Y yo? ¿Me entrego? ¿Me dejo cabalgar por las contradicciones y este deseo tristón de trascendencia? ¿O canto la oda del que-se-joda y boto mis precarios ahorros en un chalet Massó? Pero qué va. Más nunca será igual. Un pasadillo pre-tratado. Un come-back prefabricado. Episodio cerrado. ("Madera" 295–96)

[I can't believe it, they've made it into a parking lot! What a tacky destiny for my saintly home! Ay, Saint René Marqués, patron of plantation nostalgia! [. . .]

And I? Should I give in? Do I let myself be overrun by contradictions and this pathetic desire for transcendence? Or do I say what the fuck and throw away my precarious savings in a prefabricated Massó Chalet? What the heck. But it'll never be the same. A precontracted back ally memory. A prefabricated comeback. Case closed.]

In contrast to René Marqués, Vega and Rodríguez Juliá do not wish for what they know is an impossible (and undesirable) return to the past, but like Marqués, they do regret the loss of cultural traditions and the fragmentation of the community that resulted from rapid modernization and urbanization.

By recording Puerto Rico's unique features, these writers attempt to create a sense of community while recognizing the fundamental diversity of the national family. It is significant that Rodríguez Juliá's album was originally published as a series of newspapers articles, for it recalls Benedict Anderson's argument that the development of print capitalism such as newspapers and books created print communities, laying the foundation for national consciousness (22–36). Rodríguez Juliá's photographs and short evocations of traditions such as the *quinceañera* [fifteenth-birthday party] or of family events like the move to a modern suburb reached a wide readership, reminding Puerto Ricans of the many common bonds they share in a historical moment of deep divisions. An attempt to strengthen community through reading also appears in "Relevo" [Relay], a column published in the newspaper *Claridad* throughout 1985. "Relevo" was conceived as a literary relay race in which seven authors took turns contributing articles on a wide range of themes: art and literature; contemporary sociopolitical events and problems such as AIDS, crime, and pollution; and popular topics such as food, medicinal herbs, and points of interest on the island. Despite the divergent themes and points of view, read as a collection the pieces reflect the sensibility of a generation of writers (and their readers) who came of age in the 1960s and who now view their 1950s' childhood and youthful rebellions with some nostalgia (Vega, "En sus marcas" 3). Much like the "Relevo" column, Vega's short story "Cuento en camino" [Story on its way] (1991) constitutes a sort of collaborative *crónica*. In the story, the driver of a *carro público* [collective taxi] asks his passengers to tell stories to keep him from falling asleep at the wheel. The heterogeneous group narrates tales that derive from the oral tradition and create a dialogue as listeners offer their opinions and, at times, different versions of the same story. The jokes, gossip, and legends document Puerto Rican popular culture and serve to make connections among people of different backgrounds.

Performances of plays by Antonio García del Toro, Roberto Ramos-Perea, Luis Rafael Sánchez, and Myrna Casas in the 1980s and 1990s also reveal a desire to recuperate a sense of community. Following the relative absence of the family play during the 1960s and 1970s, the family unit reappears, signaling a desire to bridge rifts among ideologies and generations, past and present. The return of the family, however, does not signify a new brand of paternalist nationalist discourse. The characters in García del Toro's *Hotel Melancolía* and Ramos-Perea's *Callando amores* yearn for the past and desire to preserve tradition and cultural identity, but they critique former models of the national family. Role-playing in Sánchez's *Quíntuples* and Casas's *El gran circo eukraniano* highlight how the performance of Puerto Rican identity changes in accordance to shifting contexts. Like other artistic works of the 1980s and 1990s, the nostalgic and performative representations of the family in the plays examined in this section are in line with a postmodern outlook that consciously offers only provisional and limited answers to the problem of identity in Puerto Rico.[16]

Productive Nostalgia: Family Custodians of History and Identity

Antonio García del Toro's dramaturgy, like that of many Puerto Rican playwrights preceding him, addresses the destiny of the island.[17] García del Toro (b. 1950), who also directs and teaches theater, entered this national theater tradition in the 1980s in full dialogue with the works of René Marqués. *Hotel Melancolía* (1989) performs what Marvin Carlson calls "ghosting," for the text, the bodies of the actors who interpret the roles, and the space in which the play was produced are haunted by René Marqués (7). Textually, the play recycles Marqués's classic *Los soles truncos*. Moreover, it was awarded the 1986 Premio Fundación René Marqués and was staged in 1989 in the Sala René Marqués (Centro de Bellas Artes) with a cast that included Iris Martínez, who played the part of Emilia in a 1977 production of *Los soles truncos*. Presenting the audience with images and plots it has seen before manifests how the theater operates as a guardian of cultural memory. As I have argued, the repeating family scenario in Cuban and Puerto Rican theater records how the national community imagines itself during particular historical junctures. The memory of family that haunts this theater, however, is "subject to continual adjustment and modification as the memory is recalled in new circumstances and contexts" (Carlson 2). Thus the story of the lives of four elderly siblings who reside in an old colonial home in *Hotel Melancolía* suggests that nostalgia for the past can be productive, unlike the nihilistic outcome it produces in *Los soles truncos*. Whereas the Burkhart family in *Los soles truncos* refuses to participate in a national romance, the siblings in *Hotel Melancolía* not only break out of the confines of family to celebrate their role in the national community, they also strive to involve others in appreciating history and tradition. The introduction of an unsolved mystery, however, infuses the play with an indeterminacy that problematizes truth claims. The play values nostalgia for its capacity to maintain a sense of identity but never limits this identity by defining it precisely.

The world represented onstage in *Hotel Melancolía* consists of a realistically constructed nineteenth-century home converted into a hotel. The residents and owners, the Landrón y Rojas family siblings—Cofo (eighty-six), Filo (eighty-three), Lita (eighty-one), and Copo (seventy-nine)—rarely accept guests anymore, but during the time span of the performance, the audience itself becomes a guest in this "mundo donde gobiernan los recuerdos y la nostalgia" (13) [world where memory and nostalgia rule]. Three other characters also visit the house: a detective (Leonardo Mendoza), a journalist (Daniel), and a photographer. These characters provide dramatic tension and clarify the play's temporal framework. In the opening scene, which takes place in the present, Daniel pays a visit to the house and to Gertrudis, the housekeeper. They refer to the recent past when the siblings still lived there and witnessed a murder. This crime creates the play's little action: visits by detective Mendoza and Daniel to investigate the murder. The two acts begin in the present (the 1980s) and end in the recent past, also sometime in the 1980s, with some confluence of time throughout. The scenes in which Daniel and Gertrudis appear always mark the present, but the majority of the play's action takes place as a flashback to the time when the household became involved in the murder investigation.

Hotel Melancolía does not mirror *Los soles truncos* in terms of plot, but it does engage intertextually with the earlier play in its use of theatrical space, its characterization, and its themes. The old mansion and large second-floor window with Venetian blinds described in the stage directions immediately recall the Burkharts' San Juan residence in Marqués's play. The well-kept condition of the house and its contents, however, differentiates the two homes. Although the Landrón y Rojas family, like the Burkharts, live immersed in nostalgia, they also participate in the contemporary world. They face the reality of financial survival, and their decision to use their home as a hotel contrasts with the Burkharts' rejection of this possibility, which would open them to the "gran familia puertorriqueña" of the nation. By allowing the public access to their historical home, the Landrón y Rojas family embodies a more flexible and inclusive vision of Puerto Rico than that of the Burkharts. Furthermore, the Landrón y Rojas siblings move easily between the world of the present and their carefully cultivated world of the past. The set construction, verbal references to multiple unseen spaces within the house and outside of it, and character entrances and exits from the street mark the permeability of borders between different worlds and ideologies. Thus the first line of the play is an invitation to enter: "¡Adelante! Pase por aquí. Perdone que todo esté tan oscuro. En estos antiguos caserones, si se mantienen cerradas las ventanas, entra muy poca claridad" (15) [Come in! This way. I'm sorry it's so dark. In these big old houses, if the windows are kept shut, very little light comes in]. Unlike Emilia in *Los soles truncos*, the siblings neither avoid natural light nor veil themselves from the outside world. Despite their interest in the past, the Landrón y Rojas family does not lead a cloistered existence in the shadows of modernity.

The Landrón y Rojas siblings do share some similar life events and personality traits with the Burkhart sisters, but how they have come to live in the Hotel Melancolía indicates their fundamentally different philosophies of life. Like the Burkharts, the four remaining Landrón y Rojas siblings are unmarried and childless. Lita's failed love affair with a *capitán* and her subsequent refuge in books recalls Emilia's unrequited love for her sister Hortensia's fiancé and her predilection for poetry. Filo's divorce from her husband, after discovering he had a lover and a child, parallels Hortensia's experience with the Spanish lieutenant. Copo is a widow, and Cofo has never married. Aside from the failed romances, in each family the most beautiful sibling has died of cancer. Copo's reference to the death of their youngest sibling, Nena, strongly echoes the sisters' reaction to Hortensia's death in *Los soles truncos:* "¡Maldita enfermedad! Destruye lo hermoso y convierte en víctimas a todos por igual" (49) [Damn illness! It destroys what's beautiful and turns everyone into a victim just the same]. The Landrón y Rojas siblings, however, handle the death of their parents differently. In Marqués's play, the deaths of Mamá and Papá Burkhart signify the destruction of a world in which Emilia, Inés, and Hortensia felt safe. When they retreat from society, the sisters do so joined by fear, guilt, and resentment. In contrast, after the death of their mother, the Landrón y Rojas siblings, already in their fifties, have chosen to live together to ward off loneliness. Copo explains:

La unión, hermosa experiencia que ha sido símbolo de nuestras vidas. Aquí, en el Hotel Melancolía, nunca hemos dejado que el silencio traicione la bella melodía de la vida. Nunca hemos soñado con olvidar el dolor, únicamente hemos sabido siempre calmarlo con nuestro amor. Aquí, en esta casa, que fue de nuestros padres, hasta la melancolía ha participado en nuestra alegría de vivir. (96)

[Union, that beautiful experience that has been a symbol of our lives. Here, in the Melancholy Hotel we've never allowed silence to betray the beautiful melody of life. We've never dreamed of forgetting pain, we've only known how to calm it with our love. Here in this house that belonged to our parents even melancholy has participated in our joy of life.]

Rather than spending the previous thirty-two years alone and saddened over the death of family members or the lack of a partner, these siblings have shared their melancholy for the past in a home characterized by love, humor, patience, and hope.

Although the Landrón y Rojas siblings have converted their home into a hotel for pragmatic reasons—to maintain its expensive upkeep—the hotel also helps them to preserve contact with the community. While the siblings indulge in nostalgia for times past, they are also invested in the destiny of contemporary Puerto Rico. Unlike the Burkharts, they participate in the national economy, and they consider their house part of the national patrimony. Cofo, for example, makes his first entrance holding a pile of newspapers and magazines and listening to the news on a portable radio. He complains of crime, government corruption, and other typical Puerto Rican problems of the 1980s. Filo's exclamation indicates the depth of Cofo's obsession with the news: "¡No puedo tolerar tu continua crítica social! Cuando no hablas de la política . . . que si este partido es malo, que si este otro político es un pillo . . . invades la casa con tus noticias sobre desastres sociales y naturales" (41) [I can't stand your constant social criticism! When you're not talking about politics . . . that this party is bad, that this politician is a thief . . . you invade the house with your news of social and natural disasters]. Furthermore, to the dismay of Copo, Cofo insists on filing all the printed materials he buys. She plots with the housekeeper over how to dispose of the papers: "Le diré que los hemos regalado a la biblioteca estatal y que pondrán una placa en la entrada con su nombre. Eso le agradará" (25) [I'll tell him that we've given all of them to the state library and that they will put a plaque at the entrance with his name. That will please him]. This solution underscores the Landrón y Rojas family's respect for history and their sensitivity to opportunities to record events and information. As José Emilio González suggests, the play's main theme is the need to recognize the confluence of tradition and modernity (8). The sibling's unusual lifestyle constitutes an extreme example of cultivating a nexus between the past and the present. Copo explains: "No somos cuatro seres enajenados. No. Vivimos ocupándonos a diario del mundo que nos rodea. Aquí, en el Hotel Melancolía, establecemos las normas nosotros. Afuera el mundo gira y cada cual vive; y con su individualidad hace de la colectividad un mundo que tenemos que sostener para no hundirnos nosotros mismos" (66) [We aren't four alienated beings. No. We engage daily with the world that surrounds us. Here, at the Melancholy Hotel, we establish the norms ourselves. Outside the world goes on, each according to his own; and each makes a world out of the collectivity, a world that we have to sustain to keep ourselves from sinking].

In addition to keeping up to date on current affairs, in the past the siblings had shown their interest in contemporary society through their contact with hotel guests. In the play, a murder serves as a device to connect the siblings with people beyond their home, because at their advanced age, they no longer take in many guests. Late one evening, all four of them partially witness the murder of an actor on the street outside their home. Consequently, Copo invites detective Mendoza over to report her story about what happened. Daniel, a journalist, also comes to the house to investigate, but under the pretense of writing an article about the Landrón y Rojas family. These two characters serve as an audience for the siblings' reminiscences about the past. The detective is an ideal listener because he admits to not being very familiar with the people and customs of the capital and because he needs the information concerning the murder and must be patient with the family to receive it. Copo humorously manipulates the interview, drawing it out as long as possible in order to educate her listener about the illustrious Landrón y Rojas heritage. She points out a portrait of her uncle who was an influential politician: "Detrás del paño que lo cubre . . . hay más historia que en toda la capital junta" (28) [Behind the canvas that covers it . . . there is more history than in the entire capital combined]. She informs the detective about her family's involvement with important historical events and about how the house was once a center for writers and politicians. The siblings also describe unusual family traditions, such as moving each time that a family member dies and leaving everything behind except for Nena's piano. For Cofo, the piano embodies an important part of cultural identity: "La música es el alma de un pueblo. Es ese aliento que evita la caída final. Sin la música todo estaría perdido" (47) [Music is the soul of the people. It's the inspiration that defers the final fall. Without music, everything would be lost].[18] The detective, in contrast, mentions that he has never had time for music.

Passing on national history and family heritage has a didactic purpose. Copo tells Mendoza: "Sabe, a veces la juventud no conoce verdaderamente el porqué de tantas cosas. La historia pasada es tan importante como la que vivimos a diario" (36) [You know, sometimes young people don't really understand the whys and the wherefores of a lot of things. Past history is just as important as our daily life]. By emphasizing the relationship between the past and the present, Copo attempts to bridge the gap between generations. The magical atmosphere of the house and Copo's lessons are most effective with the journalist, Daniel. As with the Burkharts, the Landrón y Rojas's family romance has failed in the sense that they have produced no future generations. Daniel, however, becomes the grandchild the siblings never had. He admits that his initial interest was in the murder, not in the family, but he becomes so drawn to them that he drops his investigation: "Desde que entré aquí por primera vez entendí que este viejo edificio verdaderamente tenía la capacidad de conducirte por los caminos del recuerdo. Nunca imaginé, sin embargo, que después de aquella primera visita mi vida cambiaría" (55) [Since the first time I came in I understood that this old building truly had the capacity to take you down the paths of memory. I never imagined, however, that after that first visit my life would change]. For Daniel, the Landrón y Rojas family has served as a living *crónica* that passes on history to a younger generation. His newfound appreciation for the past has helped him forge a stronger sense of identity and belonging to the national community. Lita's insistence that Daniel will one day marry underscores the continuity of history, the future of the national family romance.

Although Cofo, Lita, Filo, and Copo attribute their contentment to having "sabido encontrar nuestra verdadera identidad" (66) [having known how to find our true identity], the play never makes explicit the exact nature of this identity. Contrary to many plays from the 1950s, the characters in *Hotel Melancolía* do not voice particular positions on the debate over national identity. Rather, the play suggests the importance of history in recognizing a collective Puerto Rican experience without privileging a specific vision of the island's past. Furthermore, the vagueness with which García del Toro treats historical figures and events distinguishes *Hotel Melancolía* from a traditional historical or documentary play. The audience and the visitors never see the portrait of the famous uncle because it is wrapped up in preparation for its sale to the national museum. We know that in the past, the siblings' mother fended off an angry mob that intended to destroy the painting, but no one explains the context. The play neither spells out the politics of past events nor reveals the family's ideological stance. The clues provided by *Hotel Melancolía* lead the audience to piece together a picture of the past that only provokes more questions: how and when did the Landrón y Rojas family become prominent? Who was the uncle and what did he do for Puerto Rico? This ambiguity encourages the process of historical inquiry and allows the play to celebrate history and family without using them to posit a political position or an essential Puerto Rican identity.

By raising the problem of historical truth, *Hotel Melancolía* further exemplifies a postmodern approach to family and nation in Puerto Rican drama that reevaluates totalizing accounts of identity. García del Toro's indeterminate use of history resembles what Linda Hutcheon has called postmodern historiographic metafiction. Works such as these, Hutcheon states, "enact the problematic nature of the relation of writing history to narrativization and thus, to fictionalization, thereby raising the same questions about the cognitive status of historical knowledge" (*A Poetics* 93). The play is full of history-making discourses that highlight history as a human-made narrative. Cofo compiles archives of newspaper and magazine articles that will one day form the basis of historical narratives. Similarly, the journalist's job is to seek facts that will form "true" stories, with the aid of a photographer who visually records these stories. The detective, in turn, collects evidence in hopes of building a narrative that uncovers the truth of a crime. The journalist, photographer, and detective all aim to make sense of a particular event, to shape a representation of the truth by ordering the information they receive via interviews and photographs. To expose this process implies that no one version of history exists and that the Landrón y Rojas story represents only one version of the Puerto Rican national family romance.

The murder of television actor Manolo Santini outside of the Landrón y Rojas home adds another layer of indeterminacy to these efforts to record the truth. The crime also creates dramatic tension in a play driven by memories of the past rather than by action. Much of this tension derives from the possibility that the detective has taken part in the murder. Although the audience does not know this until near the end of the play, Copo has specifically requested that Mendoza come to investigate because she suspects that he might be linked to the murder. García del Toro characterizes Mendoza with such ambiguity that his response, "¿Todo?" [Everything?], to each sibling's affirmation that he or she witnessed the murder can be viewed with suspicion or taken at face value. The detective's possible involvement in the crime underscores the bias implied in documenting events. If the detective is involved, then his report will surely hide this truth.[19] Similarly, the conflicting narrative accounts given by the siblings highlight perspectivism and the impossibility of piecing together a version of the event that coincides on each point.

Finally, whether intentionally or not, the play's ending raises questions about the supposedly solved mystery. The final scene draws together (a bit too neatly) the murder and another minor subplot, the sale of the uncle's portrait. The museum administrator's son arrives with the message that his father will not be able to buy the painting after all because he is setting up an exhibit out of town. This relieves Copo because she has secretly suspected that she saw the administrator at the crime scene (by this point, she has eliminated the detective as a suspect). She believes the museum administrator's absence gives him an alibi. The audience, however, learns that this conclusion is incorrect, because a scene in the present between Daniel and Gertrudis, the family housekeeper, clarifies the outcome of the investigation: the museum administrator had indeed committed the crime. Thus, at the end of the play, Copo's celebratory toast to faith in the truth has an ironic ring: "Y nosotros continuaremos compartiendo la dicha del recuerdo y el triunfo de la verdad" (96) [And we will continue sharing the joy of memories and the triumph of truth].

Hotel Melancolía portrays the complicated relationship between history and identity. By positing nostalgia for the past as a productive method for affirming collective experience, García del Toro reworks Marqués's *Los soles truncos*. How the families in these plays handle vertiginous sociopolitical, economic, and cultural changes depends on their ability to adapt and still retain their heritage. In this sense, from the perspective of the 1980s, García del Toro is much more optimistic than Marqués, who in the 1950s equated modernity with the destruction of traditional Puerto Rican culture. *Hotel Melancolía* advocates a living history, because the task of remembering, recording, and sharing the past affects the present and the future of the Puerto Rican community. The play's approach to history, however, suggests that there is no one unifying historical narrative on which to base a homogenous national identity. The Landrón y Rojas family and home, visited by characters in the play, and by the audience as well, embody but one family's history in the multiplicity of histories that form *puertorriqueñidad*.

"Nostalgia Rencorosa": The Performance of Errors Past

If in García del Toro's *Hotel Melancolía* nostalgia for the past promotes community building and a strong sense of identity necessary for the cultural survival of Puerto Rico, in Roberto Ramos-Perea's *Callando amores* (1995) memories endow a mother and her son with a "nostalgia rencorosa" [vengeful nostalgia] that leads them to repeat conflicts of the past. This play is but one of many works by Ramos-Perea that use historical and social themes to question what he calls "la supervivencia moral de nuestra nación" ("Escritura" 382) [the moral survival of our nation]. As Puerto Rico's most visible and prolific contemporary playwright, Ramos-Perea (b. 1959) has been involved in Puerto Rican theater as a critic, researcher, director, actor, and dramatist for over twenty-five years.[20] In *Callando amores*, he uses as a blueprint an oft-repeated situation in Puerto Rican literature—a family divided over the sale of their land—to discredit the nationalist and annexationist/colonialist discourses that have structured thinking about identity in Puerto Rico. Through intertexts and a performance that highlights the characters' self-conscious choice to resuscitate and repeat past disagreements, Ramos-Perea makes both the nationalist and annexationist positions unsatisfying options for the positive resolution of the play's dramatic conflict. *Callando amores* implies that as long as Puerto Ricans adhere to political positions no longer viable in the present, they will continue to "callar amores" [silence loves] and polarize the family and the nation.

The family conflict portrayed in the play has begun fifteen years prior to the opening scene when the father, a senator and member of the political party in power at that time, denounced the illegal sale of fertile land to a U.S. chemical company. This act alienated him from his colleagues and embarrassed his class-conscious wife, Victoria. She and one of their sons, Luis, have disowned him, whereas Mario, the other son, has stood by what he considers a heroic act. Mario, however, abandoned the ruptured family, and at the start of the play he has returned after learning that his father has died. Victoria and Luis have plotted to sell what was most sacred to the father, the family land, to a U.S. pharmaceutical company, but Mario's arrival potentially stymies their plan. With the help of Gina, Luis's wife, Mario obtains documents that would create a scandal if the family were to sell the land.[21] Victoria, in turn, produces a file on Mario that reveals he is a fugitive from a Spanish prison. Evidently this does not cause a stalemate, for the final scene shows the mother at the groundbreaking ceremony of a new factory along with Mario in handcuffs (meaning that the documents regarding the environmental impact of the sale of the land were never made public or possibly that they were but did not create enough of a scandal for the mother to renounce her plans).

Ramos-Perea's story reaches its outcome rapidly with an economy of short scenes. The stage directions are also sparse and indicate only a few items onstage: a table and chairs, a telephone, and a balcony. The dialogue communicates that the play takes place in the family home, but unlike *Hotel Melancolía* and many plays from the 1950s, *Callando amores* does not emphasize the space of the house in communicating the work's themes. Instead, intermittent monologues constitute the play's most compelling theatrical technique. They take place at the beginning or the end of a scene and are marked by a burst of light resembling a camera flash and sometimes by music. The brief stage directions in the published text leave open how these scenes are to be staged. In José Orraca's film version of the play, these scenes play out as brief press conferences during which the characters address reporters. Since they comment on the outcome of the play's action, they act as prolepses that break the linear development of time. In both versions, the characters break the fourth wall of dramatic realism and address the public directly. This joins the theatrical space of the play with the theater space of the audience, forcing the viewer to face his or her role in a national family feud that has plagued Puerto Rico throughout its history.

At the beginning of the play, Mario's voice announces, "Esta es la historia de mi país" (5) [This is the history of my country]. The story of this family divided over Puerto Rico's relationship to the United States exemplifies the autonomist and annexationist positions that have been at odds since the late nineteenth century. Ramos-Perea has asserted that the Ateneo Puertorriqueño's 1938 contest for national playwrights established the favored theme in Puerto Rican drama as "nuestra tragedia cotidiana de ser colonia de Estados Unidos" ("La dramaturgia" 161) [our daily tragedy of being a colony of the United States]. Not to address this theme, or worse, to question Puerto Rican nationalism, runs the risk of negative public reception (Dávila-López 154–55). Since the late 1960s, however, new themes have appeared on the Puerto Rican stage, and playwrights have begun to address the colonial issue by scrutinizing the discourses that support nationalist and colonialist constructions of identity. In *Callando amores*, Ramos-Perea examines these discourses by creating flawed characters with questionable motives. There is no hero or heroine in this play, nor is there a morally appealing outcome. In this regard, the audience must confront the limitations of the status options embodied by Victoria and Mario. The representation of the family in *Callando amores* provokes the audience to question the validity of the discourses espoused by the characters, whereas in the 1950s, plays tended to present these discourses as natural, downplaying their ideological and constructed character.

Victoria argues that selling the family land to a U.S. company will provide jobs for their economically depressed town. Even though the land is sterile, Mario opposes his mother and endlessly repeats his father's greatest conviction: "¡La tierra no se vende! ¡Porque si la compran, nos compran también a todos!" (53) [Our land is not for sale! Because once they buy it, they buy all of us as well!]. Mario, an *independentista* intellectual, proclaims to believe in the dignity, pride, and honor of his country, which characterizes him, in his mother's opinion, as the prototypical idealist martyr. However, Mario is neither an ideal patriot nor a particularly honorable person. Rather than confronting a family (national) crisis, he escapes to Spain and, within days of his return, ruins his brother's marriage by having an affair with his wife. In my view, Mario's sexist and condescending treatment of Gina compromises his rebellious and misunderstood poet persona.[22] Most important, as the following dialogue indicates, Mario's cynicism devalues his integrity:

Mario. Tal vez construya un castillo justo en medio del Valle. Eso. Un castillo con un gran casino, una barra, un prostíbulo, algo apestoso y sucio que nos recuerde de lo podridos que estamos.

Madre. ¿Sabes cuántas familias podrían salir de la miseria si esa fábrica se construye allí?

Mario. Ya conozco la perorata. Gina también me la recitó. Pueblo pequeño, miseria grande. ¿Qué culpa tengo yo de todo eso? Eso no tiene remedio. (30)

[Mario. Maybe I'll build a castle right in the middle of the Valley. That's it. A castle with a big casino, a bar, a brothel, something stinky and dirty that will remind us of how rotten we are.

Madre. Do you know how many families could climb out of misery if that factory was built here?

Mario. I already know the story. Gina already recited it to me. Small town, big misery. Am I to blame for all of this? There's nothing to be done about it.]

In essence, Mario's anachronistic ideals seem egotistical and fatalistic. His mother tells him that they are "mentiras que tú necesitas para justificar tu odio, tu cerrazón, y tu venganza" (36) [lies that you need to justify your hatred, your close-mindedness, and your revenge].

Likewise, vengeance for what Victoria considers her husband's "betrayal" inspires her supposed concern for the town's future. On the surface, Victoria's plan to sell the land appears practical and generous, but other details about her character make her motives suspect. Her marriage to Mario's father was political—it represented a national family romance, a wedding of aristocratic bloodlines with political power. Thus, when Victoria lost her place in the elite social circles because of her husband's political act, she sought revenge by having an affair with one of the men he had denounced. Now that her husband has died, Victoria's sale of the land, according to Mario, constitutes another form of revenge: "Es como una reivindicación. ¡Justo su Valle!, para dar la impresión de que él, desde el otro mundo, pide perdón a todos quienes hizo mal" (33) [It's like a vindication. Precisely his Valley! To give the impression that he is asking, from beyond the grave, to be forgiven by all those he wronged].

Mario also doubts Victoria's interest in the well-being of the pueblo and labels her plan "Ambición disfrazada de liberalismo" (36) [Ambition disguised as liberalism]. Certainly, her reasons for selling the land reveal her lack of faith in the Puerto Rican working class: "¡Hay que venderla porque hemos sido demasiado vagos, indolentes y cobardes y no tenemos la mínima voluntad para ponerla a producir!" (33) [We have to sell it because we have been too lazy, apathetic, and cowardly, and we don't have the least amount of will to make it productive!]. Moreover, this statement on Puerto Rican docility reveals her colonialist mentality (and implies her annexationist stance) by suggesting that foreigners will manage the land better.

A final character nuance includes Victoria's mercurial disposition toward Mario and Gina. She presents herself as a doting mother-in-law and loving mother one minute, and in the next, she verbally abuses Gina. Similarly, while she reproaches Mario for the suffering his absence has caused her, it becomes apparent that when he left, she erased his very existence from the family. In the final analysis, Victoria is equally as unlikable as her son, for her cynical pragmatism matches his cynical idealism. As her name predicts, Victoria wins this particular battle, but the damage it does to her family must disconcert the audience and lead them to question whether any of the options presented by the play are best for the nation.

To morally ambiguous characters and a questionable denouement, Ramos-Perea adds intertextuality and the theme of performance as repetition to foreground the awareness with which the characters replay a conflict that has no satisfying outcome. On a most general level, the themes of the search for identity and nostalgia for the land from earlier literary generations serve as intertexts for *Callando amores*. In particular, the play shares similar dilemmas and characters with Casas's *Eugenia Victoria Herrera* (1964) and Marqués's *Un niño azul para esa sombra* (1960). In Casas's piece, siblings disagree over the future of the family land, but she subverts the typical patriarchal identity story by having the daughter rather than the son defend the family heritage. The late-nineteenth-century "discurso de la tierra" [discourse of the land] espoused by Eugenia Victoria and her father find their counterparts in Mario and his father in *Callando amores*. Likewise, the matriarchal malice and nostalgia for the absent nationalist father in Ramos-Perea's play recalls the LeFranc family in *Un niño azul para esa sombra*. Mario stands in for a grown-up Michelín in his resentment toward his mother for her sexual and political betrayal of his (idealized) father. Both plays also contain the self-destructive nationalist character in Puerto Rican literature identified by Marqués in "El puertorriqueño dócil." One must ask, why does

Ramos-Perea, in the 1990s, restage these stories, and how are they different? The composition of the family itself has not changed in striking ways, and neither have the issues that divide it. I would suggest that Ramos-Perea "haunts" his play by recycling earlier plots to imply that the stories do not differ enough. To dramatize the same conflict in the context of the 1990s reveals the crisis of the discourses that have fueled the debate over national identity for more than a century.

Self-reflexivity distinguishes Ramos-Perea's contemporary version, for the characters are evidently aware that they are replaying a story to an audience that also already knows how it will end. In addition to the play's Puerto Rican intertexts, references to the plots of *telenovelas* [soap operas] and literary works such as *Hamlet* and Jorge Manrique's poetry foreground the characters' lack of creativity in constructing their own life plots. As Mario complains, his situation is "una historia tan conocida. Como la letra de un bolero. Como el final de una noveleta mediocre. Bah . . . la literatura está llena de historias como ésta. Uno las lee, las mofa, y de pronto, se encuentra uno en medio de ellas, tan predecibles, tan acechantes" (13) [such a well-known story. Like the lyrics of a bolero. Like the end of a mediocre novel. Bah . . . literature is filled with stories like this one. You read them, make fun of them and suddenly find yourself in the middle of them, so predictable, so imminent]. Mario is a former writer who has rejected literature because "se convierte en un vicio sin sentido, en la constante y aburrida repetición de una pervertida frivolidad" (14) [it becomes a senseless vice in the constant and boring repetition of a perverted frivolity]. However, Mario's own life and that of his family's ironically have become a repeating text. Mario believes that everything is known, that there is no surprise ending to his story, yet he continues to play the prefabricated part of the wayward son who returns home to claim his inheritance. Unlike Gina, who suggests that, as in a *telenovela*, the convoluted plot will turn out well in the end, Mario fears the real-life aftermath of his decisions. Similar to Hamlet, he begins to ponder the consequences of his actions: "Estamos en el fin del siglo, cobramos por ser idealistas" (44) [We're at the end of the century, we're paying for being idealists].

Mario's criticism of literature echoes Ramos-Perea's call for Puerto Rican writers to explore new themes in their works, and the blurring of the boundaries between art and life also denaturalizes, in a postmodern fashion, the annexationist and nationalist positions that have dominated

the status debate in Puerto Rico.²³ Similar to the use of intertexts, performance as repetition serves as a strategy that problematizes these hegemonic discourses. Repetition becomes a motif in the first scene of the
play from the moment Gina notes that Victoria repeats herself. Victoria
tells Gina: "Uno repite para reafirmarse" (7) [You repeat to reaffirm
yourself]. Gina, however, asks: "¿Y qué pasa cuando se repiten los
errores?" (7) [And what happens when you repeat mistakes?]. Similarly,
when Victoria reminds Mario that no one remembers his father, he replies: "por eso repetimos los mismos errores" (49) [that's why we make
the same mistakes over and over]. Mario associates errors with a lack of
respect for the past. For him, selling land betrays the nation and induces
historical forgetfulness. On the other hand, Mario's memories are not
particularly productive. Despite being aware that simply repeating his
father's famous credo—"la tierra no se vende" [the land is not for sale]—
means little, he persists: "Es una frase desabrida, vieja, hueca, retórica ... Sí,
una verdad tan rancia que de tanto repetirla se vuelve falsa" (19) [It's an
insipid, old, hollow, rhetorical phrase . . . Indeed, a truth so stale that it
becomes false out of constant repetition].²⁴

Although *Callando amores* does not advocate Victoria's materialist
position over Mario's nationalist stance, the play targets nationalism for
its critique by focusing on the father and son parallel. Mario's repetition
of his father's actions and ideology constitutes a performance according
to Joseph Roach's definition of the concept: "Performance [. . .] stands in
for an elusive entity that it is not but that it must vainly aspire both to
embody and to replace. Hence flourish the abiding yet vexed affinities
between performance and memory, out of which blossom the most florid
nostalgias for authenticity and origin" (3). Besides repeating his father's
political discourse, in several scenes Mario replays family episodes from
the past. Like a director, he recalls the physical arrangement of the cast of
characters and reviews the dialogue: "Y las palabras de papá . . . 'Tengo
que hacerlo, Victoria. Si no lo hago, no podré mirar a mis hijos a la cara
jamás.' ¿Lo recuerdas?" (31) [And Dad's words . . . "I have to do it, Victoria. If I don't, I will never be able to look at my children in the face." Do
you remember?]. Mario even copies his father's actions by denouncing
Victoria's sale of the land.

In Mario's attempt to be a surrogate for his father, he performs him,
but, as Roach's view of performance suggests, Mario can never really replace his father, because he only performs a selective memory of him. For

example, he remembers his father's "gran acto de honestidad" (31) [great act of honesty] and would like to replicate it, but Victoria has to remind him how his father used to criticize his adolescent attempts at poetry. Similarly, Mario tends to forget his father's role in the family rift by blaming his mother. When Victoria asserts that the breakup of the family was his father's fault, Mario avoids acknowledging his father's part in the conflict. In his desire to perform his father, Mario's memories surely construct a picture of him more admirable than reality.

Roach argues that performances never repeat themselves exactly, that "they must be invented or recreated at each appearance. In this improvisatorial behavioral space, memory reveals itself as imagination" (25). But Mario's performance of his father limits him to repeating conflicts from the past. The only difference between his father's situation and his own is the contemporary context and cynicism with which Mario pursues "¡el gran sueño de libertad por el que ya nadie quiere dar ni una esperanza!" (50) [the great dream of liberty for which no one even wants to hope!]. Memory, for both Victoria and Mario, does not yield to imagination in the sense that they never discover a way to rewrite the scenarios of the past. As the following statement indicates, Victoria has failed to recognize her part in supporting the ideological "walls" that divide Puerto Ricans: "¡Muros, hijo! Los muros del odio que ahora andan cayéndose por todo el mundo, todavía están de pie en tu corazón" (35) [Walls, son! The walls of hatred that are now falling all around the world are still standing in your heart]. Victoria's stance has afforded her economic success, but both mother and son are trapped in an old national family quarrel.

Callando amores enacts a story of familial disintegration all too recognizable for Puerto Rican audiences. Ramos-Perea's version distinguishes itself by flaunting its textual repetitiveness and staging the self-conscious performance of worn out discourses and a morally unappealing conflict. The play challenges and frustrates the audience because it locks its characters into repeating errors of the past and characterizes the annexationist-nationalist polarity that has framed Puerto Rican identity debates as unproductive. *Callando amores* puts the burden of imagining new ways to confront the issue of Puerto Rican identity on the audience. Read within the context of Ramos-Perea's involvement in the NDP movement and his other plays that have staged new perspectives on national events, the play implies the need for new texts that reflect diverse modes of perceiving Puerto Rican collective experience. The most conspicuously silent voice in *Callando amores* is that of the *pueblo* [common people] that would be most affected by Victoria's and Mario's actions. Perhaps in the absence of this perspective, the play signals the need to recognize the working class as a potential site for breaking free from an old family conflict, thus moving national history in a different direction.

Subverting the Patriarchal Family Script

Although Ramos-Perea and Luis Rafael Sánchez (b. 1938) have very different literary projects and occupy distinct roles in the development of Puerto Rican drama, their plays *Callando amores* and *Quíntuples* (1984) share an urge to examine father figures and their relation to conceptions of the family and the nation. Mario's impotent repeat performance of his father's *independentista* role suggests a need for new ways to consider identity that fit Puerto Rico's current context. In Sánchez's play, the Morrisons, a family acting troupe composed of a father and his quintuplets, stray from Papá Morrison's prewritten libretto to perform improvisational monologues. Their subversion of his script undermines the cultural authority of the paternalist family that Juan Gelpí has shown to be a key metaphor in Puerto Rican nationalist discourse of identity. Both Ramos-Perea and Sánchez reject the paternalist nationalism of former literary generations, but unlike many playwrights in Puerto Rico's dramatic tradition, Sánchez approaches the island's preoccupation with identity through humor.

Most critics consider Sánchez Puerto Rico's leading contemporary literary figure. He made his mark in Puerto Rican theater as an author, director, and actor in the late 1950s and 1960s. Since then, although only two of his new plays have been published and staged—*Parábola del Andarín* [Parable of the wanderer] (1979) and *Quíntuples* (1984)—he has continued to exert a significant presence in Puerto Rican theater and performance.[25] Sánchez's works, which intersect with the NDP movement of the late 1960s and 1970s, distinguish themselves from this political and popular theater in their focus on experimentation with language and literary traditions. Ramos-Perea has criticized Sánchez's plays for their lack of overt social commitment: "Un teatro amparado exclusivamente en la 'innovación' del lenguaje por el lenguaje mismo, muy poco servicio rinde al compromiso con la realidad que exige su correspondencia en el arte" ("De cómo" 51) [A theater based exclusively on the "innovation" of language for the sake of language itself barely responds to the engagement with reality that requires its correspondence in art]. Other

critics, however, identify a unique social perspective in Sánchez's exploration of Puerto Rico's colonial condition not only through language and
literature but also through themes of popular culture, race, class, gender,
and sexual orientation.[26]

In *Quíntuples*, Sánchez focuses explicitly on theatrical performance
and gender perfomativity to explore nation as an unstable and heterosexist construct. As many essayists argue in the collection *Nationalisms
and Sexualities* (1991), a problem of gender and sexual identity oftentimes enacts a crisis of the oppositional polarities supporting nationalist
and colonialist discourses.[27] In *Quíntuples*, the complicated sexual identities performed by the Morrison family produce what Judith Butler calls
"gender trouble," that is, they decenter and destabilize gender and sex
categories based on binaries (*Gender Trouble* x). Through improvisation
rather than repetitive performance, the children reveal problematic sexual identities that subvert Papá Morrison's patriarchal script for performing a heterosexual national family romance. Moreover, intertexts, parody,
and metatheater undermine the authority of the paternalist, authorlike
voice identified as L.R.S. in the play's prologue and expose the role of
representation in positing identities.

The two-act play presents a series of monologues delivered by the
Morrison quintuplets, Dafne, Baby, Bianca, Mandrake, and Carlota, who
form a traveling acting company led by Papá Morrison. Rather like a
circus troupe, the family itself forms the spectacle, and their performances treat "el relato de sus vidas llenas de sorpresas" (35) [the story of
their lives full of surprises]. Tonight, however, Dafne has proposed that
they improvise monologues because they have a special audience, con-
ventioneers at a Conference on Family Affairs. The spectators who form
the audience of Sánchez's play are therefore unknowingly cast as conference participants. In six separate scenes, each member of the family delivers an improvisational monologue on the themes of love and imagination
that reveals much about their individual identities and their family relationships. The audience discovers its theatricalized role when the actors'
monologues solicit its participation. The exposed stage, which contains a
table with a podium and a pitcher of water, and the same lighting onstage
as in the auditorium constitute visual signs hinting at the audience's role
in the play. The actors perform a similar double role by stepping out of
their characters (performing quintuplets) and speaking as family members, such as when Papá Morrison addresses the audience and complains

about the demands of improvisation.[28] The show's ending adds a third metatheatrical level by exposing all theatrical artifice when the actor who plays Papá Morrison exclaims: "No puedo construir más peripecias de unos quíntuples inventados y del Padre también inventado que los acompaña" (77) [I can't concoct any more adventures of some invented quintuplets and of their invented Father who accompanies them]. He and the actress who plays the three female roles then remove their makeup onstage.

Although Papá Morrison only makes his entrance onstage near the end of the play, his children's monologues have already constructed his character. He likes redundancy, however, and introduces himself as "Papá Morrison, el Gran Divo Papá Morrison, Padre de los Quíntuples Morrison, Director Escénico de las Veladas Donde Triunfa el Buen Arte de los Quíntuples Morrison. Fantaseador" (68) [Daddy Morrison, the Great Divo Daddy Morrison, Father of the Morrison Quintuplets, Scenic Director of the Soirées Where the Fine Art of the Morrison Quintuplets Triumphs. Fantasy-maker]. As this list of titles and his nickname, El Gran Semental [The Great Sperm Bank], indicate, Papá Morrison is a truly paternal figure, author of both the family and the show.[29] According to Baby, Papá Morrison's libretto addresses "las grandes ilusiones de la vida en familia, sobre la urgente necesidad de amar . . . (*Tierno y cursi.*) sobre los recuerdos de haber crecido juntos como una familia de pollitos" (23) [the great illusions of family life, about the urgent need to love . . . (*Tender and campy.*) about the memories of having grown up like a family of little chicks]. Bianca's monologue provides more information about the contents of the family show: "Ocurrencias, situaciones inverosímiles que surgen entre las personas que crecen juntas, la declamación de poemas finos de Rubén Darío, Alfonsina Storni y Luis Lloréns Torres—y poetas más recientes—integran al repertorio artístico y humano de la agrupación. Nada grosero encuentra entre ellos lugar" (35–36) [Odd events, implausible situations that arise among people who grow up together, the reciting of fine poems by Rubén Darío, Alfonsina Storni, and Luis Lloréns Torres—and more recent poets—make up the artistic and human repertoire of the group. Nothing vulgar finds its way in]. Positive family values and good taste characterize Papá Morrison's script. The actual improvisational performances, however, reveal a rather different picture of the family. Baby's description of the chaos that ensued when Dafne suggested that they improvise—"¡Todos nos salimos de las casillas! ¡Todos nos descompusimos! ¡No sé improvisar!" (24) [We all went crazy! We all fell apart! I don't know how to improvise!]—suggests the gap between Papá Morrison's dutifully performing quintuplets and their true family relations.

As Priscilla Meléndez has observed, the monologic structure of the play insinuates a lack of communication among family members ("Lo uno" 10). There are many less subtle indications of the family's problematic relationships as well. Bianca's monologue reveals that Papá Morrison censures the content of his show by excluding politics from his scripts. The children's automatic apologies when they use language that could be construed as vulgar indicate that Papá Morrison's scripts also carefully monitor their choice of words. By talking about how they once endorsed baby products, Bianca emphasizes how Papá Morrison has economically exploited his children: "Papá Morrison dijo el que no trabaja no come. Y nos puso a los quíntuples Morrison a sudar la gota gorda" (38) [Daddy Morrison said he who doesn't work, doesn't eat. And he made the Morrison quintuplets sweat their asses off]. The fact that both Baby and Dafne confess that they plan to leave the family to join the Gran Circo Antillano [Great Antillean Circus] also indicates that the family members are not as united as Papá Morrison's libretto suggests. Without the script dictating their lines, even Papá Morrison fails to uphold the facade of a happy family. He tells the audience that "el matrimonio es una institución penitenciaria. Yo lo descubrí pronto. Pero enviudé pronto gracias a Dios" (72) [marriage is a penitential institution. I quickly realized it. But I became a widower soon, thank God], and then tries to cover up his indiscretion with a coughing fit. In the end, confessions such as these lead Papá Morrison to call Dafne's plan to improvise a "locura" (71) [madness], because such variations from the script reveal marriage and family as oppressive social structures.

Improvisation involves risk because it uncovers what the patriarchal script hides. Dafne, repeating her father, says: "la improvisación corre el peligro de la dispersión, decía, . . . ¿qué decía? . . . (*Recordando de súbito.*) hablaba de los besos y decía que algunos fingimientos nos complacen, nos agradan" (6–7) [improvisation runs the risk of dispersion, he used to say, . . . what did he say? . . . (*Suddenly remembering.*) he spoke of kisses and said that some pretenses please and gratify us]. Thus improvisation unmasks the web of pretense that casts Papá Morrison as the patriarch of a close-knit, well-adjusted family. References to incest, multiple births, and a variety of sexual identity issues imply that the Morrisons embody far from the typical national family romance. Arnaldo Cruz-Malavé has argued that "the specter of homosexuality haunts Puerto Rico's hegemonic discourse of national identity" (141). Following Doris Sommer's theory of foundational fictions, he maintains that Puerto Rico represents a failed family romance in the sense that it lacks the heterosexual desire to build the nation. In literature, Cruz-Malavé argues, Puerto Rico's "queer" status as a nation-colony plays out as a failed bildungsroman, because the island never reached "manhood" or independence (142). By these terms, if the family in Sánchez's play is the "gran familia puertorriqueña" with Papá Morrison at its head, then the complicated sexual identities the Morrisons expose in their improvisations on family life foreground problematic issues of collective identity.

Dafne's and Mandrake's performances display their exaggerated beauty and sexuality. Dafne's interest in men borders on nymphomania: she has married seven times and now plans to run off with a circus dwarf. Her description of Papá Morrison as "mundanal, liviano, fiestea, mujerea" (6) [worldly, flighty, a partying womanizer] captures her own personality as well, and the recurring emphasis on their sameness is one of the play's more subtle hints at the lack of boundaries implicit in incest. Mandrake, Dafne's stunningly handsome brother, is similarly inward looking in his narcissism. In addition, his interest in Dafne may stretch a typical brotherly bond: "Le di un beso en la mejilla a Dafne Morrison cuando salía hacia el bar y la piropé [sic]: Ya quisiera la Diana Ross para sus días festivos ser tan linda como tú. (*Carcajea.*) Hay que mostrarle ternura a las hermanas" (46) [I kissed Dafne Morrison's cheek as she left the bar and I flirted with her: Wouldn't Diana Ross hope to be as pretty as you are on her good days. (*He cackles.*) You have to be tender to sisters]. To top off Mandrake's exaggerated virility, the stage directions also allude to his possible bisexuality.

While Dafne and Mandrake exude passion, Baby and Bianca, in contrast, repress their sexual identities. The empty cage Baby carries for his cat, Gallo Pelón, constitutes one sign of this repression. The stories Baby has constructed around this imaginary friend complement his childlike demeanor, seen as well in his propensity for tantrums. In a sense, Baby is asexual because he has never grown up. His underdeveloped sense of identity has tormented him since childhood, during which he and Mandrake were "tan vesiditos igualitos de marineritos que yo no sabía si yo era yo o si yo era mi hermanito" (23) [all dressed up so exactly the same as little sailors that I didn't know if I was me or I was my brother]. Bianca also struggles to assert herself among her siblings. Bianca's battle with repressing her urge to smoke, conveyed gesturally and verbally, serves as a metaphor for her attempt to conceal her lesbianism. Her gender-bending behavior and appearance and her Freudian slips, however, betray her secret.

Carlota, the last sibling to perform, is due to give birth to quintuplets at any moment. She embodies an overstated procreative heterosexuality. As John Perivolaris notes, Carlota's role as a mother figure is yet another hint at the family's complicated incestuous relationships: "A historical continuity/contiguity is suggested by an incestuous blurring of generations and relationships on the part of Carlota" ("El cuento" 355). As evidence for an incestuous relationship between Carlota and Papá Morrison, Perivolaris points out that Carlota treats her husband as if he were a child and Papá Morrison as if he were her husband. I would add that Carlota's braids also connect her to her father, for in his monologue, Papá Morrison relates the misadventure of climbing his lover's braids in an effort to enter her window (76–77).[30]

The theatrical context in which the Morrisons perform their problematic family relations and complex sexual identities underlines the scriptedness of the heterosexual family structure as well as its performativity. Butler has defined performativity as the act of repeating the norms that constitute and regulate us as subjects. In regard to gender and sexual identities, she asserts that heterosexual norms are "for the most part compulsory performances, ones which none of us choose, but which each of us is forced to negotiate" (Butler, "Critically" 26). For Butler, there is no originary or essential identity—gender, family, national, or otherwise—that exists outside its performative acts. Rather, the constant need for repeat performances to reaffirm the norms that regulate identity not only reveals its own instability and citationality but also allows for subversive repetition that exposes the norms as arbitrary and inefficacious (Butler, "Critically" 26). In *Quíntuples*, Papá Morrison's script on family unity enacts the compulsory performance of the heterosexual national family. As we have seen, Dafne's Pirandellian request to improvise opens the door for resisting a repeat performance of the patriarchal libretto. Nevertheless, improvisation does not signify that the siblings are able to invent entirely new roles for themselves, because they can never completely escape performing prescribed family roles and the many

other discourses that construct them as subjects.[31] The improvised monologues do permit the audience to witness, however, the different processes that form identity, and by focusing our attention on the subject-
in-process, the play recognizes the plurality, ambiguity, and fluidity of
individual or collective identities. Thus *Quíntuples* posits a view of the
Puerto Rican national family that highlights its diversity and changeabil-
ity, which contrasts with the more fixed definitions of national community in plays from the 1950s.

The quintuplet's dissimilar styles of improvisation, self-presentation,
and interaction with the audience help construct the identity of each
character. Baby and Bianca see themselves as inadequate improvisers, and
their awkward gestures and difficult linguistic control communicate this.
Baby obsessively asks the audience if it can hear him, and Bianca is painfully aware that she cannot compete with Dafne's theatricality. Carlota
resists improvisation by rejecting spontaneity altogether, and she scripts
and directs the scenario of her quintuplets' birth. Dafne, Mandrake, and
Papá Morrison, in contrast, revel in their outrageous physical appearance, in the facility with which they verbally improvise, and in their
ability to manipulate the audience with their gregarious and seductive
personalities. Dafne and Papá Morrison make their stage entrance demanding applause, and Mandrake goes as far as to say: "¡El cuento no es
el cuento! El cuento es quien lo cuenta" (50) [The tale is not the tale! The
tale is in the teller of the tale]. Their delivery of the story may be more
compelling than its message, but their personalities cannot dominate entirely because the stories they tell also construct them. That is, they do
not invent their identities; rather, they model themselves on film, theater,
and music icons. Mandrake's questions—"¿Cuál vida me improviso para
ustedes? ¿La del quintuple que recita *El duelo de la cañada* o *El brindis
del bohemio?*, ¿la del amante empedernido?, ¿la del jugador empedernido?" (51) [Which life do I improvise for you? The life of the quintuplet
who recites *El duelo de la cañada* or *El brindis del bohemio*? The life of
the hard-hearted lover? The life of the die-hard player?]—imply that he
can choose whichever identity he would like. These parts, however, are
not originals; they are the prewritten roles of a performing quintuplet, or
those of a stereotype. Dafne, Papá Morrison, and Mandrake may stray
from the patriarchal family script with dramatic flair, but they must
struggle for self-definition as much as the rest of the family.

The improvisations further explore subjectivity formation by highlighting how the family members define one another. As the first quintu-

plet to perform, Dafne previews her sibling's personalities: "Baby Morrison es nervioso y Bianca Morrison es hielo y esfinge y Carlota Morrison es una mujer enfermiza. Mandrake el Mago es distinto, todo lo soluciona" (9) [Baby Morrison is nervous, and Bianca Morrison is icy and unreadable, and Carlota Morrison is sickly. Mandrake the Magician is different, he fixes everything]. Carlota has a different perspective, and she presents herself as the only sane sibling. Bianca, similarly, positions herself in terms of eccentricity. She sees herself as less eccentric than Dafne, Mandrake, Baby, and Papá Morrison, but more so than Carlota. Not surprisingly, Baby, the character most vividly defined by the others, is the quintuplet with the weakest personality. Baby becomes babylike because his siblings make him so by coddling him and telling him he is timid. Baby is trapped (as his cage suggests) in a personality constructed by others: "¡Y Baby Morrison termina por ser tímido aunque Baby Morrison no lo sea! ¡Uno es, también, carajo carajete, lo que los demás quieren!" (26) [And Baby Morrison comes across as shy, even though he isn't! One is also—damn it!—what people want you to be]. Consequently, he is forced to express himself through tantrums, "Cuando chillo me impongo" (24) [When I scream, I get my way], which ironically only add to his immature character. In the final analysis, without the play's master narrative of Papá Morrison's patriarchal script controlling their performances, we witness a much more conflicted and dynamic version of individual, family, and collective identity.

Mirroring the quintuplets' subversion of their father's libretto, Sánchez ridicules authority on a metatextual level by examining the paternalism implicit in authorship.[32] The prologue by a fictionalized L.R.S. parodies the hierarchal relationship between playwright, director, actors, and public. Thus, just as Papá Morrison's script tries to control his family's performances, in the prologue L.R.S. stipulates how the *Quíntuples* script is to be performed: "De ninguna manera, bajo ningún pretexto de experimentación, distanciamiento o muestra de originalidad, deberán dichas acotaciones ofrecerse al público" (xiv) [Under no circumstance, under no pretext of experimentation, distancing, or show of originality, shall these stage directions be made available to the audience]. L.R.S. states that the long stage directions are, "pese a su apariencia, un código de señales para que la atmósfera específica que *el autor* imaginó mientras construía su pieza teatral se realice" (xiv, my emphasis) [in spite of their appearance, a code of signs so that the specific atmosphere that *the author* imagined while writing the theatrical piece can be carried out]. This insistence on authorial control becomes exaggerated in its repetition and assumes an ironic tone when L.R.S. refers to his own instructions as preachy. L.R.S. also playfully highlights his power by incorporating the audience in the fiction of the play and then pointing out that it cannot fully participate. He does this by making the descriptive stage directions miniature narratives that form part of the artistic creation that is *Quíntuples*. Not only does the audience have no access to the humorous descriptions, but Sánchez also flaunts its exclusion when he includes this detail about Bianca: "*Sus manos tiemblan aunque el público no lo sabe*" (34) [*Her hands tremble, although the audience does not know it*]. The control L.R.S. exercises through his stage directions parodies the paternalism of what Sánchez has called René Marqués's "divinas palabras" ("Las divinas" 14) [divine words]. Sánchez uses this phrase to describe the effect Marqués's brand of Christian nationalism had on audiences of the 1950s and his status as a revered playwright. Sánchez's own stage directions also make fun of Marqués's godlike attempt to control the performance text by writing long, detailed stage directions and his notorious authoritarianism in the staging of his works.[33]

Sánchez's subtle critique of Marqués's paternalism is emblematic of their contrasting views on the national family romance. In classic plays by Marqués from the 1950s, such as *Los soles truncos, Un niño azul para esa sombra*, and *La carreta*, nationalism is linked to the characters' yearning for an absent father who signifies an ordered patriarchal world in which race, class, and gender roles are clearly defined. *Quíntuples*, in contrast, presents a patriarch who cannot control the script of a traditional heterosexual national family. Sánchez, moreover, deconstructs his own paternalist authorial voice when, in the end, the two actors who once appeared to be six "unmask and question the farcical and false nature of both the family and the theatre" (Meléndez, "Lo uno" 146). The actors assert that the magic of theater is a "mentira," or a fiction, that connects "como una maroma entre ustedes, el público y nosotros, los actores" (78) [like a tightrope, you, the audience, and, us, the actors]. *Quíntuples* exemplifies the risk implicit in performance because it suggests that, like art, all forms of identity are human-made representations that must be constantly (re)performed. The improvisations by the Morrison quintuplets reveal identities to be constructed and changeable rather than seamless and fixed. In particular, the gender trouble caused by the performance of their conflicted sexual identities destabilizes the binaries that support many constructions of the family and the nation in plays from the 1950s. Through improvisation rather than repetitive performance, the Morrison family elides the patriarchal script of heterosexist nationalism and enacts instead a queer, nonessential family romance at odds with rigid colonialist/nationalist discourses of identity.

The Circus as Translocal Nation

In *Quíntuples* and in Myrna Casas's *El gran circo eukraniano* (1988), the absence of a family home represented onstage underscores the impossibility of uniting a "gran familia puertorriqueña" under one roof.[34] In contrast to countless Puerto Rican plays of earlier generations, both plays situate the family on a stage, a public performance space, rather than in a house. Presenting a bare stage rather than a realistically constructed set is one Brechtian quality Casas's play shares with *Quíntuples*. Both works also incite the intellectual participation of the spectator by rejecting an Aristotelian narrative in favor of a nonlinear plot structure and by using a self-conscious acting style that disturbs the distance between actor and character and breaks the fourth wall of realism. Furthermore, in the Brechtian tradition, both playwrights employ popular theatrical forms— commedia dell'arte, vaudeville, and the circus—to stimulate critical awareness through entertainment. By self-consciously using performance as an activity to explore identity, these plays expose the instability of the national family metaphor as a blueprint for collective identity. Casas's group of six performers, however, does not create the campy circus-like atmosphere of *Quíntuples;* in contrast, they perform thoughtful (and often satirical) monologues and skits about the locales where their circus visits. Thus, unlike the Morrisons, the goal of the Gran Circo Eukraniano is to perform others, not themselves. Their condition as a (reconstituted) family of circus performers does, however, enact Puerto Rico as a translocal nation, and the circus's migratory performances underline the fluidity of identity in general and the translocality of *puertorriqueñidad* in particular. The play deconstructs the myth of a unified Puerto Rican national family and poses instead an image of a geographically diverse collective identity. Just as in *Quíntuples*, in which serious questions lurk beneath hilarious performances of conflicted sexual identities, Casas's humorous play addresses Puerto Rico's status as a fragmented national community.

Recent studies on the Puerto Rican diaspora provide a useful framework for examining *El gran circo*. Many critics have examined how Puerto Rican writers have, since the 1960s, increasingly imagined a national identity that includes Puerto Ricans living in the United States.[35] I borrow the terms "translocal nation" and "transnation" from Agustín Lao, who theorizes Puerto Rican national identity as "a translocal historical category whose boundaries shift between the archipelago of Puerto Rico and its U.S. diaspora" (171). He argues for a conception of national community that takes into account the multiple geographic spaces and the different economic, political, and cultural settings that frame *puertorriqueñidad*. In this vein, Alberto Sandoval-Sánchez argues that the literary trope of travel in Puerto Rican literature represents this collective identity "in the context of mobility, crisscrossing, transitivity, dispersion, errantry, discontinuity, and fragmentation" ("Puerto Rican Identity" 194). Sandoval-Sánchez traces literary constructions of air migration and asserts that the generation of the 1950s (including René Marqués, Pedro Juan Soto, José Luis González, and others) relied on the myth of the return trip, whereas the generation of the 1960s faced the reality that most emigrants had become settled on the mainland. In this generation, authors such as Jaime Carrero began to represent a process of transculturation, the formation of the bicultural subjectivity of the Nuyorican (Sandoval-Sánchez, "Puerto Rican Identity" 194–95). By the 1980s, works such as Luis Rafael Sánchez's essay "La guagua aérea" [The flying bus] and Antonio Martorell's installation "House in Mid-air," based on Sánchez's notion of an airbus, represent "a creative manifesto of/for Puerto Rican identity as a migratory process, a transcultural crossroads, a border zone" (Sandoval-Sánchez, "Puerto Rican Identity" 201).[36] Through the image of the airbus, these artists open a third space, the journey between the island and the mainland, from which to envision Puerto Rican identity. In *El gran circo*, Casas interrogates this in-between space. The migratory lifestyle of the circus in Casas's play, like the images of air migration, undermines homogenous and fixed definitions of home, family, and nation in favor of fluid and hybrid versions of these institutions.

The first dialogue of *El gran circo* announces the theme of identity by foregrounding the act of naming. Gabriela José, the leader of the circus, welcomes the audience to their show. A young woman in the audience corrects her pronunciation of "Eukraniano" with "Ukraniano." This begins a discussion about names in which the woman tells Gabriela José that both her original name, Amarylis, and the name she chose for herself, Alina, derive from *telenovelas*. Alina's partiality to soap operas and her name switch preview the theme of mobile identities. As for the name of the circus, Gabriela José insists that it begins with "Eu" and that the circus has nothing to do with the Soviet Union. Both spellings, however, suggest the circus is a metaphor for Puerto Rico's transnationality because they evoke relationships between multiple spaces. "Eukraniano" calls attention to the circus's relationship to the Estados Unidos, or the United States, and as Vicky Unruh has observed: "Considering that the play was written prior to the USSR's demise, the Ukraine allusion suggests geographically-defined national or ethnic identities in tension with the larger national spaces that encompass them" (139).[37]

Individual and collective identity stories constitute an important component of *El gran circo*. They form the external play that frames the plays-within-the play, the performances related to the circus show. Each performer—Gabriela José, Sandro, Cósima, Igor, Alejandra, and Nené—has a story about his or her past that explains how each came to join the circus. Gabriela José recounts how she and Sandro left a traditional theater company to form their own group, Cósima says she joined because being a business executive bored her, and Nené tells us that Gabriela José took him in because he was homeless. Alejandra's memory of how she and Igor joined the circus places the group in an unnamed country they all remember fondly for its lovely markets, the hospitality of its people, and its good coffee. In short, each member has a past life abandoned for new roles in the circus: Sandro as a lion-man, Igor as a gorilla, Alejandra and Cósima as trapeze artists and dancers, and Nené as messenger. As circus members, they also form a new family, with Gabriela José and Sandro at its head as substitute parents.

Not only have the characters invented new lives for themselves, their task as circus members also entails performing the identity of the communities they visit. In this regard, they have a unique sort of circus that includes theatrical acts. Upon arrival at each new town, the *oídor* [the listener] (formerly Sandro, now Nené) visits offices, clubs, plazas, and restaurants to find out about local events and to speak with people of all social classes in order to bring back "el más fiel retrato de la vida del pueblo" (4) [the best description of whatever town we visited (131)]. The performers then imagine the community by dramatizing it onstage. However, when Gabriela José announces that the circus "trae hoy ante ustedes este Kalideoscopio Pueblerino o Prisma Ambarino, de tropical miopía de una IslaMetrópolis o metropolis isla," (13) [today brings you this Small town Kaleidoscope or Amber Prism, of tropical shortsightedness of an Island-Metropolis or a Metropolis-Island (141)], Alina, who represents the audience and the community performed, coughs. The cough insinuates an uncomfortable reaction to the reference to tropical shortsightedness. That is, the spectators may resist recognizing themselves and the picture of their community represented before them. The theatrical acts provided by the Gran Circo Eukraniano have much more potential to challenge its audience than traditional circus entertainment or the realist drama Gabriela José and Sandro used to perform in a repertory theater. The performances of the places the circus visits portray reality more faithfully than mimetic reproductions, for the kaleidoscopic or prismatic vision they present yields a multifaceted and contradictory portrait of a community.

The metatheatrical structure of *El gran circo* helps to convey one of its major observations on identity. Performing the communities the circus visits highlights how identities are fashioned, as do the various other kinds of performances that make up the play *El gran circo*. The frame play consists of the business of putting on the show, which includes conversations about the place the characters perform and about their personal histories. Within this frame, there is a brief introductory circus parade, several complete skits that seem to be based on the information the actors have acquired about the town, and improvisational monologues in which they adopt the voices of the locals. Throughout the play, Gabriela José announces at least four times that the show is about to begin, which confuses the multiple theatrical levels and makes it difficult to ascertain when the performances begin or end. The actors further delight in confusing the audience by mixing fiction with reality. For instance, we do not know that Cósima's impersonation of a woman she sat next to on the plane—a Puerto Rican woman flying from the United States to the island—is her "number" in the show until after she finishes. Moreover, Alina believes Cósima has based her monologue on reality until Nené comments that he—not the woman—sat next to Cósima on the plane. Gabriela José explains: "Señorita, aquí todo es inventado, invento, invención, imaginación. Esto es un teatro" (9) [Miss, everything here is made up, invented, an invention. This is theater (136)].

Even the outer frame, the moments in between the circus performances, underscores that the actors are *playing* themselves as characters who are actors. Therefore, what appear to be the characters' true life stories cannot be taken at face value. Although Gabriela José and Sandro have left their jobs in a traditional theater to pursue a different kind of performance in the circus, the discourse of bourgeois drama and soap operas contaminates their own life stories. When Gabriela José recalls how she sacrificed her own happiness by allowing her husband to leave with her son to join a more affluent circus, Sandro says, "Eso me suena a novela de televisión o a teatro" (3) [That sounds like a line in a soap or a play (129)].[38] Cósima makes a similar comment when Sandro heroically insists that, unlike Gabriela José's son and husband, he would never leave her. Furthermore, in another plot twist straight out of a soap, Sandro believes that Gabriela José has lost interest in him because she has fallen in love with a younger man, Nené. Similarly, Igor's story of how he escaped from an impoverished childhood has a prewritten ring to it. We realize Igor has invented this story as a spur of the moment improvisation when Alejandra overhears him and, puzzled, asks what he is doing. Alejandra then tells the public a completely different version that sounds equally apocryphal: Igor is a son who displeased his millionaire father by wanting to be an opera singer rather than a businessman. These are just two of the many moments during which one wonders whether any of what the characters say about their pasts is true. Just as there are never pure textual beginnings in the sense that we never know when the show is "on," this constant shifting of masks makes it impossible to discern the characters' true identities. Thus Gabriela José's brand of circus, in opposition to traditional realist theater, seems particularly apt for exploring identity as a flexible construct. As in *Quíntuples*, its improvisational style reveals identities to be disperse and decentered constructions. In highlighting process over product, the performative context of the plays links them to Brechtian dialectical theater, which insists on laying bare the mechanisms for social change.

Casas also posits the circus as a performance mode that suits Puerto Rico's specific cultural and political situation. Circuses evoke family, as they are usually composed at least partially of blood relations, and as we have seen repeatedly in Puerto Rican drama, family embodies the nation. This circus family, however, marks a change from the typical family model from the 1950s because it is not based on kinship and is led by a maternal figure instead of a paternal figure. In addition, circus families are frequently a peculiar sort of family—literally—in the sense that acts consisting of biological oddities such as unusually strong men, bearded women, and extraordinary animal species traditionally make up part of the circus attraction. Ironically, in Sánchez's play the spectacle of performing quintuplets is more circuslike than the actual circus family formed in *El gran circo eukraniano*. In both plays, however, the image of a circus family suggests aberrance and serves to foreground Puerto Rico's status as a political oddity—its anomalous condition as the Western Hemisphere's oldest colony. Moreover, the name of the circus—the Gran Circo Eukraniano—translated as "The Great US Cranial Circus" in the New York Festival Latino production (1989), implies that this strange situation is the invention or brainchild of the United States. One outcome of this colonial "experiment" has been the creation of geographically diverse communities that form Puerto Rico: the island inhabitants, the diasporic Puerto Rican population in the United States, and Puerto Ricans who migrate back and forth between these spaces. The travels of the Gran Circo Eukraniano and its particular mode of performance embody the negotiation of migratory identities as they are rescripted in a variety of scenarios.

By shifting between the audience and the stage, Alina represents a liminal character who marks the presence of different communities of Puerto Ricans. We learn about the island itself through Nené's reports and the skits created from this information. His description of the island resembles Puerto Rico of the 1980s: "Un país muy complicado. Crímenes, droga, la política los tiene enloquecidos" (10) [A very complicated country. Crime, drugs, politics are driving them nuts (137)]. Other problems Nené details include dependency on welfare, homelessness, and deficient public transportation. In the circus number "Auto de la Providencia, Sacramental metropolitano entre Carolina y Cangrejos" (97) [Miracle on Providencia Street, a Metropolitan Morality Play between Carolina and Cangrejos (163)], Casas plays with theater tradition by using automobiles for the scene of a modern-day auto sacramental. Parodying the overabundance of cars on the island, in the skit three separate couples in their cars race home late in the evening in order to beat the rain and to avoid being robbed at a stoplight. Their conversations satirize a variety of issues: materialism, class, relationships and communication between men and women, and dependency on popular culture. In a more serious skit, Alejandra and Nené tell the story of how a working-class mother lost her son in a shooting that was probably drug related. These performances portray the San Juan metropolitan area, which, according to Nené, has become like its own country apart from the rest of the island. This rural/ urban split presents yet more evidence of the diversity of the Puerto Rican experience.

Alina belongs to the metropolitan area imagined onstage, but she, too, expresses interest in joining the circus. The circus members underscore that she is not a part of their world by allowing her onstage and then teasingly revealing that she does not understand the multiple theatrical levels at play. Confused, Alina states: "Pero al principio me aceptaron. Digo, al principio no, pero después . . ." (33) [But at first they accepted me. Well, I mean, not at first, but afterwards . . . (174)]. To join the circus means Alina would leave one Puerto Rican community, the island, for another, a life of migration. The sense of nostalgia and loss exhibited by the circus family might explain why they hesitate to let Alina join them. Throughout the play, the performers insist that they have never been on this island before, yet the place produces nostalgia. Nostalgia, for Roberta Rubenstein, relates to temporality, a yearning for a period of the past, whereas homesickness refers to a locational distancing (4). Both nostalgia and homesickness in Casas's play serve to express the Puerto Rican experience of migration. José, Alejandra, and Cósima reminisce about a rainy town near the sea where they met and where generous people offered them food and wonderful coffee. Just then, Nené enters with some coffee and explains: "Lo trajo una muchacha en un thermo. Dijo que era para los artistas pero . . . ¡Qué curioso! Ahora que lo pienso, dijo que su tía lo había hecho porque a la señora Alejandra le gustaba el café. ¿Cómo sabe esa señora que a ti te gusta tanto el café?" (20) [A girl brought it, in a thermos. She said it was for the actors, but . . . how strange! You know something? Come to think of it, she said her aunt had made it because Alejandra liked it so much. Now, how does this woman know you like coffee so much? (159–60)]. She knows because she remembers Alejandra, which suggests that the circus performers have returned home. Their country of origin, however, has been so transformed by modernization and urbanization that they do not recognize it.

The circus demonstrates what Sandoval-Sánchez views as the false promise of the round-trip ticket and dispels the myth of the eternal return to a rural and utopian place of origin ("Puerto Rican Identity" 192). The circus performers can never take a return trip to the Puerto Rico they left behind because that place no longer exists, and at the same time, they can never really go back because they, too, have become something else.

Still, Alina is unaware of the cultural amnesia a migratory lifestyle has produced for the circus members and is puzzled by their reluctance to let her participate in what she believes to be an exotic job: "Me parece fascinante lo que hacen. Viajar, conocer gente de distintos países" (34) [What you do seems fascinating. You travel, meet people from different countries (175)]. The circus members' visit to this place they feel a connection with, but do not recognize, produces a sense of sadness and loss beneath the traditional surface gaiety of a circus. Gabriela José misses her son, Sandro worries that he might lose Gabriela José's affection, and Alejandra wishes she could have a baby. Alejandra even wonders out loud why they pursue this line of work. Gabriela José's answer is less than reassuring: "[N]o hacemos otra cosa" (17) [Because it's what we do (156)]. Nevertheless, the group's constant performance of identity stories—fictional or not—indicates a preoccupation with origins and a desire for a less nomadic life. Wishing for a house and a family, Alejandra says: "No, esto no es normal. Andareguear por el mundo pretendiendo ser otra y otros" (17) [No, this is not normal. Roaming around the world pretending we're other people (156)]. Gabriela José issues a more direct warning and tells Alina: "Señorita, esto se hace con sangre. Con sangre" (36) [Listen to me. This takes blood, sweat and tears and guts, you hear me, GUTS (178)]. The pain Gabriela José refers to is twofold: first, the precarious existence of an independent, traveling theater, and second, the sense of homelessness suffered by the circus troupe.

Thus, in addition to highlighting the creative possibilities of constant self-invention in the mobile boundary space occupied by the troupe, the play exposes Casas's anxiety about such an existence as well. Joseph Roach writes that "improvisation is an art of collective memory as well as invention" (286). The performers in Gabriela José's circus are master inventors, but the circus's cultural amnesia suggests the need to recognize themselves in one of the collective memories they perform. In this regard, the troupe makes manifest what Arcadio Díaz-Quiñones calls "la memoria rota" [the broken memory], the ruptures in Puerto Rico's historical memory created by the experience of colonialism. For Díaz-Quiñones, a major lapse in traditional narratives of the nation has been emigration, one of Puerto Rico's central historical processes ("La memoria" 46–51). I would argue that the cultural disorientation of the circus troupe and the play's theme of misrecognition illustrate this broken memory. On the one hand, by embodying onstage the complexities of a transnational identity, Casas implicitly does her part to repair Puerto Rico's ruptured memory. On the other hand, the existential bewilderment of the troupe and its longing for a more rooted lifestyle betrays Casas's apprehension about viewing Puerto Rican identity as portable and free of geographical boundaries. That is, the play stops somewhat short of celebrating the migratory space as an interstitial site of new meanings, relations, and cultural practices.[39] Yet by stepping out of the bourgeois living room and onto the stage, the plays by Casas and Sánchez show that new meanings can be ascribed to the family as metaphor for the nation. Their plays' exploration of performance as a space to "house" identity counters some of the more static and totalizing interpretations of the nation seen in predominantly realist Puerto Rican family plays from the 1930s through the 1950s.

The Oscar-nominated film *Linda Sara* (1994), written and directed by Jacobo Morales, captures the paradoxical longing for the past that colors many Puerto Rican artistic works from the 1980s and 1990s. In the film, four siblings in the genteel but financially troubled Escudero Defilló family must find a way to pay for their father's funeral and hold on to the family home for Sara, their elderly widowed mother. Much like in *Hotel Melancolía,* family history fills their colonial home, and when it dawns on one brother that the house is virtually "un almacén de antigüedades" [a storehouse of antiquities], the siblings decide to auction off its contents to save the family from ruin. At the auction, a stranger appears and offers to buy all of the contents provided the family agrees to leave them in the house. Ironically, this mysterious man is Alejandro, Sara's lost love who was rejected long ago as a suitor because he was a working-class *independentista*. A black-and-white film-within-the-film narrates Alejandro and Sara's doomed love story, providing a glimpse of Puerto Rico during the first half of the twentieth century. The auction brings the lovers together again, and the last shot of the movie shows them riding off in a carriage as the film turns from color to black and white. In the final shot, we hear a voiceover of Sara as she turns to the camera and waves: "Anoche soñé que mi vida se había convertido en una película y que las cosas pasaban de la manera que yo quería y nada y nadie podía alcanzarme" [Last night I dreamed that my life had turned into a movie and that everything happened the way I wanted it to and that nothing could touch me].

If events had turned out differently for Sara, how would her family's history have played out differently? That is, by looking at the Puerto Rican past, what is it that Morales wishes could be different? Alejandro and Sara's failed romance seems to replay a national identity story perhaps most famously portrayed in René Marqués's *Los soles truncos*. The movie has many links with Marqués's play; in particular, the family's financial situation, the theme of unfulfilled romance, and the visual images of windows in the style of *soles truncos* evoke the classic drama.[40] In 1958, through the saga of the bankrupt Burkharts, Marqués laments the displacement of the criollo landowning class by U.S.-led modernization. The Burkharts choose to commit suicide rather than confront modernity and cultural change. At the end of the century, Morales dramatizes the ruin of a family with a similar background. This family also ends up bankrupt, although it did survive much longer by adapting to the neocolonial economy. In these stories, holding out against the Americans or selling out to them each results in a similar outcome. However, Morales's recycled version presents some variations that offer an alternative to the colonialist/nationalist binary that limited Marqués's thinking on Puerto Rican identity.

In my view, the film's nostalgia for an idyllic agricultural past is suspect. Sara's wave good-bye to the contemporary world as she rides off to a past epoch can be interpreted as an ironic gesture if one asks what it would really mean to return to this world. The film-within-the-film presents a hierarchical national family ruled by European landowners. Even the film's brief depiction of this paternalist rural utopia reveals that it was stifling for women and offered limited opportunities to the working class and to people of mixed racial heritage. This world denied a marriage that might have strengthened Puerto Rico against North American colonialism by creating a bond between the agricultural proletariat (Alejandro) and the upper class (Sara). The film seems to portray the missed opportunity for such a national romance in terms of regret, for had Sara married Alejandro she would have had more personal fulfillment; likewise, perhaps the family's fortune would have played out differently.[41] Nevertheless, the film also includes other romances that metaphorically suggest alternate spaces from which to imagine Puerto Rican identity. For example, the biracial character Tita is the product of a Nuyorican union between one of the Escudero Defilló brothers living in New York and an African American woman. The characterization of Sofía, the only daughter of the family, as high-strung and in desperate need of control, recalls Bianca, the repressed lesbian in *Quíntuples*. At the end of the film, Sofía's decision to leave the family home and to move in with another woman hints at her homosexuality. The failed marriage between Gustavo, the proudest and most conservative sibling, and his more open-minded and pragmatic wife, Pilar, has produced a bond of friendship and partnership.[42] Unlike Marqués's destructive solutions to cultural change, these relationships that foreground subjectivities constituted by migration, sexuality, and fellowship are indicative of the many possible organizers of Puerto Rico's collective identity.

In the 1980s and 1990s, the legacy of social and economic problems and deep political divisions led many writers to reminisce about what seemed to be a more stable era. Nevertheless, as in *Linda Sara,* this nostalgia never emerges as unproblematized or overly facile. Like in Rodríguez Juliá's album of family photographs, *Linda Sara* visually pays homage to Puerto Rican history at the same time that words and actions deconstruct this idealized past. In the theater, plays like *Hotel Melancolía* and *Callando amores* are nostalgic in their desire to preserve tradition and cultural identity, but they also suggest that the Puerto Rican historical archive be open to reinterpretations of old identity stories and the invention of new ones. By positing the translocality and the "queerness" of *puertorriqueñidad,* plays like *Quíntuples* and *El gran circo eukraniano* offer ways to conceive of identity beyond the discourses of colonialism and nationalism. Although these plays regard paternalist constructions of the family and the nation with suspicion, they do reveal some yearning for the sense of community and stability of the past implicit in earlier portrayals of the national family. In the context of postmodernity, however, it is understood that there are no originary good old days to which to return or any totalizing definitions of Puerto Rico's past, present, or future collective experience. The families represented onstage in recent Puerto Rican drama instead guide audiences to imagine a collective identity informed by difference and change.

Scene 2

• ◆ •

Ties That Bind

Staging the New Family in Revolutionary Cuba

The 1959 Revolution led by Fidel Castro set the Cuban family and nation on a new course. If in prerevolutionary plays generational conflict highlights a Cuban identity repressed by political authoritarianism and neocolonialism, then the Revolution's quest to build a socialist society and the ideal citizen—the "new man"—further exemplifies the imperfect or mutable quality of the Cuban character. The Revolution thus adds another layer to a national identity characterized by transculturation, a process by which contact between various cultures produces a distinct, syncretic culture.[1] While the revolutionary goal of reshaping Cuban identity exposes its constructedness, the idea that the "new" way to be Cuban would rectify a mistaken, bourgeois identity also suggests a fixed (static and perfected) identity envisioned within Marxist terms. In revolutionary society, to be Cuban is to show *conciencia*, the socialist values of dedication, selflessness, cooperation, and loyalty. Mass organizations, schools, the media, and the workplace form this new Cuban identity and redirect loyalties from the family, the Catholic Church, Afro-Cuban religions, and other components of traditional Cuban culture to the nation—now synonymous with the Communist state.

In an effort to change people's consciousness and create a socialist culture, Castro's government has also invested in cultural projects. The theater, for example, has served for many years as a public arena for discussing the problems encountered in constructing a new nation. As a part of this building process, it has been crucial for the Revolution to imbue the family, the basic cell of society, with socialist values. This chapter argues that the family play in post-1959 Cuba both assumes the didactic goal of enacting the changing role of the family in revolutionary society and operates as a barometer of the Revolution's performance, serving as a space from which playwrights examine critically the status of their nation. *La emboscada* [The ambush] by Roberto Orihuela and *Ni un sí ni un no* [No arguments] by Abelardo Estorino stage the formation of new socialist subjectivities in the mid-1960s and mid-1970s. These plays participate in the state's project of transforming traditional conceptions of the family and clarifying the role of the family in the Revolution. The collapse of the Soviet bloc (1989–91), however, has forced the Cuban government to focus on economic survival and on refashioning a political ideology that distances itself from Marxist-Leninist socialism. Thus plays from this period, such as *Manteca* [Lard] by Alberto Pedro Torriente and *Vereda tropical* [Tropical path] by Joaquín Miguel Cuartas Rodríguez, portray the family in a much more fragile state than in the earlier works. These later plays reveal the toll the Revolution has taken on the family unit and a turn toward familial self-sufficiency. If the state is no longer in the paternalist position of being able to provide for "la gran familia cubana," or the nation, then it must allow individual families increased autonomy. At the same time, a more open cultural climate in the 1990s enabled dramatists to express more contentious views of the Revolution.

The relative use of realism in family plays by Orihuela, Estorino, Pedro, and Cuartas provides diverse ways of communicating with the spectator/reader. Although the regime has never enacted a formal policy stipulating a revolutionary aesthetic such as social realism, most plays from the late 1960s through the late 1980s use realism to represent current Cuban themes from the perspective of legitimizing the Revolution. In recent years, though, some playwrights have employed the more experimental techniques rejected in the late 1960s to criticize the government subtly and evade censorship. Conversely, plays that depict Cuba's contemporary problems too directly may meet with more official resistance. In the use of realism, then, we can see how Cuban playwrights negotiate with shifting contextual factors, including what Pierre Bourdieu calls the "field of cultural production," in order to send their messages, whether supportive or critical of the Revolution. For Bourdieu, "to speak of 'field' is to recall that literary works are produced in a particular social universe endowed with particular institutions and obeying specific laws" (163). In Cuba's social universe, the fields of literature and culture are inextricably linked with state socialist institutions.

A New Family for a New Cuba

When Fidel Castro and the 26 of July revolutionary movement triumphantly reached Havana on January 1, 1959, they moved swiftly to effect radical political and economic changes. By 1961, Castro had strained relations with the United States and many middle- and upper-class Cubans by signing an agrarian reform act that expropriated farmlands over a thousand acres and prohibited foreign ownership of land, by nationalizing all U.S. business and commercial property, and by signing a trade agreement in which the Soviets would supply the island with crude oil and other products for Cuban sugar.[2] In this same year, the United States broke diplomatic relations with the island, and Cuban troops defeated the invasion of anti-Castro exiles—supported and trained by the United States—at Playa Girón. With the Revolution, Cuba had finally achieved the national sovereignty and self-determination so fundamental to its concept of national identity.

The notion of a new Cuban citizen played an important role in the ideology that fueled the early years of the Revolution. Rather than following the socialist precept that cultural change must follow the construction of a solid economic foundation, the revolutionary leaders sought to forge a Communist *conciencia* simultaneously with the material base of their society.[3] Ernesto "Che" Guevara, a major figure in the revolutionary vanguard, provided the concept of the *hombre nuevo* [new man] that would guide the creation of revolutionary *conciencia*.[4] Che's theory of a new citizen emerges from several speeches and essays. In "The Duty of a Revolutionary Doctor" (1960), for example, he calls specifically for medical professionals to join the revolutionary movement and generally for Cubans to examine their lives "with critical zeal in order to reach the conclusion that almost everything that we thought and felt before the Revolution should be filed and a new type of human being should be created" (258). In a 1965 essay, Guevara alludes to how the new Cuban must be constructed: "it is necessary to develop a consciousness in which values acquire new categories. Society as a whole must become a gigantic school" ("Socialism" 159). The state will educate the new men and women, but Cubans must also commit to a process of self-education to rid themselves of defects of the past. The new Cuban, affirms Guevara, will reject the past by redefining concepts such as individualism to reflect revolutionary values ("Duty" 260). Thus collective advancement rather than personal gain will motivate the new citizen, providing him or her with "great inner wealth and many more responsibilities" ("Socialism" 167). In short, Guevara and other revolutionary leaders envisioned a new socialist ethic that would transform Cuban society by liberating the island of capitalist cultural ills such as materialism, selfishness, elitism, corruption, sexism, and racism. This ideological idealism motivated the revolutionary movement's initial goals of dismantling the capitalist system and introducing socialist values and institutions.

The failure to meet the all-important goal of a 10-million-ton sugar harvest in 1970, however, forced the Revolution to take a more pragmatic turn. In this decade, Cuba solidified its relationship with the Soviet Union by adopting a similar political and economic system, by signing trade and aid agreements with the superpower, and by sending troops to Africa to support Marxist internationalism. At the same time, to correct the overcentralization that had developed during the crucial first years of the Revolution, the regime emphasized popular participation in decision making and made reforms to give mass organizations more power. These changes institutionalized the Revolution and culminated in the 1976 constitution. The 1974 national meeting of the Federación de Mujeres Cubanas [Federation of Cuban Women] (FMC) and the subsequent involvement of this organization in drafting the Cuban Family Code exemplifies how the government encouraged mass participation in resolving problems that had evolved in the transition from a bourgeois Republic to a socialist state.

Women's integration into the Revolution began in the early 1960s with their participation in literacy campaigns, counterrevolutionary militias, and Comités para la Defensa de la Revolución [Committees for the Defense of the Revolution] (CDR). The economic mobilization of the late 1960s involved women in the national economy on a massive level for the first time. As many studies have shown, rapidly changing gender roles strained the traditional Cuban family to the breaking point. Alfred Padula and Lois Smith point out how the Revolution put pressure on women who were "now called upon to excel at work, to volunteer, to study, to participate in sports and politics, and to raise families—to be super women" (79).[5] Conjugal tensions mounted as many men resisted adapting their role in the family to help with housework and child rearing. The increased participation of the state in the socialization and education of children through day care, boarding schools, and government-sponsored recreational activities also altered family relations by weakening the formerly powerful roles of the patriarch and matriarch. Parents were expected, in turn, to become further involved in the Revolution by studying at night school or working in distant provinces and foreign countries.[6] Participation in revolutionary activities forced behavioral changes that impacted Cuban family life, but, as we will see, prerevolutionary attitudes toward gender roles persisted.

In 1974, the Cuban government presented a draft of the new Cuban Family Code that began a nationwide discussion on the changing relationships between husband and wife and parents and children at meetings of the FMC and the Confederación de Trabajadores Cubanos [Confederation of Cuban Workers] (CTC), at block meetings, and on the streets. The code, adopted on February 14, 1975, implicitly acknowledges the difficulty of creating a new Cuban family. In contrast to some Marxist views of the family, by labeling the family "the elementary cell of society," the code recognizes its beneficial role in the socialization of new generations (Cuba Council of Ministers 217).[7] The code also implies that, realistically, the state cannot fully socialize the household through laundries, cafeterias, and day care. Therefore, it must regulate family relations so that the domestic sphere reflects socialist principles.[8] Article 26 of the code illustrates well the revolutionary vision of the family and the relationship between the sexes: "Both partners must care for the family they have created and each must cooperate with each other in the education, upbringing, and guidance of the children according to the principles of socialist morality. They must participate, to the extent of their capacity or possibilities, in the running of the home, and cooperate so that it will develop in the best possible way" (Cuba Council of Ministers 222). Furthermore, the code stipulates that both partners must share housework and child care even when one of them stays at home and the other provides the family's financial support. Cuban couples must agree to the above article, as well as several others, as a part of their marriage contract. Although the code has undoubtedly made a great impact on Cuban society, cinematic and theatrical representations of Cuban families suggest that the process of creating a Cuban family that embodies the *conciencia* of the new Cuban is slow, because social attitudes toward gender roles and the family are resistant to change.[9]

Similarly, the Cuban government overestimated the degree of revolutionary zeal that a supposedly "malleable" young generation formed under socialism would display.[10] In 1980, over 10,000 Cubans stormed the Peruvian embassy in hopes of receiving political asylum, forcing Castro to allow a mass departure of refugees from the port of Mariel. Of the 125,000 Cubans who left, 41 percent were under the age of twenty-seven, which placed the success of political socialization of young people in doubt (Fernández, "Youth in Cuba" 198). The mass departure also contradicts official representations of a united socialist national family. The visit of 100,000 exiled Cubans in 1979 might have contributed to the exodus because it made the island population more aware of its limited access to consumer goods (Skidmore and Smith 274).

To alleviate the people's impatience for a higher standard of living, and in an effort to enhance economic performance, the government responded by permitting some market-type activities. By 1986, however, Castro ended the experiment with market mechanisms because it sparked inequalities and corruption. Abolishing the markets formed part of a government campaign to rectify negative trends such as bureaucratic inefficiency, profiteering, and lackluster political participation. The rectification campaign also attempted to re-ignite revolutionary fervor by calling for ideological purification and the return of moral incentives and volunteerism. Even though the regime showed some flexibility and tolerance for contending perspectives, it is doubtful that invoking Guevarian ideals had much resonance with young people.

To complicate matters, the ideological collapse of socialism in Eastern Europe in 1989 and the subsequent dissolution of the Soviet Union placed Cuba in a politically and economically unstable position. Cuba entered what Castro has called the "Special Period in Times of Peace" in which the rapidly deteriorating economy—upon the breakup of the Soviet Union, the island lost about $6 billion in annual subsidies and a very favorable trade policy—has forced Cubans to endure strict austerity measures. The state can no longer provide some basic necessities and social services, and it has become harder to justify deprivations in the name of socialist principles. For political survival, yet still within the parameters of an authoritarian regime, Castro has softened some of the constitution's totalitarian features.[11] As the father figure of the paternalist state, Castro must entrust his children, "la gran familia cubana," with more autonomy. Consequently, the family, as Smith and Padula explain, "is again emerging as the preeminent social institution in Cuba. Family networks will grow in importance as food and other resources become scarce. They are already serving as the fulcrum of nascent resistance to the Castro regime" (*Sex and Revolution* 167). What kind of Cuban family and nation will emerge from the crisis of the Special Period remains to be seen, but the postrevolutionary generation's critical view of the regime suggests major changes on the horizon.

Theater and Revolutionary Culture

Louis Althusser's theory on how the state achieves social control locates both the family and the theater in what he calls an ideological state apparatus. These are institutions (cultural, religious, political, and so forth) that control subjects through ideology as opposed to state apparatuses such as the army, the police, and prisons that operate through violence (Althusser 145). Cuban plays that focus on the family to depict the conflict of coexisting prerevolutionary and new socialist values, then, represent a particularly potent tool in shaping a new national family. In order for cultural activities such as theater to make an impact on people's revolutionary consciousness, however, the Cuban government first had to create a popular culture. Its initial task was to eradicate illiteracy, as this would not only create an audience for the new Cuban art but would also benefit the entire revolutionary process. In 1961, society literally became the giant classroom Guevara had envisioned, for an estimated 270,000 volunteers divided in different programs worked in all areas of the country to raise Cuba's adult literacy to 96 percent (Pérez 358–59).[12] The state next sought to democratize culture by making it accessible to all. For many years, government-funded, neighborhood Casas de Cultura have offered free cultural activities, such as classes in photography, art, and dance, and have sponsored art exhibits and theatrical and musical performances. Mass organizations such as unions have also encouraged adult participation in amateur theater and in music and dance groups.[13] At the same time, to facilitate the work of the intellectual vanguard, within the first three years of the Revolution important cultural institutions such ICAIC (Cuban Institute of Cinematographic Arts and Industry), Casa de las Américas [House of the Americas], Unión de Escritores y Artistas de Cuba [Union of Writers and Artists of Cuba] (UNEAC), and a national school of fine arts, the Cubanacán, were established.

As the infrastructure of cultural institutions developed, so did a cultural policy that made it difficult for artists to address critically the changing nature of the nation and the family. In a 1961 speech to intellectuals, Castro stated that culture should be the patrimony of the people, and he called on the intelligentsia to support the Revolution. His famous statement, "Dentro de la Revolución, todo. Fuera de la Revolución, nada" (Castro 18) [Within the Revolution everything. Outside the Revolution, nothing], addressed the problem of artistic freedom. A shift in cultural policy took place between the early 1960s and the 1970s, and by 1968 the line between what was "within" the Revolution and "against" the Revolution had become rigid. Officials cracked down on writers such as Antón Arrufat and Heberto Padilla for the "counterrevolutionary" nature of their work, and some went so far as to advocate socialist realism as the appropriate revolutionary aesthetic.[14] At the 1971 First National Congress on Education, Castro lashed out against "pseudo-leftist" intellectuals and homosexuals, and statements from the 1975 First Congress of the Communist Party reinforced a hard line on the political purpose of culture. Revolutionary cultural policy has been volatile and has changed in accordance with how editorial committees define "against" the Revolution. Moreover, the degree of confidence of the revolutionary regime itself determines what is considered counterrevolutionary. The ambiguity of what constitutes an appropriately revolutionary stance is the policy's greatest strength because it forces artists to censor themselves.

Gerardo Mosquera affirms that, at the end of the 1970s, a new generation of artists formed in the postrevolutionary period broke with the dogmatism of the cultural politics of the late 1960s and early 1970s (60). Furthermore, the relationship between artists and intellectuals and the bureaucrats of cultural institutions has become less tense in the 1980s and 1990s. The 1988 UNEAC congress proposed cutting bureaucratization in the artistic sphere, creating more dialogue between the official cultural apparatus and Cuban writers, and distancing the UNEAC from the Communist Party (P. T. Johnson 157). The congress reflected a political climate more open to pluralist visions of the Revolution. Arturo Arango maintains that Cuba's release from its ideological bond with the Soviet Union has further contributed to a new sense of freedom (125).

Cuba's profound domestic crisis—the Special Period—to some extent has forced government officials to be more lenient with critical interpretations of Cuban society because of the gap between the media's "official" representation of the situation and reality.

Rather than producing art oriented toward forming the new Cuban's revolutionary *conciencia,* in the 1980s and 1990s artistic works are more apt to examine the imperfections of the new national family formed by the Revolution. Less focused on direct communication and functionality, writers are freer to experiment with language and form and to write on topics not explicitly revolutionary. Conversely, they have been able to address formerly taboo topics more directly, such as homosexuality in Senel Paz's story "El lobo, el bosque y el hombre nuevo" [The wolf, the forest, and the new man"] (1991), which was the basis for the screenplay of the successful film *Fresa y chocolate* [Strawberry and chocolate], directed by Tomás Gutiérrez Alea and Juan Carlos Tabío (1993). Writers who grew up in the 1970s and 1980s and had experienced the disjunction between official history and their daily life experiences were uninspired by the values embodied by the Guevarian *hombre nuevo,* "a profoundly humanistic ideal which subsequently exposed them to empty slogans and schemas, clichés devoid of any real meaning" (Mateo Palmer 161–62). Many of these artists display a postmodern mistrust of the mythical *hombre nuevo* and the master narrative of scientific communism, an obligatory subject in school they have renamed "ciencia ficción" [science fiction] (Mosquera 61). While young artists may feel frustrated with the regime and the failings of socialism, their commitment to Cuba shows in their special interest in national culture and history. Moreover, their postmodernism is unique to their national experience, because many of their works still communicate faith in history and the utopia of social justice (Mateo Palmer 166).

On numerous levels, theatrical performance chronicles the different phases I have outlined in the creation of a new Cuban society and culture: euphoric idealism, pragmatism and orthodoxy, and decentralization and self-sufficiency. During the first decade of the Revolution, state sponsorship finally offered playwrights and theater groups the support to produce a national theater movement. In these early years characterized by experimentation and creativity, the Cuban stage saw productions of classic and avant-garde plays by international dramatists, as well as works by a new generation of Cuban authors.[15] By 1967, however, the climate of ideological orthodoxy had permeated the theater, and plays that did not represent a recognizable social reality came under suspicion as decadent, elitist, and potentially counterrevolutionary. This oppressive environment hampered the staging and publication of works by some of Cuba's best playwrights, such as Antón Arrufat, Virgilio Piñera, and José Triana. At the same time, at the 1967 Primer Seminario Nacional de Teatro [First National Theater Seminar], theater practitioners examined the role of their art form in a budding socialist society. Rine Leal writes: "acogieron el principio de que el arte [. . .] esté al alcance del pueblo, pero no a través de lo populachero o el paternalismo. El nacimiento de un teatro popular (realmente del pueblo) se ligó al surgimiento de públicos masivos, y muy especialmente a la formación integral del hombre nuevo" (152) [they embraced the principle that art [. . .] should be within the reach of the people, but not fall into vulgarity or paternalism. The birth of a popular theater (truly of the people) was linked to the emergence of massive audiences, and very particularly to the integral formation of the new man]. In this spirit, Sergio Corrieri initiated the Cuban Teatro Nuevo [Cuban New Theater] movement by founding Grupo Teatro Escambray in 1968. This movement offered artists a forum for exploring, from a prorevolutionary stance, the changing identity of the Cuban nation.

Like the New Dramatists movement (NDP) in Puerto Rico during the 1960s and 1970s and similar popular theater movements in other Latin American countries, the Cuban groups abandoned the proscenium stage in search of new spaces and audiences for their collectively created pieces. Specifically, the label "Teatro Nuevo" in Cuba applies to a popular, anti-bourgeois theater that emerged from an interactive relationship between the theater groups and their public. Corrieri's group worked in a province in the remote Escambray mountains, as did Flora Lauten's Teatro La Yaya. Other groups performed in working-class neighborhoods in urban Havana and Santiago de Cuba. Teatro Nuevo plays dealt with immediate issues relevant to the island's socialist transformation: land reform, the struggle against counterrevolutionaries, the changing role of women, and the clash between new and old morals and behaviors.[16] By using a particular area as a base, the groups oftentimes had prolonged relationships with their public and became invested in resolving the problems they represented in their plays. This linked their interest in improving their art with the development of a strong revolutionary *conciencia*. Likewise, by involving peasants, workers, and students as actors, the plays not only engaged the audience in a critical reflection on the difficulties of constructing a new society but also allowed those affected the most by the changes literally to become "actors" in the revolutionary process of creating a new Cuban citizen, family, and nation.

The Teatro Nuevo movement participated effectively in officially sanctioned cultural production because the artists evidently understood what Bourdieu calls a "space of possibles," that is, "all that one must have in the back of one's mind in order to be in the game" (176). The movement coincided in large part with the period of ideological orthodoxy now referred to as the "Quinquenio Gris" [Gray Five Years] (1971–76). To be in the game during the 1970s, the theater produced accessible art for the masses from a socialist perspective. The purpose of the Teatro Nuevo movement was to gain a larger audience, as Leal puts it, to turn Cuba into "una inmensa plaza teatral" (151) [an immense theatrical space]. The Revolution would receive ideological validation through theatrical performances, assuming that the public grasped the play's message. Such a grasp, as Bourdieu argues, depends on the divergence between the level of emission (the complexity of the code required to access the work) and the level of reception (the degree to which the public masters the code required for understanding the work) (224–25). By writing plays with clear conflicts and using uncomplicated forms and colloquial language, Cuban playwrights from the late 1960s to the 1980s kept the level of reception high and the level of emission low. In Bourdiean terms, the plays produced cultural capital (forms of cultural knowledge, in this case, socialist competency) because the audiences had to be trained to decipher them. In this regard, the works served as a form of consciousness-raising as they instructed the spectator on how to become a good member of the new family of socialism.

Teatro Nuevo represents the most innovative Cuban theater in the ideologically charged climate of the 1970s, for few memorable works were produced outside of the movement.[17] The 1981 graduation of the first class from the Instituto Superior de Arte [Higher Institute of Art] (ISA) marked the beginning of a new theater generation. The students' creative reinterpretations of Cuban classics contrasted with the overuse of realism, popular language, schematic formulas, and didactic messages that had invaded the island's stages. Institutional reorganizations further contributed to a livelier theater movement. In 1989, the theater wing of the Consejo Nacional de Artes Escénicas [National Council of Scenic

Arts] (CNAE) initiated a system that funds, for a limited duration, projects proposed by artists who wish to work together on developing a creative vision. By freeing artists from being permanent members of a group, the CNAE shifts "the emphasis from building theatrical institutions to making available the resources for creating theatre" (Martin 54).[18] The autonomy from cultural state apparatuses and the flexibility of working in different collectives have fostered creativity and have produced more diverse theatrical representations of the new Cuban family and nation.

Rather than focusing on immediate social conflicts, in the 1980s plays have included complex character sketches, individual problems, and the study of connections between Cuba's past and present.[19] In addition, Lilian Manzor-Coats and Inés María Martiatu Terry note how new theater collectives such as Flora Lauten's Teatro Buendía and Víctor Varela's Teatro del Obstáculo "began a theatrical renovation which transformed theatre into a public forum for an audience that felt 'marginalized': young people. These young people, having lived through the achievements of the Revolution, demanded a form of expression that was different from those characteristic of the 'official voice of the revolution'" (39). The unresolved conflicts, ambiguity, and violence in recent performances by such groups effectively dare to suggest that socialism does not exempt the new Cuban from alienation and frustration (Correa 77). In the 1990s, playwrights continued to renovate theatrical form and content through a postmodern poetics of fragmentation with respect to history, myth, language, and dramatic structure. Rosa Ileana Boudet also notes a synthesis of diverse theater traditions, as well as the use of metaphor and parody ("New Playwrights" 32). These new approaches reveal a shift in the field of cultural production. On the one hand, audiences are better educated and can decipher more complex codes, and on the other, the space of possibles has wider parameters, which allows the artists more liberty to express their ideas in singular ways. The survival of Cuban theater in spite of the difficult conditions for performances in the Special Period— the lack of materials, electrical blackouts, and the problem of transportation—testifies to its strength and commitment to staging the problems of national and cultural identity. In spite of dire economic conditions, the interaction between the theater and the Revolution is as rich and complex as it ever has been.

For the past four decades, government officials have used education, the arts, and new revolutionary laws to shape attitudes and behaviors in accordance with socialist principles. The family structure, resistant to change, has been a crucial target in this project of forming a new Cuban citizen and nation. In order to instruct proper revolutionary behavior and perhaps diffuse further conflicts, earlier plays were didactic and performed conflicts with which audiences could identify. The family torn apart by conflicting values in Roberto Orihuela's *La emboscada*, for example, implies the need for a new socialist family. Corrieri signals a different type of revolutionary theater in which playwrights shift their focus from those having difficulty integrating into the Revolution to "los problemas que tenían aquéllos que estaban haciendo la Revolución" (Luzuriaga 52) [the problems faced by those participating in the Revolution]. *Ni un sí ni un no* by Abelardo Estorino exemplifies this approach by addressing one of the challenges faced in forming a new society, the changing gender roles and their effects on the family. The fragile state of the family in plays such as *Manteca* by Alberto Pedro Torriente and *Vereda tropical* by Joaquín Cuartas Rodríguez, in contrast, raises questions about the Revolution itself, and its shortcomings in creating a new Cuba. These playwrights embody a critical stance "within" the Revolution, that is, a more nuanced position no longer immediately labeled as counter-revolutionary. In all four plays, the playwrights' approach to the theme of family provides important clues about Cuban cultural politics and the Revolution's distinct stages in shaping the new national family.

The Family of Socialism: New Loyalties in Revolutionary Cuba

Teatro Escambray first performed Roberto Orihuela's play *La emboscada* in 1978.[20] The play subsequently shared the 1979 UNEAC prize for drama and has received several notable stagings, including a 1980 production at the annual Theater Festival in Havana and a 1981 free version by Flora Lauten's students at the ISA. Although *La emboscada* marks the close of the Teatro Nuevo era, it pays homage to an important issue from an earlier historical moment during which the Revolution and the Teatro Nuevo movement intersected. Corrieri and his group went to the Escambray Mountains in search of a new audience to involve in the revolutionary process. The region had proved to be a difficult area to integrate into the Revolution and was the seat of organized counterrevolutionary activity from 1960 to 1965. *La emboscada,* which takes place in this context, enacts the inevitable clash between two brothers, one a member of the revolutionary army (Lorenzo) and the other, a counterrevolutionary

(Jacinto). On the surface, the conflict and dramatic structure appear simple, and the didactic message of the play is unmistakable: family loyalties should take second place to one's commitment to the Revolution. Orihuela's play, however, goes beyond sketching a Manichean fraternal conflict to explore carefully a convulsive, transformational moment for the family in revolutionary Cuba.

The works of Orihuela and Teatro Escambray dramatists reached a wide audience during the most repressive period for the arts since the Revolution. Corrieri states that if theater is to fulfill what he considers its double function, to entertain and provoke critical reflection, "tiene que haber una comunicación colectiva" (Luzariaga 56) [there must be collective communication]. The Revolution demanded a popular theater that communicated its ideology to the masses. Successful playwrights (that is, those who did not encounter trouble staging their work in the politicized climate of the 1970s) understood this code and expressed revolutionary ideology in such a way that a broad public was able to read it. For some critics, the accessibility (simple form) and instructive content make the artistic value of these plays limited. A Brechtian approach to realism, however, makes some works more transcendent than others, for some of these plays achieve collective communication without sacrificing innovative techniques.

In his essay "The Popular and the Realistic," Brecht uses the term "popular" to refer to "a people that is making history and altering the world and itself" (108).[21] For Brecht, the popular and the realistic go hand in hand: "It is in the interest of the people, the broad working masses, that literature should give them truthful representations of life; and truthful representations of life are in fact only of use to the broad working masses, the people; so that they have to be suggestive and intelligible to them, i.e. popular" (107). Brecht's realism does not ascribe to the conventions of a particular model of realism, such as the detailed representations of reality in nineteenth-century novels. For Brecht, realism entails laying bare the mechanisms of society that oppress the masses and "writing from the standpoint of the class which has the broadest solutions for the most pressing problems afflicting human society" (109). Brecht argues that realistic/popular representations of society can and should be achieved by diverse approaches because reality constantly changes, thus "to represent it the means of representation must alter too" (110).

In revolutionary Cuba, the theater movement has suffered because some believed that avant-garde works necessarily alienate popular audiences. Brecht, in contrast, suggests that as long as the work is realist, that is, truthful, its form can be as inventive as the playwright would like and the people will understand it. Although revolutionary playwrights have produced few experimental pieces, by seeking out popular audiences and making them the subject, as well as sometimes the performers of plays, the Teatro Nuevo movement added a new dimension to Cuban theater. In the spirit of Brecht, Teatro Nuevo plays both dramatized the changing reality of revolutionary Cuba and contributed to forming the new society under construction. The most memorable works have been those like Orihuela's *La emboscada,* which poses a nuanced revolutionary conflict in a thought-provoking manner.

The development of the dramatic action in *La emboscada* suits the dynamism of the epoch it depicts. The brief episodic scenes have the cinematic quality of capturing simultaneous events in different locations. They break the classic unities of time and place and propel the action forward quickly, just as the Revolution set in motion rapid changes in society. In the play, a rural family feels the effects of these changes as their family falls apart. Lorenzo, a *miliciano* [militiaman], discovers that his brother, Jacinto, has rebelled against the government, and Zoila (their mother) makes him promise that he will not act against his brother. This places Lorenzo in a difficult position when the Capitán asks him to lead a mission against his brother's band of rebels. Although Lorenzo is the ideal person to lead the attack, as he is the most familiar with the terrain, he refuses because of his pledge to his mother. His friend Camilo offers to lead the operation in his place. In the meantime, one of Jacinto's principal collaborators, Pancho (his cousin), has ceased his subversive activities and has denounced Jacinto to the authorities. The play reaches its climax when Jacinto and his *bandidos* murder Pancho and his wife, Prima. Family loyalties break down further when Lorenzo discovers that the rebels also have killed Camilo. These events catapult Lorenzo into action. He reveals a new level of commitment to the revolutionary family by avenging Camilo's death and leading the ambush in which Jacinto is killed: "¡El que quiera vengar a un hermano, que me siga!" (97) [Whoever wants to avenge a brother, let him follow me!].

Orihuela complicates the dramatic structure by placing virtually identical scenes at the beginning and end of the play. In scenes 1 and 30, a divided stage shows the rebels marching in circles on one side and *milicianos* planning an ambush on the other. Scenes 2 and 3, which lead to the confrontation between the two groups, are replayed almost identically in scenes 31 and 32. In the early scenes, however, the audience does not know that the rebel leader, El Muerto, is Jacinto's alias, and it does not know that the body Lorenzo finds after the attack is his brother. Throughout the play, there are clues that lead the audience to realize that it has witnessed the play's ending in the opening scenes. By framing the play's conventional rising-falling action with these scenes, Orihuela hands the audience an active interpretive role. Knowing the outcome allows the spectator to consider analytically the steps that led to it and invites the audience to speculate on possible different courses of action. Consequently, viewers may examine critically how they participate in the revolutionary changes going on around them.

Orihuela creates the spaces in which the play's action takes place by rearranging basic objects and pieces of furniture that one would find in a rural home or military camp. Lighting changes and flexible props such as stools, a table, and a bunk bed designate shifts between scenes in the homes of Zoila and Pancho, military camps, and *bandido* hideouts. Unlike the set dominated by a realistically constructed house that signifies oppression in earlier Cuban plays, the absence of an onstage house fits the play's theme of forming a new Cuban family. This period of change suggests homelessness, for the family has been torn apart by the Revolution and must rebuild in the context of a socialist society. *La emboscada* implies that various levels of family need to become more interconnected as the Revolution develops. In the play, two families are related by blood: the immediate family of Zoila and her children and their extended family, which includes Pancho and Prima and other relatives. Strong community ties also form a kind of extended family. In this relatively remote area, family and community allegiances have hampered implementing revolutionary values and policies. Lorenzo's place in the army, however, has exposed him to a new kind of family bound by socialist ideology. Pancho, Prima, Camilo, and even Jacinto ultimately die because Lorenzo's loyalties are caught between a family of blood relations and a family of revolutionary *compañeros*. Through Lorenzo's predicament, the play suggests the need to redirect one's allegiance from the individual family to the larger family of the socialist nation.

How Zoila, Lorenzo, and Jacinto view the family highlights their position with respect to the Revolution. Zoila serves as an audience for

Lorenzo's and Jacinto's opposing stances on the revolutionary government. She rejects both positions because they pit family members against each other: "usted tendrá sus ideas y el tendrá las suyas, pero antes que todo, ustedes son hermanos. La familia está ante to las cosas, ante to los gobiernos, sean buenos o malos. ¡La familia es sagrada!" (20) [you'll have your ideas, and he'll have his own, but first and foremost, you're brothers. Family comes first, before any government, whether it be good or bad. Family is sacred!]. Nevertheless, the play shows that the family is subject to change, that it is not sacred or impervious to the historical process. As a widow with seven children and a sick father to care for, Zoila wants whatever is best for her family: "Lo que tiene que pasar es que ustedes se recuerden que los dos son hermanos y que debían jalar pal mismo lao, pal lao que beneficie a la familia" (28–29) [What must happen is that you remember that you two are brothers. You should work on the same side, the side that benefits the family]. In a country mobilized for mass transformations, Zoila's profamily stance represents a reactionary mentality. From a Marxist perspective, trying to obtain what is good for the family encourages its members to think in individual terms. In doing so, it weakens the bond between the individual and the collectivity and becomes an obstacle in the process of constructing the socialist nation. Thus Zoila's supposed "neutrality" is almost as detrimental to the Revolution as an outright counterrevolutionary standpoint. Through Zoila, *La emboscada* encourages its audience not to remain passive spectators to the Revolution.

The characterization of the brothers makes it clear which position the play would have its audience emulate. The audience learns that both Lorenzo and Jacinto were involved in the movement to topple the Batista dictatorship, but Jacinto distanced himself from the Revolution when its Marxist orientation became clear. Personal gain motivated Jacinto's participation in the Revolution; therefore he is unsatisfied with his rewards: "Fuimos nosotros los que tumbamos a Batista, los que nos jodimos. Pues bien, es a nosotros a los que nos toca la mayor parte de las cosas que se repartan. Pero no, ¿qué hicieron? Los cachitos de tierra pa'los guajiros y to lo otro pa'l estado" (50) [We were the ones who overthrew Batista, the ones who busted our asses. Well then, we should be the ones to get the largest share. But no, what did they do? The small pieces of land for the *guajiros*, and all the rest for the state]. The Revolution has not fulfilled his modest materialist dreams of owning enough land to pay others to work on it, as well as possessing some oxen, a truck, and a house. Instead of climbing the socioeconomic ladder as he had hoped, Jacinto finds himself in the middle of a revolution that seeks to destroy class distinctions. Jacinto, like many other campesinos, lacks revolutionary *conciencia*, and his exclamation, "¡El comunismo es del carajo! ¡To es pal gobierno: las tierras, las casas, los hijos, las mujeres, to se lo cogen!" (52) [Communism is shit! Everything is for the government: land, houses, children, women, they take everything!] echoes the ideological confusion and anxiety produced by political change in the Escambray zone in the early 1960s. In spite of its hyperbolic tone, Jacinto's statement contains some truth because the revolutionary government does socialize the private sphere of the home, altering gender roles and the relationship between parents and children. For Jacinto and Zoila, then, who have lived in an isolated area neglected by the government and the church, state intervention represents a threat to the family, the only social institution that organizes the lives of campesinos.[22]

Lorenzo, in contrast, sees the ideological change as beneficial for his family and others. He has learned to read thanks to the Revolution, and he shows a growing revolutionary *conciencia*. In his opinion, "La revolución nos dio la tierra y no a nosotros solos, sino a to'l mundo; a to'l que la trabajaba. La revolución se hizo pa'que los muertos de hambre como nosotros vivieran como personas, no pa'que to'l que estuvo alzao se hiciera rico" (28) [The Revolution gave us land and not just to us, but to everybody; to everyone who worked on it. The Revolution was fought so that the dirt poor like us could live like people, not for those who revolted to become rich]. Moreover, Lorenzo points out that Jacinto's dream of paying others to work on his land would perpetuate the same oppressive economic system against which they both rebelled. Unlike Zoila and Jacinto, who focus on their own family's well-being, Lorenzo insists that they think about other people as well. Lorenzo's collectivistic thinking manifests the social consciousness of a developing *hombre nuevo*.

Exposing the process of forming a new Cuban—with all its uncertainties and errors—moves *La emboscada* beyond an overly schematic conflict between the brothers, or on a more general level, between old and new Cuba. Whereas Jacinto and Zoila are representative of plays that portray characters having difficulty integrating into the Revolution, Lorenzo exemplifies works that investigate the conflicts that arise for those involved in building a new nation. The references in *La emboscada* to the errors of the Instituto de Reforma Agraria [Institute of Agrarian Reform] (INRA) in implementing agrarian reform show, as Guevara admits, that "socialism is young and makes mistakes" ("Socialism" 165). Similarly, Lorenzo, when pressed by Jacinto to define Communism, admits that he does not entirely understand the ideology of the Revolution: "¡Yo qué coño sé! ¡A mí las cosas de la política no me entran en la cabeza! Pero tengo los ojos bien abiertos y miro" (52) [What the hell do I know! I don't get politics! But my eyes are wide open, and I can see]. Like the Revolution, Lorenzo learns as he gains experience. Jacinto's rebellion and Lorenzo's subsequent pledge to Zoila place him in a situation in which he must define what he understands as revolutionary behavior. Lorenzo concludes that he cannot help with the operation against his brother:

> Mire, capitán, yo quisiera ayudar, pero si yo engañara a la vieja, si yo ahora les ayudo a ustedes, ¿con qué cara iba a mirar después a mi madre? Yo creo que pa'ser revolucionario lo primero es respetarse uno mismo, si yo ahora les ayudara estaría incumpliendo algo que prometí por la memoria de mi padre, dejaría de tenerme respeto, dejaría de ser revolucionario. (75)

> [Look, Captain, I'd like to help, but if I betray my old lady, if I help you now, how could I face her afterward? I think that to be a revolutionary you've got to respect yourself; if I help you now, I'd be breaking a promise I made in memory of my father, I'd lose respect for myself, and I'd no longer be a revolutionary.]

Orihuela sets up a moral dilemma because self-respect undoubtedly constitutes an admirable revolutionary quality. On the other hand, Lorenzo's loyalty to his family shames him in front of his *compañeros*. Lorenzo's problem raises several unanswered questions: If Lorenzo had not made the pledge to his mother, would he have fought his brother? What would Lorenzo have done if the Capitán had ordered him to lead the attack against Jacinto? Should Lorenzo have been less loyal to his own family for the benefit of the common good?

The play answers this final question by showing how kin relationships fall apart and by offering an alternative family. In the beginning, Jacinto relies on knowing that, although Lorenzo is in the army, "él no se va a virar contra mí, es mi hermano" (27) [he's not going to turn against me, he's my brother]. Jacinto, however, does not expect himself to respect the same rules and turns against his blood relations. When Jacinto finds out that his cousin Pancho has accepted money from the INRA, he tells him that he has orders to burn the homes of any campesino who accepts help from the government. He warns: "No cojas mucho a cuenta de la familia, Pancho, que se me puede olvidar que somos parientes" (72) [Don't count too much on the family, Pancho, because I could forget we're relatives]. Jacinto does disregard their kinship, and after he kills Pancho, Prima cries: "¡Tú lo mataste, ya tú no eres familia . . . !" (90) [You've killed him, you're no longer family . . . !]. At the same time that these traditional family relationships based on blood ties break down, a new revolutionary family is being born. Various scenes highlight the camaraderie of Lorenzo's military *compañeros*, and as the Capitán explains to Lorenzo, "Aquí todos somos hermanos. En ocasiones más hermanos que los que llevan nuestra propia sangre" (36) [We're all brothers here. Sometimes closer than those who share blood]. Lorenzo understands this only after Jacinto betrays their family and Camilo is killed by the *bandidos*. Consequently, when Zoila seeks his support, rather than comforting her over the impending ambush he will lead against his brother, Lorenzo shows her Camilo's body and says: "Llore, vieja, llore por Camilo; ese es el hijo suyo que merece esas lágrimas" (97) [Cry, mother, cry for Camilo; he's the son who deserves those tears]. In the final line of the play, Lorenzo identifies another dead body: "Sí, era mi hermano" (101) [Yes, he was my brother]. Significantly, Lorenzo uses the past tense to refer to Jacinto not only because he is dead but because he no longer considers him a brother.

La emboscada reflects a Brechtian approach to realism in its realistic, that is, truthful, construction of the character Lorenzo. Rather than the embodiment of a rigid ideological position, he is a character who makes errors and learns. Orihuela's model of the *hombre nuevo* is flawed and unfinished, which enriches the basic conflict between the brothers and presents a far more challenging dramatic conflict for the audience to interpret. Typical of the theater of the period, however, the play's revolutionary message is clear. It asks its audience to abandon the individualism characteristic of capitalism in favor of the Guevarian ideal of collectivism. This entails a socialist redefinition of the family in which the individual household is "socialized" to benefit the collectivity, the larger family of the Revolution. In terms suggested by Edward Said, in this play a new Cuban identity emerges as affiliative ties (identification through culture) replace filial (heritage or descent) ones (16–24).

Performances of *La emboscada* by different theater groups in the late

1970s and early 1980s mark the close of the Teatro Nuevo movement and the emergence of a new generation of artists interested in taking Cuban drama in new directions. Although I have argued that the form and content in *La emboscada* is far from simplistic, its didactic lesson is clear. Raquel Carrió notes that the 1981 interpretation of the play by the ISA's graduating class offered "un nuevo camino, una experiencia que lograba sintetizar, con un nuevo lenguaje, las búsquedas más fértiles de la escena nacional durante dos décadas de teatro revolucionario" (2) [a new path, an experience that synthesized with a new language the most fruitful quests of the national stage during two decades of revolutionary theater]. The new version used richer images and less revolutionary discourse to communicate with an increasingly complex and demanding audience (Carrió 3–4). In the late 1960s, the Teatro Nuevo groups found the uninitiated audience they had been looking for, and by the end of the 1970s this audience reached a level of sophistication ready for new representations of Cuban reality. This shift coincided with the end of the orthodoxy of the Quinquenio Gris and an opening in cultural policy. In Bourdiean terms, the ISA's production was able to raise the level of emission, first, because the Teatro Nuevo movement had helped elevate the level of reception, and second, because the space of possibles had been altered. *La emboscada* captures the rupture of the individual bourgeois family institution and the birth of a larger national family bound by socialism rather than blood. At the same time, the play's flexibility, seen in its contrasting performances, presages fresh approaches to representing this new family and society under construction.

Gender Relations in the New Family

From the chaotic early years of the Revolution portrayed in *La emboscada*, the scene of Abelardo Estorino's *Ni un sí ni un no* (1980) shifts to the institutionalization of the new socialist system in the 1970s. While Orihuela's play signals the dawning of a new Cuban family, Estorino's piece addresses the challenges encountered in instilling egalitarian, socialist values in this family. Like the ISA's groundbreaking production of *La emboscada*, *Ni un sí ni un no*, staged by Cuba's most prestigious theater collective, Teatro Estudio, and directed by Estorino, experiments with realist forms.[23] This break with realism, along with the play's urban setting in Havana, marks a departure for Estorino, but in the themes of marriage, machismo, and family, *Ni un sí ni un no* is well within the playwright's typical dramatic universe. The play traces the evolving relationship of a young couple, Él [He] and Ella [She], in the 1970s. His father and her mother, as well as two "others" who play alternate romantic partners for Él and Ella, round out the cast and provide more perspectives on the issue of sexual equality.

In *Ni un sí ni un no*, Estorino's examination of the impact of changing gender roles on the family in revolutionary Cuba posits a dialectic notion of Cuban identity. By employing metatheatrical and Brechtian techniques, Estorino questions Cuban values and traditions associated with family relations assumed to be immutable and given, suggesting that the only essential quality of Cuban identity, or *cubanía*, is its constant transformation. To stage this changeable reality, the theater must reject superficial, realist representations inclined toward resolution and finality. Describing the play, Estorino states: "La obra trata la transformación, el movimiento anímico, vivo, dinámico de esos personajes y la estructura de la obra va transformándose de la misma forma. Están imbricados el contenido y la forma que no puede ser de otra manera" (qtd. in Martínez Tabares, "Morir" 29) [The play is about the transformation, the psychic, live, and dynamic movement of those characters and the structure of the play transforms itself in the same way. The content and the form are inextricably imbricated]. In its focus on the transformation of Cuban family values, *Ni un sí ni un no* enacts the spirit of Cuba's 1975 Family Code, the preamble of which states that discriminatory bourgeois norms "must be replaced by others fully in keeping with the principles of equality and the realities of our socialist society, which is *constantly dynamically advancing*" (Cuba Council of Ministers 217, my emphasis).

The first scene of *Ni un sí ni un no* establishes the play's central problem by linking the themes of transformation and gender. As Él sorts rice for dinner, he recites passages from Engel's *Anti-Dürhing* (1878), a materialist interpretation of Hegelian dialectics. Él reads: ". . . 'de la humanidad, o nuestra propia actividad mental, se nos ofrece en primer lugar el cuadro infinito de un tejido de relaciones, de acciones y reacciones en las que nada queda como era'. . ." (290) [". . . concerning humanity, or our own mental activity, we are first given the infinite picture of a web of relationships, actions and reactions in which nothing remains as it was . . ."]. This dialectical vision of the world leads him to ponder how his relationship with his wife has changed. Él illustrates his reading by throwing grains of rice on the floor, assigning them a gender, and proclaiming: "Este macho crecerá, éste no se transformará, machos desperdiciados, lanzados al piso de una cocina en el Vedado donde no tendrán oportunidad de cumplir el proceso diálectico de la naturaleza" (290) [This male will grow, this other one won't; wasted men, thrown to a Vedado kitchen floor where they won't have the chance to realize the dialectical process of nature]. While Él's musings are lighthearted, it becomes apparent when his wife comes home that their relationship is strained precisely because his attitude toward gender roles has not evolved enough to meet her expectations of a new Cuban husband. In contrast, he believes she has changed too much. The two-act play, therefore, begins near the end of their story, for they are no longer the same people they married eight years ago, and divorce seems imminent. The rest of the play backtracks and shows the evolution of their relationship. We witness their wedding, their early years of marriage, how they grow apart and meet new love interests, their separation, and finally, what appears to be a reconciliation.[24] Metatheatrical scenes in which the actors step out of character to discuss the play or to experiment with different modes of representation break up the linearity of the story.

In line with the thematic focus on the new family, Estorino abandons the well-made family drama to experiment with new ways to represent the story of Él and Ella. In this regard, Estorino implicitly questions the efficacy of realism in portraying a world in transition and challenges the Cuban theater movement to resist superficial *costumbrista* [folkloric] representations of Cuban society. He strays from the typical orderly unfolding of the plot with flashbacks, improvisation, and characters who wander in and out of scenes or step out of their roles to discuss the play's structure and action. The stage directions indicate that scene and costume changes, as well as the shift between character and actor, should be made visible. The house, a standard fixture in realist theater and a traditional site for representing the family, also highlights the play's artifice. On the one hand, the kitchen is so authentic that it includes food, utensils, and running water; on the other hand, the walls move when the actors bump into them, and smashed plates lose their dramatic effect because they are made of cardboard. Estorino plays with realist conventions, dismantling them to underscore that what the audience views onstage is a constructed and changeable world rather than a seamless representation of a fixed reality. This has the Brechtian effect of distancing the spectators emotionally from the play and encouraging them to consider analytically the attitudes and events represented onstage.

Various uses of metatheater serve to expose gender stereotypes and encourage the audience to examine male-female relationships. Él and Ella's decision to pull down the walls of their flimsy house signifies a rejection of the vestiges of the family formed with prerevolutionary values. If Él and Ella's marriage was built on a shaky foundation, then they must tear it down and build a new revolutionary family. Tearing down the set also parallels laying bare realist conventions, as the following dialogue indicates:

> Él. Hicimos bien en echar abajo las paredes.
> Ella. Sí, que nada sea falso.
> Él. Ni las paredes ni los personajes.
> La Madre. Que todo sea real, como la vida.
> Ella. Como la vida y el arte. (297)
> [He. We did well in ripping down the walls.
> She. Yes, nothing should be fake.
> He. Neither walls nor characters.
> The Mother. Everything should be real, just like life.
> She. Like in life and art.]

The play mixes different levels of fiction and reality to highlight the connections between life and art, suggesting that the roles we play in life may be as constructed as those in the theater and that art expresses many truths about life. Self-conscious performances in the style of old movies and *comedias costumbristas* [comedies of manners] parody superficial and stereotypical representations of *cubanía*. El Otro [The Other Man] suggests that they do "una escena cubana de verdad" (317) [an authentic Cuban scene], and the actors improvise two scenes that highlight *machista* behavior, one that exaggerates the sexual banter and linguistic characteristics of Afro-Cuban types and another in which a jealous husband chides his wife for leaving the house. In the context of the play's goal of altering sexist attitudes, these scenes should strike the audience as outmoded representations of Cuban culture. A more overtly didactic use of metatheater is seen when the actors step out of their roles to comment on the characters. The actors who play Él and Ella, for example, note how much their characters have changed:

> Él. ¿Pero te fijaste bien cómo son?
> Ella. *Eran* más jóvenes.
> Él. Me refiero a las actitudes. No se parecen en nada a los de la cocina. (301)

[He. But did you really notice how they are?
She. They *were* younger.
He. I mean their attitudes. They don't seem at all like the ones in the kitchen.]

Similarly, when the characters stop to redirect the action of the play, they underscore, as Él puts it, that "Ningún libreto es definitivo" (381) [No text is final]. Just as the actors stray from the script, the play suggests that spectators reject prescribed sex roles and create new ones suitable for Cuba's revolutionary context.

Él and Ella's relationship embodies the changing script of Cuban identity. The characters are representative of a generation of Cubans who have had to negotiate between the traditional values of their parents and the new force of the Revolution that has entered the private family space to inculcate socialist values. This is most visible in a recording of the Family Code, which plays over the pantomime wedding of Él and Ella. A scene from early in their marriage, however, hardly shows a revolutionary couple. Ella, pregnant, fetches water and turns the television on and off for her pajama-clad husband. Ella depends on her mother for decision making, and when Él receives orders to leave for a military mobilization, she insists on going to stay with her because she is fearful of staying home alone. These behaviors change, however, because in her husband's absence, Ella is obliged to become more independent; instead of staying at her mother's house to avoid being alone at night, she volunteers to participate in a special night course in pediatrics.

The relationship between Él and Ella is never the same after he returns from military service. Él seems pleased with Ella's new endeavors, and he surprises her as well by having learned to do his own laundry. They appear to be a maturing new Cuban couple until Él exposes a double standard when Ella announces that she must leave for class: "Me parece bien que quieras superarte. [. . .] Pero debes atender a tu marido. ¿Está claro? Por lo tanto, hoy no vas a clases, porque yo acabo de llegar de una movilización y he estado fuera cuarenta y cinco días. Y tu deber es atenderme" (332) [I think it's good that you want to improve yourself. [. . .] But you should take care of your husband. Is that clear? So, today you aren't going to class, because I just came back from a mobilization and I've been away for forty-five days. And it's your duty to take care of me]. She tells him that he should be a true revolutionary and accept her commitment, but he replies: "¿Revolucionario de qué, chica? Esto es un asunto de

marido y mujer. ¿Qué tiene que ver la Revolución en la cama?" (332)
[What kind of revolutionary, girl? This is a matter between husband and
wife. What does the Revolution have to do with us when we're in bed?].

Throughout the play, Él and Ella's work and study responsibilities reveal that the Revolution really does enter the bedroom because they have
less free time to spend with each other. The integration of women in the
revolutionary process has altered traditional characteristics of family
roles and relations, because as a student, a worker, and a wife, Ella cannot
attend to her husband and the home as a traditional Cuban wife would.
They have come to share household tasks, and Él prides himself on being
a "marido evolucionado" (291) [evolved husband]. His reference to the
Family Code, however, has an empty ring to it: "Yo soy un humilde
esposo que acata el Código de Familia porque ha entendido la igualdad de
derechos y deberes de ambos cónyuges" (294) [I'm a humble husband
who obeys the Family Code because he's understood the equal rights and
duties of both spouses]. Él has not evolved as quickly as Ella, and her
achievements outside of the home create tension within it.

Not only do Él and Ella feel the effects of the Revolution on their
married life, they also must contend with the influence of their parents,
who embody prerevolutionary culturally defined male and female roles.
The play's title—*Ni un sí ni un no*—refers to traditional authoritarian
families in which the wife obeyed the husband without question. El
Padre says that with Candita, his wife, "no tuvimos ni un sí ni un no. Yo
decía, y ella decía: así es" (306) [we never had an argument. I would say
something, and she would agree: that's the way it is]. El Padre upholds
a sexual/spiritual dichotomy by praising her subservience and lack of
sexual instincts: "No era una mujer, era una santa" (297) [She wasn't a
woman, she was a saint]. In contrast, El Padre is a stereotypical *machista*
dominated by his sexual drive. He attempts to instill male chauvinist behavior in his son by advising him to never marry the women he success-
fully seduces. When La Madre finds out that Ella is pregnant, however,
she acts swiftly to save her daughter's reputation by pushing her to
marry and to lie about the due date: "Y cuando nazca, ¡sietemesino! Y si
hay que ponerlo en la incubadora, lo ponemos, aunque pese doce libras"
(309) [And when he's born, we'll say: premature! And if we have to put
him in the incubator, we'll do so, even if he weighs twelve pounds].
Rather than break a cycle of marriages built on material values and lies
instead of love and respect, the mother draws on her protective instincts

and sets up her daughter's marriage to be just as unhappy as her own has been. La Madre's unquestioning perpetuation of cultural attitudes, such as the social stigma of an unwed mother, is consistent with El Padre's philosophy of parenting: "Yo eduqué a mis hijos como me educaron mis padres y mi hijo educará a los suyos como lo eduqué a él. Y así seguirá la historia" (356) [I educated my children as my parents educated me, and my son will educate his own as I raised him. And that's how history will continue].

The Family Code, in contrast, aspires to redirect inherited attitudes and in fact grants full rights and equal status to all children, whether legitimate or not. Through Él and Ella, Estorino shows how the Revolution has attempted to modify the cultural codes passed through generations. Ella says her mother educated her one way but that she turned out another because "a mí no me educó sólo ella, sino también el trabajo, la escuela, el cine, los libros, las concentraciones y la milicia" (356) [she's not the only one who educated me. Work, school, movies, books, political gatherings and the military also played their role]. Similarly, El Padre watches in disbelief as Él ignores his advice and takes responsibility for the pregnancy, marries Ella, and, above all, washes his own socks. At times, how Él and Ella handle their relationship baffles their parents, which suggests that the couple learned revolutionary values mostly outside of the home. As Ella explains to El Padre: "Esta es otra época, con otras leyes y con otros conceptos morales, igual que hay otras modas y otra música. Y el que no lo vea así está momificado" (356) [These are other times, with other laws and other morals, just like there are new fashion trends and music. And whoever doesn't see this is mummified].

Ultimately, El Padre and La Madre learn from the younger generation, and the play portrays the formerly private space of the multigenerational family adjusting to the new revolutionary ethics advocated by the state. Although La Madre initially appears to be a typical bourgeois mother, the play shows her willingly participating in the Revolution, and she approves of the advances in women's rights. By the play's end, she has learned not to meddle in her daughter's affairs, and she stops deferring her own happiness and fulfillment by remarrying. Her class-consciousness has changed as well, because her new husband is a mason, whereas earlier she encouraged her daughter not to marry a working-class man. On the surface, El Padre never stops resisting the Revolution, which, in his opinion, robbed him of his business and is destroying his son's macho sensibilities. In a vulnerable moment, however, El Padre reveals that he has cancer and admits that he came to appreciate some benefits of the Revolution, but to save pride, he did not publicly acknowledge his change of perspective: "Yo cambiaba y me daba cuenta, pero seguía viviendo y repitiendo las mismas palabras. Me daba pena que me vieran cambiar, me parecía una debilidad, y los hombres deben ser firmes, dicen" (379) [I realized that I had started to change, but I kept living and repeating the same words. I felt bad about letting them see me change, it seemed like a weakness, and men must be firm, or so they say]. Now, El Padre admits to his son that he approves of Ella and that he is pleased with the opportunities in education, work, and travel that the Revolution has provided his son.

In the play's final scene, Él and Ella also unmask themselves by removing the carnival costumes they were wearing when they first met and recognizing the people they have become rather than the couple they once were. They had found the costumes while dividing up their things in preparation for their divorce. Nevertheless, they do not become another statistic in the skyrocketing divorce rate of the 1970s, for, as Salvador Arias notes, their conflict is transcended dialectically (21). After pursuing others—El Otro and La Otra—whose personalities and values are ironically similar to the younger versions of Él and Ella, the couple reunites with a deeper understanding of the transformational nature of relationships. Thus Estorino ends his piece optimistically, suggesting to audience members that the dialectical resolution of the conflicts in their own home can lead to revolutionary *conciencia* as opposed to divorce and family instability. The recognition scene and subsequent happy ending has the flavor of a Golden Age *comedia,* which Estorino accentuates by summing up the moral of the play in verse. When Él suggests storing the costumes, Ella says not to bother because they will constantly play new roles in life. Él wonders whether anything is unchangeable or eternal, and Ella replies: "¡Claro que sí! / El deseo de cambiar, / Cuando una historia termina / Otra está por empezar" (394) [Of course! / The desire to change / When one story ends / Another one is about to begin]. As if to prove this point, Estorino avoids the closed dramatic structure of realism by ending the play with a new beginning, as Él and Ella reunite as a stronger couple and El Otro and La Otra prepare to perform the same scene that opened the play. By challenging the notion of timeless national characteristics that include the values of the prerevolutionary Cuban family, *Ni un sí ni un no* implies that the great web of relationships that constitutes the Cuban national family will continue to evolve in consonance with changing social and economic realities. In form and in content, Estorino's play strives to represent *cubanía* as a process.

Endangered Species: Socialism and the New Family

In Cuban plays from the mid-1950s to the mid-1960s by Rolando Ferrer, Virgilio Piñera, Abelardo Estorino, and José Triana, children rebel against their parents in an effort to redefine the family and the nation. *La emboscada* and *Ni un sí ni un no* center on this young generation in the 1960s and 1970s and their mission to build a revolutionary society. As young people gain revolutionary *conciencia*, they confront the problems that emerge in forming a new Cuba and negotiate with the resistant values of an older, prerevolutionary generation. Plays of the 1990s, by contrast, invert this generational conflict. In *Vereda tropical* (1994) by Joaquín Miguel Cuartas Rodríguez, women nearly in their sixties play steadfast revolutionaries, and the characters who doubt the Revolution are their children and grandchildren. The play treats the aging of the Revolution in the context of Cuba's Special Period. Given the resurgence of experimental theater in the late 1980s and 1990s, the realist detail of Cuartas's piece "le da cierto aire de teatro de una época anterior" (Monleón 112) [gives it an air of theater from another epoch]. Ironically, after years of a cultural policy that favored staging tangible social realities over artistic experimentation, the play's frank portrayal of the difficulties the new Cuban family has faced following the breakup of the Soviet Union may have resulted in censorship. In 1994, *Vereda tropical* and Abilio Estévez's *La noche* shared the prestigious Tirso de Molina prize for Hispanic theater. Nevertheless, *Vereda tropical* has been neither published nor produced in Cuba, and its title has scarcely been mentioned in Cuban theater publications. It is possible that the play remains unstaged in Cuba because Cuartas does not work in a subsidized theater collective or because the play is simply too difficult to produce in Cuba's current economic conditions, but its unperformed status might very well relate to the play's portrait of the socialist family in decline.[25] *Vereda tropical* suggests that not only has the Revolution failed to erase traces of the prerevolutionary family but that the new family, built over the foundation of the older model, is on shaky ground as well.

The central character in *Vereda tropical* is fifty-eight-year-old Buenavista Rufino Ruiz (Bururú). She lives in a *solar* [tenement house] in Havana with her mother, Engracia (eighty); her daughter, Caridad (thirty-eight); and her granddaughter, Purita (twenty). Each time the city suffers a blackout, their elderly neighbor Romualdito sings the song "Vereda tropical" to fight the sensation that he is alone in the world, as he puts it: "El último ser de una especie que se extingue" (47–48) [The last member of a species on the brink of extinction]. With the Special Period as its backdrop, *Vereda tropical* reveals socialism and the new Cuban family to be endangered species. Faced with losing her family, Bururú must reconcile her revolutionary idealism with the ideological and economic crises in Cuba. Each act proves to be a downward spiral for Bururú: she breaks her leg in a blackout at the end of the first act, and in the second, her home catches fire (Romualdito is killed), and Gladis La Jabá, her mortal enemy from Miami, returns home. In the third act, Bururú is disappointed by love and discovers that her commitment to the Revolution has alienated her from her family. The play ends with Bururú alone in the dark singing "Vereda tropical," aware that she will indeed become extinct if she does not adapt to the changing face of Cuban reality.

Through the daily life of the characters, the play dramatizes the economic realities of an island that has suffered a trade embargo for over forty years and has recently lost its main subsidizer and trading partner. Bururú's crumbling home visually evokes the deterioration of the socialist family and nation in Cuba. Realistically constructed onstage, the living space that Bururú shares with her three family members constitutes a sign of national economic hardship. Their home is so cramped that there is not enough space for a rocking chair to rock, the kitchen is outfitted poorly, and they have no bathroom of their own. Due to the island's lack of construction materials and replacement parts, it is unlikely that the characters will be able to move or improve their quarters. If Romualdito dies, they could expand into his space but, typical of the play's dark humor, Caridad laments: "(*Suspiro.*) Pero el viejo tiene buena salud, aunque de la cabeza está un poco mal, ya sabes" (16) [(*Sigh.*) But the old man's in good health, even though he's a little confused in the head, you know]. Energy shortages have caused everyday tasks to become complicated. Oil lamps clutter the house because of long, scheduled blackouts, and Engracia, speaking to Caridad, describes crossing the city as an arduous odyssey: "al regreso no había guagua y cuando se apareció una la empujadera fue grande, ni porque es vieja la respetan. No, y se rompió a las cuatro paradas. Mi nieta, he tenido que caminar 20 cuadras" (30) [on the way back there were no buses, and when one finally came, there was a lot of pushing and shoving—they don't even respect old ladies. No, and then it broke down after four stops. My dear, I had to walk 20 blocks]. Other indications of Cuba's dire situation mentioned by the characters include medical and food shortages. The Cuban pesos the women earn are virtually worthless, and Caridad understands that to survive, they need to find a creative way to earn dollars.

While the younger generation scrambles to gain capital in a changing socialist system, Bururú is unfailingly supportive of the Revolution and stoically suffers the brunt of the economic crisis. As a woman of African heritage and a single mother, Bururú represents those who have ben-efited the most from the Revolution's advances in eliminating sexual and racial discrimination and its achievements in socializing medical care, day care, and education. Her faith in the socialist system, therefore, is well-founded, and with Bururú, Cuartas creates a memorable character that embodies the new Cuban. Indeed, she differs notably from the dependent and self-abnegating middle-class Cuban mother we have seen in pre-revolutionary plays by Ferrer, Estorino, and Piñera. Before the Revolu-tion, Bururú was a maid; now she is a community leader who has held a position in the Ministerio de Cultura for twenty-five years.

Bururú has been an exemplary revolutionary. On the wall facing the public, a gigantic picture of Che Guevara surrounded by medals and di-plomas dominates the family's cramped home. Antolín, her gentleman caller, is duly impressed: "Usted tiene toda su vida colgada de la pared, Bururú" (45) [You've got your whole life hanging on the wall, Bururú]. On the wall, one can read the history of the Revolution in Bururú's life, from her participation in the underground movement against Batista to her efforts in the 10 million–ton harvest in 1970, her work in Africa, and her devotion to the neighborhood CDR. The many diplomas recognizing her blood donations suggest that she has literally sacrificed her life for the Revolution, even, as Antolín points out, in the current period of poor alimentation. Bururú's wall, a living example of Guevara's doctrine of volunteerism and moral incentives, contrasts with the material impover-ishment of the home. The Revolution is the focus of meaning and com-mitment in Bururú's life, and, given how her quality of life has improved from the creation of a more egalitarian society, it is easy to understand her revolutionary zeal. But for Caridad and Purita, born after the Revolu-tion, it is more difficult to justify problems such as material shortages and the lack of personal freedom.

Marching down the street dressed in their *miliciano* uniforms, Bururú and her sixty-year-old friend Adarcisa present a striking image of the aging Revolution. Unlike the works we have seen thus far, here characters between the ages of fifty-eight and eighty dominate the action of the play. The builders of the Revolution have aged, and the younger generation brings with it a new attitude toward the revolutionary society. Elderly widows populate the shooting range, honing their skills should they need to defend their nation, while Caridad and Purita socialize with friends. The older generation gladly does its patriotic duty and participates in Preparación Combativa [Combat Preparedness] sessions, but the instructor does not bother to appear. Adarcisa complains about his flimsy excuse and the general lack of desire to serve the Revolution: "¡Gripe, gripe! ¿Te has fijado cómo últimamente todo el mundo se enferma o busca alguna excusa para no cumplir?" (21) [The flu! Have you noticed lately how everyone gets sick or looks for an excuse not to do their part?]. Worse than indifference is the lack of respect young people show toward symbols of national pride. On their way home, Adarcisa and Bururú encounter the decapitated bust of José de la Luz y Caballero, an important nineteenth-century Cuban educator, in the dilapidated park they had built doing voluntary work. Disheartened by the vandalism and the economic crisis, Adarcisa wonders if, "después de tantos años de lucha todo se está haciendo sal y agua" (21) [after fighting for so many years, everything is slipping through our fingers]. After all, it looks as if the nation is selling out to capitalism: "Ya tú ves todas las empresas y corporaciones que se han inventado, ¡y como llaman a los capitalistas a invertir! Chica, ni las putas que existieron en el barrio de San Isidro llamaban tanto a los machos" (21) [You can already see all of the companies and corporations that have sprung up. And the way they kiss up to the capitalists! Girl, not even the whores from the San Isidro neighborhood pestered men as much].[26] They rally their spirits by remembering the good old days and cheerfully shouting out the names of North American companies nationalized by the Cubans. Later, they erect a new bust, showing the perseverance ingrained in their generation.

To younger Cubans, Bururú's and Adarcisa's enthusiasm for the Revolution seems anachronistic. Bururú's family brings a generation gap into relief when Bururú returns from Preparación Combativa to find Caridad in bed with Pititi, the son of Gladis la Jabá. Their families had been friends until Gladis la Jabá betrayed the Revolution fourteen years earlier by leaving Cuba on the Mariel boatlift. Unlike her mother, Caridad holds no grudge against the family, and she tells Bururú that the neighborhood will welcome Gladis la Jabá back because of the dollars she will bring. She laughs when Bururú retorts: "No va a ser. La gente no se arrastra por un dólar, la gente tiene dignidad" (30) [It's not going to be like that. People aren't won over by a dollar, people have dignity]. Caridad knows that in Cuba's current circumstances, dignity is not most people's main concern and points out: "el que no se dedica a algún negocio o a algún trapicheo no vive hoy en Cuba, chica" (50) [if you don't find some business or money making scheme, you can't live in Cuba these days, girl]. Nevertheless, any business involved with U.S. dollars is immoral from Bururú's perspective, and she waits for official channels to improve her situation. She expects that any day she will receive a new apartment in return for her many years of service to the Revolution. Caridad, in contrast, complains, "Bururú. Siempre ha sido como una línea recta. Pero el mundo es redondo, coño; el mundo es redondo. No cuadrado" (39) [Bururú. She has always been straight as an arrow. But the world is round, damnit; the world is round, not square]. Their different world-views reach a climax when Bururú discovers that Caridad has received gifts of shoes and clothing from Gladis la Jabá and Caridad tells her that she plans to marry Pititi and move with Purita to an apartment his mother has bought for them.

Bururú has never confronted Caridad's and Purita's progressive distancing from the family, because over the years she has perfected the art of daydreaming as a means of avoiding unpleasant realities. The set includes a space to the side of the apartment marked with a sign stating: "El Lugar donde se sueña" (12) [The place where one dreams]. In this magical space, Bururú lies on a pink hammock between two phosphorescent palm trees and watches her dreams play out. One of her long-term fantasies involves her relationship with Caridad's father. When she conjures him up, he appears as a handsome white chauffeur, and they dance. She has created a whole mythology about their relationship and his heroic death fighting against Batista in order to deny that Caridad was the product of a brief affair. This subconscious desire for a traditional family headed by a (white) male offers a vision of the family more in line with bourgeois ideals than the revolutionary family represented in the play. The fantasy therefore seems to suggest that the Revolution cannot erase traditional models of the prerevolutionary family and that Cuba's new family and nation have more links with the past than some revolutionaries would like to admit.

In another dream, Bururú's wish for Purita to become a doctor mixes with her anxiety about the Special Period and Gladis la Jabá's visit. In this fantasy, Purita announces that she has won the Nobel Prize for discovering the vaccine for AIDS and that she plans to give all the rights to her discovery to the revolutionary government. Bururú exclaims: "Purita, mi nieta, salvaste a Cuba. Mija, salimos del periodo especial gracias a ti. Ya no necesitaremos los dólares de la gusanera. Ya no van a dejar venir a Cuba a Gladis la Jabá. (*Purita se retira. Bururú queda sola en la hamca, meciéndose con alegría.*)" (35) [My dear, we made it out of the Special Period thanks to you. Now we don't need the money from the traitor exiles. Now they aren't going to let Gladis la Jabá come to Cuba. (*Purita leaves. Bururú remains alone in the hammock, rocking happily.*)[27] Bururú resolves another problem in a humorous fantasy in which Caridad rejects Pititi in favor of an exemplary revolutionary worker. She tells Bururú:

Caridad. Mamá, nunca más va a tener que ver a Pititi en cuero en tu cama. Te lo prometo.
Bururú. Gracias, mija, un hombre en cuero no es nada edificante.
Caridad. (*Amorosa.*) Mamá, haré lo que tú digas. (53–54)
[Caridad. Mom, you're never going to have to see Pititi naked in your bed again. I promise.
Bururú. Thank you, dear, a naked man is never edifying.
Caridad. (*Lovingly.*) Mom, I'll do whatever you say.]

In reality, Caridad does not obey her mother, and Purita has doubts about a medical career. Bururú's conflicted fantasies help her ignore the fact that her household embodies neither the ideal prerevolutionary family nor the exemplary new family.

As Bururú's misfortunes add up, it becomes harder for her to evade reality, and she begins to recognize how she has alienated her family. She breaks her leg, her house is damaged in a fire, Gladis la Jabá comes home in a blaze of material glory, and she discovers that Antolín is interested in Adarcisa, not in her.[28] Perhaps worst of all, the union awards her yet another medal and treats her to a dinner for six instead of a much-anticipated new apartment. The realization that her family is slipping away, however, truly jolts Bururú from her dreamworld. When Caridad announces that she and Purita are moving out, Purita delivers Bururú another shock by telling her that she has decided to leave medical school to work at a hotel. Bururú cannot believe that Purita does not want to become part of a tradition that has been a source of pride for the Revolution: "Vas a ser Premio Nobel. Además, además, tenemos uno de los por cientos de mortalidad infantil más bajos del mundo. Tenemos los médicos de la familia. Tenemos más maestros por habitante que cualquier país del mundo. (*Desesperada.*) Tenemos . . ." (130) [You're going to be a Nobel Prize winner. Besides, besides, we have one of the lowest infant mortality rates in the world. We have family doctors. We have more teachers per capita than in any other country in the world. (*Desperate.*) We have . . .]. But Bururú's frantic list of the Revolution's accomplishments means little to young people who cannot afford to buy shoes. In Cuba's skewed economy, Purita points out that she can earn more from tips in a hotel than as a doctor: "Una profesional suelta el piojo y lo que gana no le alcanza ni para un ajustador. La empleada de un hotel come bien y con las propinas se viste mejor que la profesional" (130) [A professional works her ass off and what she earns can't even buy a bra. A hotel maid eats and dresses better than a professional]. The character Purita is representative of what Enrique Baloyra calls an "internal brain drain" in which overqualified professionals and technicians seek jobs in the dollarized sector of the economy (36). For Purita's generation, the satisfaction from having gained revolutionary *conciencia* does not match the desire for a higher standard of living. In general, according to this play's perspective, the state's ideological orientation has not been as effective shaping the behavior of young people as it was with Bururú's generation. Consequently, the image of the family in recent plays such as *Vereda tropical* contradicts any official rhetoric of a united socialist family and nation.

In the meantime, Engracia has considered moving to a retirement home where she can live in greater comfort. She tells Bururú that the home is like a five-star hotel: "No te falta el buen desayuno, ni la merienda, hay televisor en colores, excursiones, y te dije, hasta un grupo de teatro, un médico que viene a verte" (68) [You never miss a good breakfast, or lunch. They have a color television, excursions—there's even a theater group and an on-call doctor]. It is heartbreaking for Bururú to accept the fact that she cannot take care of her mother adequately, and the realization that her family is leaving leads her to renounce her illusions. She physically destroys her dream space and announces that there are no more dreams left in Cuba. Engracia asks, "Y ¿quién te dijo a ti, mija, que un país vive de sueños? Vive de realidades, y las realidades siempre son duras" (132) [And who told you, my dear, that a country lives on dreams? They live on realities, and realities are always tough]. Bururú understands the difficult reality of everyday survival in Cuba, but what she must confront is the rigidity of her worldview and the changing nature of Cuban socialism. Ultimately, her hard work and devotion to the Revolution have given her dignity, but to avoid extinction, the play implies that she and the revolutionary government must find new ways to hold the national family together.

Although the pressures of the Special Period strain Bururú's family, Engracia stands by her daughter, and together they will weather the economic crisis. In the end, old-fashioned mother's advice guides Bururú rather than revolutionary principles. This empowerment of the private sphere, a return to a source of knowledge long considered detrimental to the official indoctrination of revolutionary *conciencia*, suggests that the older models of the family that have persisted in Cuba may contain values useful to the new family. It also constitutes a sign of the times, for the loss of Cuba's main ideological referent, along with the economic emergency, has forced the socialist state to step back and allow alternative ways for Cubans to resolve problems. The regime's antireligious stance, for example, has eased because the state knows that the island needs the support of other institutions in this time of crisis. Engracia assures Bururú that God will reward her goodness. This confuses Bururú, who points out that for thirty-five years the Revolution has said that God does not exist. Engracia replies: "(*Sonriendo con gran sabiduría.*) Eso también está cambiando, Bururú. También está cambiando. Mi madre, que en paz descanse, siempre decía aquello de que todo lo que pasa conviene" (133) [(*Smiling with great wisdom.*) That's also changing, Bururú, that too. My mother, God rest her soul, always said that everything happens for a reason]. Again, motherly advice evokes generational continuity and underscores how the Revolution might draw upon traditional Cuban resources to resolve the national crisis of the Special Period.

Crisis management and experimentation have characterized the operational mode of the Cuban regime and helped ensure its longevity. To preserve her family, Bururú must adapt to the changing times. The new family will survive, but as Estorino argues in *Ni un sí ni un no*, it will constantly take on new forms; likewise, *Vereda tropical* makes evident that in the changing Cuban family, different models of family coexist.

Engracia tells Bururú, "A veces en las familias tienen que pasar cosas así. Las familias son como los países, que de vez en cuando necesitan un sacudión" (134) [Sometimes families have to go through things like this. Families are like countries; sometimes they need a little upheaval]. In the shake-up of the family dramatized in this play, we have seen utopian dreams dashed, a socialist aperture toward capitalism, and young people motivated by consumerism rather than by revolutionary ideals. The presence of multiple generations in Bururú's family reveals the persistence of some values and traditions from an epoch that the Revolution had purportedly eradicated. The prize-winning play's failure to generate interest suggests that, similar to Triana's experience with *La noche de los asesinos* (1966), perhaps Cuban officials found that *Vereda tropical* did not maintain a sharp enough contrast between past and present national families.

Of Lard and Family: Surviving the Special Period

Alberto Pedro Torriente's *Manteca* (1993) is a darkly humorous play that, in the tradition of Piñera and Triana, combines realism with elements of the theater of the absurd and Artaudian cruelty to form a distinctly Cuban representation of the family. Like *Vereda tropical*, *Manteca* treats a new family's endurance of the Special Period, but the play's synthesis of styles and discursive density make its presentation of this crisis much more ambiguous than the *costumbrista* realism of the other work. As in Cuartas's piece, *Manteca* challenges the Revolution's perennially optimistic rhetoric by showing some of the negative effects of the current socioeconomic crisis on the Cuban family; consequently, the play was initially censored. The theater collective Teatro Mío eventually played *Manteca* over fifty times to audiences that reportedly greeted the play "with passion, heated applause, and raucous laughter" (Martínez Tabares, "*Manteca*" 46).[29] Akin to Brecht's view of realism as truthful, for Pedro, sincerity defines the most revolutionary plays. He affirms that "si las obras no consiguen generar una fricción con la sociedad en que vivimos, si no se provoca un rozamiento, un conflicto con la época, entonces algo funciona mal en esa escritura" ("Todo esto" 77) [if the plays don't generate friction with the society in which we live, if they don't provoke disagreement or conflict with the period, then something is not working in that writing]. Despite the play's challenging form, or indeed, perhaps because of it, *Manteca* clearly struck a chord with audiences eager to experience honest portrayals of the difficult circumstances in which they live.

As in *Vereda tropical*, the family theme in *Manteca* serves to assess the island's changing national identity after the demise of Marxist socialism. Because of Cuba's relationship with the United States during the first half of the twentieth century and its ties with the Soviet bloc in the second, Pedro argues that Cuba has not fulfilled the potential of its unique identity: "I think we have not yet become all that we are, with all the dignity that is required" (Martínez Tabares, "Theater" 63). In *Manteca*, the characters turn to the family, not the state, as a means of surviving Cuba's economic crisis. This reliance on kinship and appealing to one's own "metonymically introduces into the discourse, from another angle, the focus on Cubanity (*cubanía*)" (Muguercia, "The Gift" 56–57). That is, according to this play, to orient themselves in a world undergoing great ideological shifts and to achieve self-sufficiency, Cubans must look to themselves for answers. In this regard, the play's scrutiny of the Cuban family and national identity forms part of an artistic trend in the 1990s that counters the precariousness of the present by examining national values and traditions.

The dramatic action of *Manteca* is uncomplicated. To alleviate the shortage of food, three adult siblings, Pucho, Celestino, and Dulce, have shut themselves in their fifth-story apartment in Havana to raise an illegally purchased pig. It is New Year's Eve, the day they have agreed to slaughter the pig, and they have trouble doing the deed because the animal has become like one of the family. When Celestino does kill the pig, they realize that they must raise another because it has come to represent a utopia that provides them with a sense of purpose. Part of the play's dramatic tension derives from the fact that the action that the siblings have to take does not become clear until well into the play. Their unwillingness to act, a strong odor permeating the apartment, and the presence of a knife create a somewhat menacing ambience.

The majority of the one-act play, however, does not treat violence. It consists of the siblings' daily rituals of survival and their conversation, which is often entertaining. Dialogue rather than action dominates the play and includes logical comments about their absurd situation; rationally expressed memories of the past; bizarre proclamations about Cuba, the world, and themselves; intertextual references; and the rhythmic enumeration of, among other things, English verbs and days of the week.

Over their disconnected conversations, the song "Manteca" intermittently blares throughout the play. The abusive music contributes to the anxiety of the cloistered atmosphere of an apartment so cluttered that it looks like a storehouse of junk.[30] The trio of siblings, their ritualized daily activities, and the possibility of a bloody sacrifice in *Manteca* obviously recall the murderous siblings in José Triana's *La noche de los asesinos*.[31] Here, however, the survival of "la gran familia cubana" depends on the siblings coming together to reconstruct what's left of their family, whereas in Triana's play, the children wish to destroy their family unit in hopes that a less oppressive version might emerge. Nonetheless, as in the earlier play, the incarcerating atmosphere of the family apartment in *Manteca* suggests the repression of personal freedom in revolutionary Cuban society, which highlights the similarities between the pre- and postrevolutionary families.

The economic crisis has brought three very dissimilar siblings to live together in the small apartment their parents have left them. Celestino is a macho Communist who has married a woman he met while studying engineering in Leningrad. He refers to the breakup of the Soviet Union as the "desastre" (171) [disaster] and insists that, to him, Russia will always be the Soviet Union. Pucho is a gay, frustrated writer who has lost his position as a university professor for introducing taboo subjects in his classroom. The brothers' antithetical personalities make their relationship tense, and at one point Pucho comments, "No es fácil convivir con un hermano como tú" (181) [It isn't easy living with a brother like you (31)]. He adds that he is only living with Celestino because he has no other option. Dulce is a domestic motherly type who tries to smooth things over between her brothers; she amusingly delivers offbeat comments about the world in a tone of conventional wisdom. Overall, in spite of their differences, the siblings show concern for one another and cooperate to make the best of their situation.

Life in the apartment has a ritualistic, timeless quality. The passage of time acquires meaning only inasmuch as it relates to sustenance. The beginning of a New Year, for example, is meaningful only because it is when the siblings plan to slaughter the pig. On a daily basis, the siblings ask each other if it is an odd or an even day because this determines when they leave their home to wait in line for rations: "Hay que estar los días impares, de madrugada, con los recipientes" (175) [You've got to be there first thing in the morning on odd-numbered days, with your containers

(26)]. Thus days of the week matter only in terms of portioning their rice adequately. Dispensing rations becomes a ritual for Dulce, who sorts rice, divides the daily bread into three servings, and passes out glasses of sugar water. Repetitive tasks also occupy Celestino's and Pucho's time: Celestino repairs makeshift objects, and Pucho searches for an essential lost page of his novel. Even Celestino's attempts to commit suicide are on their way to becoming a ritual to fill time. He informs Pucho and Dulce that he would like to be run over by a truck, but they point out that he has already tried this twice before, at the same corner, in front of the same truck driven by the same driver. The incongruency of Celestino's suicide attempt and the detached logic with which the siblings treat the pathetic act make it almost seem funny. The play's dark humor recalls Piñera's treatment of the family in *Aire frío*. Just as Luz Marina understands the absurdity of waiting in her stifling family home for *aire frío*, or change, as the siblings in *Manteca* portion, fix, search, and, most of all, wait for the pig to fatten, they are struck by the absurdity of their situation: "Estamos criando un puerco en los umbrales del año dos mil, a escondidas, en un edificio de apartamentos, desafiando las leyes sanitarias que han hecho posible el florecimiento de las ciudades del planeta, porque necesitamos proteínas, proteínas y manteca" (186) [We're raising a pig on the threshold of the year 2000, secretly, in an apartment building, defying the sanitary laws which have made it possible for the cities of the planet to flourish, because we need protein, protein and lard (34)].

This family's isolation in their battle for survival, by extension, embodies the situation of the Cuban nation. Pucho's bewildered questions, "¿En qué acabará todo esto? ¿Hasta donde vamos a llegar?" (177) [Where will this all end? What is it all coming too? (28)], refer to his family's plight as well as to the ideological vacuum and economic crisis Cuba faces with the loss of Soviet support. As unstable as the Revolution's early years were in terms of Cuba's position in the world, especially after Castro declared himself a Marxist, Dulce associates stability with the good old days when the Soviet Union became part of Cuba's extended national family. She remembers fondly Nikita Khrushchev and the missiles, the circus, and the canned meat sent to Cuba by the Soviets: "Aquella carne que tenía una vaca pintada en la latica y que la gente decía que era un oso y que aquello era carne de oso, aquella carne que nos salvó, cuando ningún país quería mandarnos nada, aquella carne a mí me caía bien" (173) [That meat with the cow painted on the wrapper, that people said was a bear, and that the meat was bear meat; that meat that saved us, because no country wanted to send us anything—I really liked that meat (24)]. Although Castro has led a uniquely Cuban revolution, the Soviets provided an anchor that helped Cubans define their place in the world order. The certainty of having Soviets as allies and the North Americans as enemies, even if it meant teetering on the brink of a nuclear war, seemed to Dulce a more stable time: "Cuando la crisis esa de los cohetes, como le llaman, estábamos mejor. Al amanecer podíamos ser barridos de la faz de la tierra, pero estábamos juntos todos aquí. Mamá, papá, nosotros, mis hijos, la familia" (192) [When that missile crisis, as they call it, happened, we were much better off. When daybreak came we could have been wiped off the face of the earth, as they say, but all of us were together right here: Mama, Papa, the three of us, my children, the whole family (38–39)]. Dulce also identifies stability with a different kind of family than the one she is living with now, which suggests that the Revolution has altered the family in important ways.

For Martínez Tabares, "*Manteca* defends the space of the family as the individual's last recourse and refuge from the arduous and relentless process of transformation opened up by the Revolution" ("Manteca" 45). I would argue, however, that the Special Period marks a return to the family as a refuge from state intervention only because the state can no longer support "la gran familia cubana." As we have seen in other plays, the Revolution's attempt to create a socialist family has greatly affected this institution by modifying relationships between parents and children and between husbands and wives. Through the family, playwrights have explored how the regime has attempted to instill revolutionary values in Cuban society and to what extent it has been successful. In the case of *Manteca*, all that is left of the new Cuban family is a fragment: two brothers and a sister. After the initial years of installing a socialist system in Cuba, the Revolution looked abroad in the 1970s and became involved in Marxist movements in other countries. Dulce maintains that with the geographical dispersion of the Cuban family, "empezó la locura" (192) [the craziness started (39)]. In Dulce's case, service to the Revolution has destroyed her marriage and weakened her ties with her sons: "Un hijo en Africa y otro en el Polo Norte. Y no puedo culparlos porque el primero que empezó fue mi marido. Por eso se acabó nuestro matrimonio, porque vivía más tiempo en el lugar donde lo mandaron que en su propia casa y por supuesto allá encontró otra y por allá se quedó" (191–92) [A son in

Africa and another at the North Pole. And I can't blame them because the first one to get started was my husband. That's why our marriage ended, because he spent more time in the place they sent him than in his own home, and of course he met another woman and ended up staying there (38)]. Celestino's marriage has also ended in divorce. He married a woman from the Soviet Union and brought her to Cuba. Although their children seemed to grow up comfortably Cuban—they rejected their mother's borscht in favor of their Cuban grandmother's black beans—their mother never adapted to her new country, and she left Celestino and took the children back to the Soviet Union. With these divorces, the death of the siblings' parents, and no mention of other relatives, only a piece of the family remains.

Celestino's failed marriage evokes the end of Cuba's Soviet romance and the beginning of a period of great uncertainty for the island. The characters in *Manteca* are very aware of how the fall of Marxist socialism has ushered in a period of shifting world borders and alliances, as well as renewed national and ethnic movements. Dulce's chaotic enumeration of these changes matches the disorienting feeling of the epoch:

> Y los bosnioherzegovinos bomba viene y bomba va. Y vaya sangre y venga sangre. Y de África ni hablar. Con tanta vaca suelta que hay en la India. Y ahora en Alemania, ni negros, ni turcos. ¿Habrán podido tumbar aquella estatua? Vamos a ver, porque están los vietnamitas, los chinos y los coreanos. (176)

> [And the Bosnians, bombs here and bombs there, blood flowing every which way. And don't even talk about Africa. And all of those cows running loose in India. And now in Germany: no blacks, no Turks. So they were able to knock down that statue? Let's see now, there're Vietnamese, Chinese, and Koreans over there. . . (27)]

Whatever the future of Communism may be, for Celestino, one thing is certain, its collapse in Eastern Europe and the Soviet Union signifies more than a simple transition to capitalism: "Mucha gente piensa: 'Se acabó el comunismo y para la tienda,' lo que no saben es que lo que viene si no es fascismo se parece bastante" (188) [A lot of people think, "Communism's finished, let's go Capitalist," but the way it looks, if what's coming isn't fascism it sure looks a lot like it]. Likewise, Pucho's comments reveal his concern about recent waves of racism, xenophobia, and fundamentalism.

Manteca portrays the worldwide tendency to decentralize through a renewed autonomy of the individual Cuban family. After decades of experimenting with the construction of a new society based on collectivist ideals, Dulce concludes: "Al final con lo único que cuentas es con tus padres, tus hijos, tus hermanos, con tu sangre" (189) [In the end the only people you can count on are your parents, your children, your brothers, your blood (37)]. As the state cannot provide for the nation in this period of scarcity, citizens have turned to their own individual families to find creative ways to survive the economic crisis.[32] In light of the food shortages, it is fitting that in *Manteca*, a pig, which recalls the tradition of a family gathered together for holiday pig roasts, has reunited what remains of the siblings' family.[33] The totemized pig objectifies their kinship and recalls a more primitive existence in which basic survival determined human groupings. The ritualistic quality of the siblings' daily tasks and the spilled blood of the pig, which constitutes a visual image of blood ties, adds to the ambience of primal survival. As Dulce affirms, the pig underscores the primacy of the family: "Ese animalito mantuvo unida a la familia y la familia es lo principal" (191) [This little animal kept the family together and the family is the main thing (38)]. This change in priorities in which loyalty to one's family takes precedence over commitments to the collectivity implies a more lenient approach to difference and individuality in Cuban society. As Pucho says, "El integracionismo es excluyente" (189) [Integration is exclusivist (37)]. The regime's project of integrating Cubans in the Revolution has required sameness; the new Cuban family has included those who emulate revolutionary qualities, and Pucho's homosexuality automatically has excluded him from this national family. In the 1990s, the Revolution can ill afford to exclude members of the Cuban family. This is evident in the fact that the regime has allowed exiles to visit in order for Cuba to gain U.S. dollars. This opening toward a more diverse Cuban family, one that includes components new to both traditional and new families, coincides with a reexamination of all things Cuban.

Part of Cuba's survival depends on its resourcefulness and adaptability. In the post-Soviet period, the Revolution has had to de-emphasize the Marxist foundation of the Cuban constitution and tone down the official rhetoric that alienates young people. In addition, the regime has understood the importance of maintaining a strong national identity and a sense of cultural belonging in order for Cubans to draw from their own experiences to find ways to resolve their problems. Rather than looking to the state or to another country, Cubans must now look to the family for answers. In *Manteca*, the siblings implicitly reflect on national identity when they discuss Cuba's place in the world. For instance, Dulce's amusing theory of how the world is dominated by those countries that had dinosaurs refers to Cuba's problematic lack of oil: "Y aquellos que tuvieron dinosaurios siempre han hecho de los otros lo que les ha dado la gana, como esos siete que siempre se están volviendo a reunir por allá, por Europa" (170) [The world's divided into countries who had dinosaurs and countries who didn't have them. And the countries who had dinosaurs always did what they wanted with the others, like those seven countries always busy having meetings over there in Europe (22)]. Whereas Dulce defines Cuba by its lack of natural resources, Celestino distinguishes Cuba from other countries affirmatively. For example, while thinking of his ex-wife in Russia, he defends Cuba's brand of Communism: "Yo soy de aquí. Allá ella con sus mundos y sus problemas. ¡Yo soy de aquí! ¡Comunista de aquí! Sí, comunista. Cada día soy más comunista, más comunista de aquí" (188) [I'm from here. She's over there with her worlds and her problems. I'm from here! A communist over here, yes, a communist, every day I'm more of a communist, more of a communist from here (36)].

In the play, some of the characteristics that describe this "aquí," however, include machismo, racism, and intolerance. Dulce's humorous remark about Cuban men being incapable of monogamy and Celestino's obsession with failing to stop his ex-wife from taking the kids—"No tuve cojones, no tuve cojones!" (174) [I didn't have the balls, I didn't have the balls! (25)]—parody the aggressive virility of Cuban men. Celestino repeats "cojones" so many times it begins to lose its shocking effect, and Pucho further deflates his exaggerated masculinity by suggesting that all his bravado may be a cover-up for repressed homosexuality. The play underscores that the Revolution has not welcomed homosexuals in the new Cuban family/society. Pucho has lost his job and has trouble publishing, and Celestino has felt obligated to look out for him because he has known that Pucho could get into trouble with the authorities. Celestino's refusal to pose nude for an artist friend of Pucho's makes fun of Cuban male anxiety about homoeroticism. The pose planned by the artist—Celestino, naked, with a crown of laurel on his head and a hammer and sickle in his hand—also expresses the challenge of being an artist in a Communist society. Dulce's exaggerated surprise at the fact that the artist is black parodies obvious racial stereotypes: "¡Qué pena, un muchacho tan decente y tan fino, a pesar de su color! Si cuando lo vi por primera vez, pensé que era un deportista, un basquetbolista de esos, y en cuanto habló me dio una vergüenza porque era artista. ¡Un artista a pesar de su tamaño y su color!" (180) [What a shame, such a decent and elegant young man, in spite of his color. Sure, when I saw him for the first time, I thought he was an athlete—one of those basketball players—and the minute he opened his mouth I felt so ashamed because he was an artist. An artist in spite of his size and his color! (29)].[34] The play also mentions the Cuban inclination for socializing and celebration and alludes to a jocular but satirical attitude summed up as *malicia,* which is similar to *choteo,* the national habit of mocking figures of authority and serious occasions. *Manteca* parodies some of these supposedly Cuban attitudes and prejudices to encourage Cubans, in this moment of self-examination, to rely on humor, tolerance, and camaraderie to survive this difficult period.

Without Soviet support, Cuba has looked hard at itself to determine the best ways it can secure a stable economy without betraying the principles of the Revolution. *Manteca* represents this recent search for self-sufficiency in its examination of *cubanía,* in its portrayal of the desire to define Cuba's place in the world, and in its focus on the renewed responsibilities of the individual family. The siblings' decision to raise another pig maintains their illusions of utopia and holds the family together. They do, however, brainstorm about other ways to survive. Pucho proposes the capitalist venture of selling the slaughtered pig and, with the profits, making sweets to sell outside of children's hospitals. Dulce is more creative and imagines a fifth-story garden paradise in which they would cultivate their own fruits and vegetables in large pots in their apartment. Martínez Tabares affirms that these other options show "the need in Cuban society for personal initiatives, for individual involvement in the search for paths out of the crisis and solutions that will move the country forward" ("*Manteca*" 45–46). That is, in contrast to the socialist ideal of a collective revolutionary family, the state must entrust unique groupings of individual families with more liberty to determine their destiny.

Manteca suggests that as the dominance of the state in Cuban society weakens, another new Cuban family emerges that is more comfortable with heterogeneity and that seeks innovative solutions to difficult national problems. At the same time, on an aesthetic level, Pedro's playful absurdist techniques signal a new trend in the arts that permits more diverse explorations of the Cuban family and nation. Just as the family must become more self-sufficient, officials have granted more autonomy to the arts because they cannot afford to fund them and because they understand the importance of allowing an outlet for Cubans to express their discontent with the island's present circumstances. Since the Revolution, Cuban playwrights have had to negotiate with a space of possibilities that has shifted in accordance with a rather slippery revolutionary cultural policy. Therefore, in portraying Cuban social realities, the diverse approaches of the playwrights examined in this chapter have varied in motivation and in responses from government officials and the public. Each play, however, examines how Cuban identity has evolved since the Revolution by emphasizing changes in the family. Che Guevara, a central figure in the project of revolutionizing Cuba, maintained that the construction of socialism and the birth of the new Cuban was an ongoing process: "His [the new man's] image is as yet unfinished; in fact, it will never be finished, for the process advances parallel to the development of new economic forms" ("Man" 160). From *La emboscada*, which teaches its audience that the bonds of socialism are stronger than blood ties, to *Manteca*, which reaffirms kinship as a mode to strengthen the revolutionary family in a time of great uncertainty, the theater has performed the constantly changing identity of the Cuban family and nation.

Exit

•◆•

From the House to the Stage

Haunted Family Scenarios in Cuban and Puerto Rican Drama

> "It has become an essential ritual of our societies to scrutinize
> the countenance of the family at regular intervals in order to decipher
> our destiny, glimpsing in the death of family an impending return to
> barbarism, the letting go of our reasons for living; or indeed, in order
> to reassure ourselves at the sight of its inexhaustible capacity for survival."
>
> —Jacques Donzelot

Family and Identity in Contemporary Cuban and Puerto Rican Identity
is a study of variants on one theme: the story of national identity embodied by family conflicts. Although this book follows a trajectory that is not
strictly chronological, by focusing on two crucial moments of the production of family plays I am able to trace not the progress but the historical
articulation of the concepts of nation and identity in the theater. The theater, as Martin Esslin observes, "is the place where a nation thinks in
public in front of itself" (101). I have argued that the dynamic of national
theatrical self-reflection is particularly evident when plays present audiences with family scenarios. The contiguous spaces of the stage, frequently configured as a family home, and the auditorium compel spectators to ponder questions of affiliation, encouraging them to identify or
dis-identify with the "national family" represented onstage.

In plays from the 1950s and 1960s, the physical space of the house,
which stands for the nation, attains a protagonism that rivals its human

inhabitants. In Puerto Rican theater, the physical state of the family home and the characters' perceptions of their place within it signify conflicting interpretations of national community. Plays by Francisco Arriví, René Marqués, and Myrna Casas manifest a preoccupation with Puerto Rico's changing national character under the newly adopted political status of the Commonwealth. Their family plays enact a historically pivotal moment that heralds displacement for some groups and, for others, the forging of a more inclusive Puerto Rican national family. The many failed love matches in these plays suggest that the island's nation-building romance never produced a hegemonic vision of the Puerto Rican people. The characters portray dissenting views on what should constitute *puertorriqueñidad* and in some metatheatrical scenes imagine alternative identities to those available for performance in the world created by the play and in the cultural field of the 1950s. While Puerto Rican drama in the 1950s is primarily realist in its theatrical form, the metatheatrical moments in these plays signal subsequent dramatic methods for exploring national selfhood, prefiguring the performative representation of the Puerto Rican family in the 1980s and 1990s.

In Cuban plays from the 1950s, in contrast, there is more consensus on national identity in the overwhelming dissatisfaction with what Cuba had become since its independence. The family quarrel in this country plays out as a generational conflict in dramas by Rolando Ferrer, Virgilio Piñera, José Triana, and Abelardo Estorino. The younger generation portrayed in these works seeks to create an autonomous nation and a more just society, a task their parents' generation had failed to achieve during the Cuban Republic. In the act of rebelling against parental authority, the dismantlement of the house suggests the need to reconstruct the institution of the family as a form of rebuilding the nation itself.

In the 1980s and 1990s, the reevaluation of the conceptual category of the nation both alters what is understood by national community and requires different ways of doing theater to express newer, more flexible models of family and nation. In the process of creating a new, socialist national identity, and in the case of Puerto Rico, in the process of debunking nationalist myths, dramatists in the 1980s and 1990s are thus inclined to abandon the realist tradition of using the house to create an onstage world that (re)presents ideologies as natural and enduring. The arrangement of theatrical space takes on new meanings and forms, and playwrights are less apt to build an onstage structure that "houses" a particular view of the national family. The use of metatheater and other anti-illusionist techniques also calls into question essentialist nationalist discourses and highlights the constructed and contingent nature of imagined national communities. By reworking identity stories from the 1950s, plays by Roberto Ramos-Perea and Antonio García del Toro reveal the necessity of new paradigms to debate Puerto Rican national identity. In pieces by Luis Rafael Sánchez and Myrna Casas, families leave the home and display themselves on actual stages. This performance context presents families as mobile and their members as forever reinventing their roles within them.

In a similar vein, the task of forming revolutionary subjectivities has situated the private space of the family on the national stage in Cuban plays of the 1980s and 1990s. These plays register how the Revolution has entered the home in order to ideologically orient the private and individual character of the family unit toward the larger family of socialism. I have argued that Cuban drama at midcentury portrays a self-conscious awareness of *cubanía* as a process. That is, by challenging the politics of their parents, the children show an awareness of the alterable condition of Cuban identity. It is no surprise, therefore, that the Revolution's endeavors to mold yet another national identity have characterized the plays of the post-1959 period. In the 1980s, plays by Abelardo Estorino and Roberto Orihuela contribute to discussions about a new Cuban family by staging the conflicts that arise between prerevolutionary traditions and values and new ones. The revolutionary optimism of transcending these conflicts translates spatially as a set free of the realistically constructed house that had signified oppression during the prerevolutionary period. The desire to build a different sort of house or national family and the problem of housing shortages contribute to the new connotations of Cuban family space as well. By the early 1990s, plays enact the erosion of the new family under the precarious social and economic conditions in post-Soviet Cuba and propose that the family in contemporary Cuba is really a palimpsest of new and old models. The plays imply, in fact, that the national family has survived precisely because Cubans have inventively synthesized old and new traditions.

In charting a genealogy of the family play, this study has crossed national borders and juxtaposed dramatic texts with other forms of artistic and symbolic production in order to develop an understanding of how drama engages with the problem of collective identity. The analysis of how the family scenario repeats itself across cultures and over time brings into focus the singular functions of the human activity of performance. One of the operations of theater illuminated in much recent criticism is its role as preserver of cultural memory.[1] For Marvin Carlson, the theater is a cultural activity characterized by repetition, for the "ghosts" of the stories as well as the materials and bodies used to tell these stories "haunt" their retelling. Carlson writes: "Drama, more than any other literary form, seems to be associated in all cultures with the retelling again and again of stories that bear a particular religious, social, or political significance for their public. There clearly seems to be something in the nature of dramatic presentation that makes it a particularly attractive repository for the storage and mechanism for the continued recirculation of cultural memory" (8). If, as Carlson suggests, ghosts frequent all theater, then this study has shown that theater in Cuba and Puerto Rico is particularly haunted because of its fixation with the family plot. As we have seen, in this dramatic tradition, family plays allegorize narratives of national identity. Such stories have particular significance for these two Caribbean islands, since they form part of a region constantly engaged in the processes of decolonization. Puerto Rico's uncertain status as a Commonwealth of the United States and the Revolution's convulsive reorganization of Cuban society have prolonged debates on the problem of self-definition well beyond the nineteenth-century era of national formation in other areas of Latin America. On the one hand, re-presenting already familiar stories of family conflicts such as failed love relationships and generational rifts guides audiences to respond to certain storylines in predictable ways. Puerto Rican audiences come to understand the drama of selling land, for example, as a battle between autonomy and annexation, while Cuban audiences recognize generational conflicts as a battle against ideological intransigence. On the other hand, recycling stories encourages audiences to compare contrasting versions of the same story. Spectators become actively involved in the cultural politics of representation when their awareness of discrepancies leads them to recognize that different family compositions and outcomes to their conflicts signify dissimilar ways of understanding collective identity.

The haunted quality of Cuban and Puerto Rican family drama makes evident the theater's capacity both to generate and preserve cultural memory. Just as a ghost constitutes an apparition, a materialization of something unseen, staging the image of the family and the spaces it inhabits concretizes and makes present discourses and ideas that might otherwise seem abstract or distant. The reappearance and reexamination of the family on the Cuban and Puerto Rican stage at particular historical junctures is part of the ritual "to decipher our destiny" referenced by Jacques Donzelot in the epigraph to these concluding remarks (4). Some plays depict the termination of family lines or the rupture of family relations, but the persistence of the family as a mode for assessing the status of the nation suggests not the death but the "inexhaustible capacity for survival" of both (Donzelot 4). The playwrights included in this book are representative of the many voices in Cuban and Puerto Rican theater history that have confronted the destiny of their nation. When brought into dialogue with one another, we see how repeat performances of the family trope leave an imprint of a polemical search for self-determination and identity on the Cuban and Puerto Rican cultural memory.

Notes

Curtain-Raiser. A Family Affair: Theater and Nation in Cuba
and Puerto Rico

1. The dates following the titles of the sixteen plays that form the corpus of this
study refer to the year of their premiere. I note cases in which there is a significant
gap between the dates of writing, publication, and production of the play.

2. For a useful review of the many methods of theorizing the family, see the
collection of essays edited by David H. Demo, Katherine R. Allen, and Mark A. Fine.

3. For my purposes, "nineteenth-century realism" implicitly includes naturalism; these movements in the theater emerged in the 1880s and continued through
the first decade of the twentieth century, although many of their features still in-
form theatrical conventions today. Christopher Innes makes a helpful distinction
between the two terms that many treat as synonyms: "It would be logical to use
'Naturalism' to refer to the theoretical basis shared by all dramatists who formed the
movement, and their approach to representing the world. 'Realism' could then apply
to the intended effect, and the stage techniques associated with it" (6).

4. Louis Althusser uses the term "interpellate" in his theory of the subject. He
argues that ideology transforms individuals into subjects "by that very precise operation which I have called *interpellation* or hailing, and which can be imagined
along the lines of the most commonplace everyday police (or other) hailing: 'hey,
you there!'" (174). The matrix of subject positions constructed in language and in
discourse that produces identity, or subjectivity, is an effect of ideology that conceals
the role of language in the construction of the subject and induces the individual to
(mis)recognize himself or herself as a unified and coherent self.

5. On another level, the erotic disappointments of the protagonists and the construction of the nation depend on one another: "Once the couple confronts the obstacle, desire is reinforced along with the need to overcome the obstacle and to consolidate the nation. That promise of consolidation constitutes another level of desire
and underscores the erotic goal, which is also a microcosmic expression of nationhood" (Sommer, *Foundational Fictions* 49). In some of the foundational romances
Sommer describes, the obstacles are too great for the lovers to overcome, and the

romance fails on both a personal and a national level. The public venue of the theater and the pressure of providing a "happy ending" might be factors in dramatic renditions of national romances.

6. Similar to scholars of the family who contest the normative view of the nuclear family unit as natural, Donzelot looks at the family as a historically contingent ideological construct. Donzelot posits the family "not as a point of departure, as a manifest reality, but as a moving resultant, an uncertain form whose intelligibility can only come from studying the system of relations it maintains with the sociopolitical level. This requires us to detect all the political mediations that exist between the two registers, to identify the lines of transformation that are situated in that space of intersections" (xxv). Donzelot shares with his friend and mentor Michel Foucault a genealogical approach to history (more on this historical method in the following pages). I would like to thank Sharon Magnarelli for introducing me to Donzelot's work on the family.

7. I am referring to Catharine MacKinnon's famous statement: "to say that the personal is political means that gender as a division of power is discoverable and verifiable through women's intimate experience of sexual objectification" (21). The "personal is political" rallying cry defined the feminist project that emerged in the 1960s. For more on the public/private distinction in feminist theory, see essays by Joan Landes, Carole Pateman, and Nancy Fraser in the collection edited by Landes. Many of the writers of this collection analyze the unthematized gender subtext in Jürgen Habermas's theory of the public sphere.

8. By naming the presence of a character in space and time as the basic components of drama, I am following Charles Lyons's argument in his article "Character and Theatrical Space."

9. Foucault writes that heterotopias "create a space of illusion that exposes every real space, all the sites inside of which human life is partitioned. [. . .] Or else, on the contrary, their role is to create a space that is other, another real space, as perfect, as meticulous, as well arranged as ours is messy, ill constructed and jumbled. The latter would be the heterotopia, not of illusion, but of compensation" ("Other Spaces" 27).

10. Thus, by "collective identity" I mean Anderson's conception of nation as an "imagined political community" (6). One's personal identity, constituted linguistically and discursively, may be fashioned in connection with various collectivities such as class, race, gender, region, political party, religion, or sexual practice, but the central discourse I examine in these plays is the nation. In some way, each play grapples with what it means to be Cuban or Puerto Rican.

11. For an incisive study on the relationship between the power of performance in manipulating what we see, see Diana Taylor's book *Disappearing Acts* on gender and nation as spectacle in Argentina's "Dirty War."

12. In determining the scope of this study, similar historical experiences and literary developments make Cuba and Puerto Rico a natural pair for a comparative study. I have reluctantly left out the Dominican Republic because although historically the three islands of the Greater Antilles share the experience of Spanish colo-

nialism and North American imperialism, the Dominican independence process—particularly the timing and the nations involved—and the country's complex relationship with its French-speaking neighbor, Haiti, set the island apart from Cuba and Puerto Rico. Moreover, theatrical production in the Dominican Republic in the 1950s–90s has been scarce, and those plays staged and published tend to pose individual, existential questions and contain Greek mythological and Christian intertexts that explicitly have little to do with Dominican realities (Iván García Guerra, Franklín Domínguez, and Héctor Cabral Incháustegui have written important plays representative of this style). Undoubtedly, Rafael Trujillo's extended dictatorship from 1931 to 1960 stifled the development of a dramatic tradition characterized by an overt interest in national affairs, while, on the contrary, this was precisely the period when Cuba's and Puerto Rico's national theater movements coalesced.

13. In order to limit my study, I have included plays that combine the following criteria: each work includes a combination of two or more characters from an immediate or extended family, and each work is set in the historical present. In addition, most take place in the house. I have excluded plays that treat solely a married couple and have focused instead on works with multiple siblings or generations. I have also excluded plays that follow the blueprint of Greek myths, since in the Greek tradition, plots almost automatically treat the family. See William García's and Javier Martínez de Velasco's unpublished doctoral dissertations for more on the use of myth in the drama of the Hispanic Caribbean.

14. Diana Taylor characterizes the plays produced between 1965 and 1970, roughly the period between the decades I investigate, as a "theatre of crisis" (*Theatre* 6). In Cuba and Puerto Rico, as in much of the rest of Latin America, the practice of collective creation and of generally popular and politicized dramatic forms dominated the theater of the late 1960s and 1970s. Rather than portray the national family, many plays confronted specific local social and political crises as well as international events like the war in Vietnam. The focus on very local or international issues placed debates on national identity on hold, and as a result, while the family play in Cuba and Puerto Rico did not entirely disappear during these years, it did not dominate.

15. Joseph Roach's brilliant study of the relationship between history and memory and between document and performance in *Cities of the Dead: Circum-Atlantic Performance* (1996) signals the disparities between discursive history and enacted memory (25–31). His work on genealogies of performance has been a source of inspiration for my own.

Act I, Scene 1. Four Failed Puerto Rican Family Romances

1. I use the Spanish term *"puertorriqueñidad"* to signify Puerto Rican identity throughout, because its English translation, "Puerto Ricanness," is somewhat awkward.

2. Teresita Martínez Vergne writes: "Puerto Rico's landowning, merchant, pro-

fessional, and intellectual groups participated in politics only through the formulation of very localized demands consonant with circumstances in the mother country. It is not surprising, then, that the constant attempt at reform culminated in plans for autonomy, not independence" (192). The strongest nationalist challenge to Spanish domination was the 1868 Grito de Lares led from Saint Thomas by Puerto Rican–born and French-educated doctor Ramón Emeterio Betances.

3. According to Blanca G. Silvestrini, by 1928 "U.S.-owned *centrales* controlled approximately 80 percent of the sugar lands and processed more than 60 percent of the sugar exported. The peso devaluation and scarcity of currency made it very difficult for Puerto Rican *colonos*, the sugarcane growers who supplied the *centrales*, to expand or modernize their farms in competition with foreign investors" (149).

4. Ángel G. Quintero Rivera states that this formed a triangular political conflict between the agricultural workers, the hacendado class, and the colonial power (217). Later, however, "it had become clear to the island's proletariat that its real class enemies were the great absentee North American corporations which controlled the sugar industry" (221). The triangular relations created by colonialism created class conflicts and weakened the bonds between Puerto Ricans, perhaps making the island more vulnerable to North American domination.

5. For example, the United States sought to Americanize schools by imposing a new calendar that dropped traditional Puerto Rican holidays, by prohibiting religious instruction in public schools, and by requiring mixed-gender classrooms and the study of North American history and English (Morris 28; Oróñoz Echeverría 20).

6. In *Insularismo e ideología burguesa* [Insularism and bourgeois ideology], Juan Flores places *Insularismo* within the philosophical and ideological currents of its time, such as José Enrique Rodó's Latinist *arielismo*, José Ortega y Gasset's elitism, and Oswald Spengler's racism, in order to explain how Pedreira's vision of Puerto Rican identity "es ejemplo clásico de la ideología burguesa" (107) [is a classic example of bourgeois ideology].

7. For more on the debate on which cultural values were chosen to represent *puertorriqueñidad*, see Dávila (43–59). Ultimately, the PPD's definition of national culture was very similar to the Generation of 1930 writers. The PPD promoted a spiritualist, romanticized vision of Puerto Rico's agricultural past that included the harmonious blend of the Indian, black, and Spanish cultures as the building block for Puerto Rican national identity.

8. Of course, the nationalist violence of the 1950s was not a new phenomenon. Throughout the 1930s there were several violent events. In 1936, the chief of insular police was killed, and Puerto Rico's most famous nationalist leader, Pedro Albizu Campos, was tried for sedition and sentenced to a federal penitentiary in Atlanta. The following year, police opened fire on a nationalist parade in what is referred to as the Ponce Massacre.

9. The dedication to Marqués's essay is as follows: "A la juventud puertorriqueña de hoy, con la esperanza de que el contenido de este volumen, [. . .] pueda aclarar

algunos problemas fundamentales que a esa juventud (debido a condiciones arti-
ficialmente creadas por otros para ella) despista, desorienta o confunde" ("El puertorriqueño" 11) [To the Puerto Rican youth of today, in the hope that the contents of
this volume, [. . .] might clarify some fundamental problems that (due to conditions
artificially created by others) mislead, disorient or confuse them].

10. Rodríguez Castro argues that in narrating the nation, authors such as Pedreira
and, more recently, José Luis González build a discursive house that contains the
national culture. The spatial metaphor of the house implies a sense of internal cohe-
sion, a common identity, and conversely, exclusiveness, because the centralizing
image legitimates its version to the exclusion of others (37).

11. Puerto Rico's geographic position between two continents and its status as a
small island are major factors that contribute to what Pedreira terms its *insularismo:*
"No somos continentales, ni siquiera antillanos: somos simplemente insulares que
es como decir insulados en casa estrecha" (51) [We are neither continental nor Antillean: we are simply insular, which is like saying we are insulated in a small house].

12. For more on Luisa Capetillo, see Julio Ramos's *Amor y anarquía: Los escritos
de Luisa Capetillo* (1992) [Love and anarchy: The works of Luisa Capetillo]. See also
Rubén Dávila Santiago's anthology *Teatro obrero en Puerto Rico (1900–1920)* (1985)
[Working-class theater in Puerto Rico (1900–1920)].

13. Marqués's essay "Pesimismo literario y optimismo político: Su coexistencia
en el Puerto Rico actual" [Literary pessimism and political optimism: Their coexist-
ence in Puerto Rico today] elaborates on the political interest in national culture.

14. I have found Montes Huidobro's volumes on Cuban and Puerto Rican drama
to be particularly useful because his historically situated formal and thematic expli-
cations illuminate cultural idiosyncrasies. Act I, scenes 1 and 2, of this book will refer
frequently to these studies.

15. In his historically contextualized reading of *La cuarterona*, Aníbal González
suggests that setting the play in Havana also had to do with the fact that the plot
details regarding the acquisition of social status made more sense in the context of
Cuba, given that, in Puerto Rico, there were few persons with titles of nobility during the nineteenth century (52).

16. *Vejigantes* forms part of a trilogy of plays including *Bolero y Plena* (1956) and
Sirena [Siren] (1959). The trilogy, entitled *Máscara puertorriqueña* [Puerto Rican
mask], develops the mask motif and the theme of race.

17. Juan Flores's essay "Cortijo's Revenge: New Mappings of Puerto Rican Culture," in his book *Divided Borders: Essays on Puerto Rican Identity*, examines how
writings from the 1980s on Puerto Rican identity valorize African and working-
class culture. Arriví's interest in this aspect of Puerto Rican identity predates this
trend by two decades, but, inexplicably, Flores does not include him as a precursor.

18. As Puerto Rico's leading actress of the time, perhaps it is not surprising that
Lucy Boscana was cast as both mothers of the Puerto Rican nation: Doña Gabriela
and Mamá Toña. The fact that the same actress enacted remarkably different national identity stories stands as a powerful reminder of the multiplicity of identities

that form *puertorriqueñidad* precisely during a period when some intellectuals and politicians attempted to promote a reductionist version of Puerto Rican identity.

19. The tourist industry was just beginning to develop during this period. The legalization of gambling in 1948, the construction of the Caribe Hilton in the 1950s, and the diplomatic rupture between the United States and Cuba in 1962 all contributed to jump start the island's tourist industry.

20. Arriví's use of race to distinguish Puerto Rican identity from North American cultural values echoes Tomás Blanco's earlier essay, *El prejuicio racial en Puerto Rico* [Racial prejudice in Puerto Rico] (1937). Among Blanco's conclusions are that racism is more prevalent in the United States and that the colonial mimicry enacted in response to the North American presence in Puerto Rico exacerbates Puerto Rican racial prejudice (63–65).

21. The *locas* destabilize the perceived fixity of gender binaries. The presence of *locas* and the absence of the Puerto Rican male in the play could be usefully examined in light of Arnaldo Cruz-Malavé's theory of how the island lacks a heterosexual desire to build the nation. For more on Cruz-Malavé and on the crisis of gender categories, see Act II, scene 1.

22. *Palm Sunday* (1949), *La carreta* [The oxcart] (1953), *Juan Bobo y la Dama de Occidente* [Juan Bobo and the Lady of the Occident] (1956), *La muerte no entrará en palacio* [Death will not enter the palace] (1956), *La casa sin reloj* [The house without a clock] (1961), *Carnaval afuera, carnaval adentro* [Carnival within and without] (1964), *El apartamiento* [The retreat] (1964), *Mariana o el alba* [Mariana or daybreak] (1965), and *Sacrificio en el Monte Moriah* [Sacrifice on Mount Moriah] (1970) all deal with Puerto Rico's political situation on some level.

23. Marqués's dramatic works have provoked much critical discussion. Since my analysis of *Un niño azul* and *Los soles truncos* focuses on the themes of family romance and national identity, I will not examine in depth many elements of these complex plays. For more on the evolution of the themes and techniques in Marqués's plays, as well as his artistic influences, his staging techniques (lighting, music, and use of multiple temporal planes), and his use of ritual, Christian symbolism, and myth, see studies by Howard M. Fraser, Tamara Holzapfel, Eleanor J. Martin, Angelina Morfi, and Bonnie Hildebrand Reynolds.

24. For more on the narrative of trauma in Puerto Rican literature, see Rubén Ríos Ávila's essay "El relato del trauma" [The story of the trauma] in his book *La raza cómica del sujeto en Puerto Rico* [The co(s)mic race of the subject in Puerto Rico].

25. Thomas Feeny, for example, in his article on female characters in Marqués's works, writes that because "Marqués's male protagonists who share his dedication to Puerto Rican autonomy inevitably fail, he inflicts shame upon them as a form of retribution for their inability to gain independence" (193).

26. Michael Issacharoff develops the concepts of mimetic and diegetic dramatic space in *Discourse as Performance*. See especially chapter 5, "Space in Drama."

27. This is the opposite effect of what Austin Quigley suggests in his theory of

the world motif in theater. He maintains that as characters are dramatized in contrasting spaces both they and the audience members are drawn to envision their worlds as permeable and changing (10–12).

28. Díaz-Quiñones's essay "La vida inclemente" [The inclement life] from his book *La memoria rota* [The broken memory] recalls how, under the banner of progress, the PPD and university officials silenced the dissenting voices of socialists and nationalists (see especially 23–31).

29. The "*sombra*" from the play's title has multiple meanings. It refers to Michelín's dreamworld as well as to living trapped between his parents' ideologies and, finally, to the island's situation beneath the shadow of the United States.

30. Bessel A. Van Der Kolk and Onno Van Der Hart write about how psychologists can use memories to alleviate trauma. For trauma victims, the "intrusive past" can become an obstacle to recuperation, but the ability to imagine an alternative scenario to the past that would replace the traumatic memory can help victims move forward with their lives (175–79). I am arguing that neither Marqués nor his fictional character Michelín are able to imagine a productive response to Puerto Rican colonialism.

31. The image of castration as a metaphor for Puerto Rico's colonized status is also important in Marqués's prose fiction, such as his short story "En la popa hay un cuerpo reclinado" [In the stern there lies a body] (1970) and his novel *La mirada* [The gaze] (1975).

32. Quotes in English are from *The Fanlights*, Richard John Wiezell's translation of *Los soles truncos* published in the collection *Modern Stage in Latin America* (1971) edited by George Woodyard.

33. Since the decade of the 1960s, Myrna Casas has written over a dozen published and unpublished plays that range from traditional realism-naturalism to absurdism and to postmodern metatheatricality and intertextuality. Critics have examined her works from a variety of approaches, noting their experimentalism, female protagonism, and concern for Puerto Rican identity. Most relevant to my approach is the work done by Sandra Messinger Cypess, Matías Montes Huidobro, and Vicky Unruh that focuses on the issues of cultural and national identity in plays that address this theme explicitly and implicitly. For criticism less centered on the cultural specificity of Casas's work, see Raquel Aguilú de Murphy's study of the absurdist elements in her plays and Luz María Umpierre's feminist-semiotic reading of *Absurdos en soledad* [Absurdities in solitude].

34. In an interview, Casas explains why she has not received as much critical attention as her fellow national playwrights: "Por ser mujer y un poquito más allá, el no pertenecer a la claque intelectual, pro independencia de este país, que es la claque que controla la crítica seria, las revistas" (Pánico 418) [Because I am a woman and, moreover, do not belong to the proindependence intellectual claque of this country, the one that also controls serious criticism and journals].

35. Myrna Casas has two other plays from this period that also could be examined from the perspective of family romance: *Eugenia Victoria Herrera* (1964) and

La trampa [The trap] (1963). Cypess's study of *Eugenia Victoria Herrera*, in which she examines how Casas redefines the male-dominated discourse of the nation, has inspired some of my thinking about family romance and house/nation in *Cristal roto*.

36. Cypess, for example, writes, "The Voice accuses the women of cowardice as the explanation for their pitiful situation" ("Women Dramatists" 34).

37. Critics have pointed out evidence of an incestuous relationship between Hortensia and her father in *Los soles truncos* as well. This aspect of the play is very subtle, but it does support the idea that the Burkharts were too "inward" looking in their relationships.

Act I, Scene 2. Tearing Down the House: The End of an Epoch in Cuba

1. The excellent collection of essays on Cuban national identity edited by Damián J. Fernández and Madeline Cámara Betancourt, for example, offers many insightful readings of Cuban identity, but none of the authors address the particular role of theater in the articulation of discourses of collective identity.

2. Pérez Firmat points out that in Puerto Rico, Antonio Pedreira drew exactly the opposite conclusions, that Puerto Rico's excessive *insularismo* or isolation impeded the development of a strong sense of national identity (3).

3. The Grupo Minorista's 1927 declaration demands national renovation and makes clear the group's anti-imperialism and solidarity with other Latin American nations. For an in-depth study of intellectuals and the activities of this group, see Ana Caro's study.

4. The Platt Amendment, in effect until 1934, gave the United States the right to intervene for the preservation of Cuban independence, the right to maintain a naval base at Guantánamo Bay, and the right to oversee Cuba's economy. The amendment also curbed Cuba's ability to conduct foreign policy (Skidmore and Smith 250).

5. Under the leadership of university professor Ramón Grau San Martín, in four months the revolutionary government abrogated the Platt Amendment and passed more social legislation than in all the previous history of independent Cuba.

6. Some of the longer-lasting groups were Teatro Universitario (1941) [University Theater], Patronato del Teatro (1942) [Theater Council], Teatro Popular (1943) [Popular Theater], and the Academia de Artes Dramáticas (1945) [Academy of Dramatic Arts] (ADAD). For a complete list, see Muguercia (*El Teatro cubano* 44–45).

7. Over 70 percent of the plays produced between 1936 and 1950 were foreign (Muguercia, *El teatro cubano* 70).

8. Critics commonly divide Ferrer's dramatic works into two stages. Before the Revolution, Ferrer wrote several three-act poetic plays from a psychological perspective, whereas following the Revolution, he wrote politically committed one-act dramas. Although many of Ferrer's post-Revolution works have been popular with audiences, most critics agree that the plays from his second period are poorer in dramatic quality and tend to overstate the playwright's sociopolitical intention

(García Abreu 290; Montes Huidobro, *Teatro cubano* 206–7). I find that the tendency to divide Ferrer's works into separate periods downplays the themes the plays share, particularly the sociopolitical concerns of his early works.

9. In his book on socialist theater, Randy Martin discusses a much-transformed 1986 production of *Lila, la mariposa* by Teatro Buendía. He notes that the new production "acknowledges the history of Cuban national dramaturgy in its struggle for independence in the 1950s" (171). I would add that the 1950s' version embodies this struggle as well.

10. The three Fates, Clotho, Lachesis, and Atropos, were goddess too old for anybody to remember where they came from, and they determined how long each mortal would live by snipping off a thread they had spun to measure the mortal's life span (Graves 20).

11. See Jill Netchinksy's study of madness and colonization in Rosario Ferre's story "La bella durmiente" [Sleeping Beauty] for her theory on the connection between dance and colonialism.

12. To evoke what Jorge Duany calls "the rhetoric of roots," Marino remains planted in his home country (18). This kind of nationalist discourse tends to exclude diaspora communities from discourses of Cuban identity. Duany proposes that scholars "move away from the customary distinction between the nation and emigration, where the former category is firmly rooted in a fixed territory with a stable core of culture and the latter is uprooted from its ancestral origins with a displaced sense of self" (19). My genealogy of the performance of the family focuses on the theater produced in Puerto Rico and Cuba, but by no means do I mean to suggest that the diaspora communities fall outside of the nation as "imagined community." I view the experiences of exile and emigration that occasionally surface as themes in the plays discussed in this book as part of the many pieces that constitute Cuban and Puerto Rican identities.

13. Raquel Aguilú de Murphy's book-length study on Piñera's dramatic works discusses his early use of absurdist techniques.

14. In the late 1980s and throughout the 1990s, Cuban critics and theater practitioners have shown a renewed interest in Piñera's drama. The 1990s, in fact, were named "la década Piñera" by Cuban theater publication *Tablas* 64.2 (April–June 2001). This is partly due to a more lenient cultural policy that allowed for the publication of Piñera's unedited manuscripts *Teatro inconcluso* (1990) and *Teatro inédito* (1993).

15. *Aire frío* was written before the Revolution but not staged until 1962 because of its critical vision of Republican society. Not surprisingly, the play's primarily realist dissection of prerevolutionary Cuba has made it Piñera's most frequently staged work. In contrast, because of the tendency to focus on Piñera's absurdist style, the body of criticism on the work is disproportionately small. What makes *Aire frío* a fine play, however, is precisely its combination of absurdist elements and realism.

16. In this sense, I depart from Elías Miguel Muñoz's vision of the play: "El texto criticará, primero y principalmente, los gobiernos corruptos que pasaron por Cuba a

lo largo de tres décadas" (41) [the text criticizes, first and foremost, the corrupt governments that passed through Cuba over three decades].

17. Angel is the first to say this to Oscar in act 1. At some point, all of the inhabitants of the house use the phrase. With regard to Angel, please note that I am remaining consistent with the *Aire frío* text included in Piñera's *Teatro completo* in which his name appears without an accent.

18. The play serves not only as the Shakespearean trick to "catch the consciousness of the king" but also as a commentary on the state of theater during this period. Many theater practitioners were concerned with the effects of the invasion of radio and television on the theater in the 1950s. A neighbor present during this conversation automatically assumes *La malquerida* must be a *radionovela* [radio drama].

19. On the historical context, Pedro Bravo Elizondo writes: "Batista desata en mayo de 1958, la única y mayor ofensiva contra los rebeldes en la Sierra Maestra y la eliminación sistemática de sus opositores en la Habana. Esta situación histórica justifica la huida de Adela de la capital, la indecisión del pueblo de sumirse a la revolución, la persecución de los enemigos del régimen y la brutalidad represiva de la policía" (80–81) [In May of 1958 Batista deploys the only significant offensive against the rebels in the Sierra Maestra and the systematic elimination of opposition groups in Havana. This historical situation justifies Adela's flight from the capital, the reluctance of the townspeople to join the Revolution, the persecution of enemies of the regime, and the repressive police brutality].

20. Scolnicov's use of the terms "perceived" and "conceived" space, or the theatrical space within and the theatrical space without, is similar to Issacharoff's diegetic and mimetic space. Perceived space is onstage, within the field of vision of the spectator, and conceived space is offstage (Scolnicov, *Woman's Theatrical Space* 3).

21. This pattern of behavior and attitudes has been identified as *marianismo*, "the cult of feminine spiritual superiority, which teaches that women are semi-divine, morally superior to and spiritually stronger than men" (Stevens 91). Cristóbal embodies the opposing phenomena: machismo. According to Evelyn P. Stevens, "The chief characteristics of this cult are exaggerated aggressiveness and intransigence in male-to-male interpersonal relationships and arrogance and sexual aggression in male-to-female relationships" (90).

22. *El robo* was first performed on August 21, 1961, at the Sala Hubert de Blanck. Therefore, it is possible that the play's title also alludes to the failed U.S.-supported counterrevolutionary attack, the Bay of Pigs invasion (Bahía de los Cochinos), which took place on April 17, 1961. In this case, the greedy United States was robbed of its opportunity to destroy Fidel Castro's revolution.

23. Since 1980, Triana has lived in exile in Paris.

24. Translated quotes with page numbers refer to *Night of the Assassins*, Sebastian Doggart's 1996 translation of *La noche de los asesinos*. All other translations are my own, such as the following opening stage directions that refer to the siblings' age: "*y sin embargo conservan cierta gracia de adolescente, aunque un tanto marchita*" (138) [*they nevertheless conserve a certain adolescent grace, al-*

though a bit wilted]. The text also indicates that Lalo is thirty and that Beba is twenty. It is important to note that they are not children, for Triana states that the characters are from his own generation: "Escribí *La noche de los asesinos* cuando tenía 33 años, es decir que a partir de esta edad es que creo que debe concebirse a sus personajes" (Escarpanter 2) [I wrote *Night of the Assassins* when I was 33 years old, in other words, it's at about this age that one should envision the characters].

25. The criticism on *La noche* generally falls into three lines of inquiry. The first focuses on the play's anti-illusionist techniques and themes with little emphasis on its sociohistorical context. For example, studies by Anne C. Murch, Frank Dauster, and Isabel Álvarez-Borland and David George have examined the play's use of myth, ritual, and games. In addition, Kirsten F. Nigro and Priscilla Meléndez have analyzed from a semiotic perspective how the structures of the play communicate its meaning. Other critics focus on the work in relation to the Cuban Revolution. Matías Montes Huidobro and Eduardo Lolo, for example, consider the play a critical commentary on revolutionary Cuba, whereas Román de la Campa sees it as a condemnation of prerevolutionary society. He does not view *La noche* as a prorevolutionary play, however, for "La visión crítica del pasado pre-revolucionario que Triana mantiene es vista como algo estático, que no evoluciona y le impide reflejar la realidad social transformada por el nuevo sistema" (14) [Triana's critical vision of the prerevolutionary past is seen as something static, that doesn't evolve, and that impedes the social reality transformed by the new system to be reflected]. Finally, recent studies by Jerry Hoeg and Diana Taylor examine how the play is about revolution in general rather than limiting its stance as either pro- or contrarevolutionary.

26. In a 1967 interview, Triana stated that he began the piece in 1958, put it away until 1963 when he attempted again to work on the text, and then in 1964 finally finished it (Estorino, "Destruir" 6). Triana also speaks of the process of writing *La noche* in a 1993 interview with Sebastian Doggart.

27. In this respect, I find Diana Taylor's reading of the *La noche* helpful because she maintains that the play cannot be seen in isolation from its revolutionary context since it is an examination of the very concept of revolution from neither a clear pro nor contra position (*Theatre* 66–67).

28. Dauster, along with other critics, examines the play's family conflict on a more existential or universal level than I do: "Obviously, this is not simply a presentation of the unpleasantries of a single family but a dramatic metaphor of a decaying institution, a great blasphemy against the foundations of social life. [. . .] This is no social drama in the usual political sense but rather in the sense that it presents in almost unique fashion the terrible conflict of generations that is literally shaking the roots of society in our world" ("The Game" 182). I see the generational conflict as a particular dramatic metaphor that defines a series of plays during a particular period in a specific culture.

29. Taylor argues that the children are unable to define themselves because they exist in a context of crisis: "The blurring of boundaries and the collapse of the frame-

works that would allow for differentiation, associated with the objective systematic rifts in crisis, are accompanied by the subjective, personal experience of crisis in *Assassins*. Lalo, Cuca, and Beba try to define themselves in the absence of a concrete, objective other, either individual (parents) or social" (*Theatre* 74).

30. It is important to note that parody does not always serve to ridicule. Hutcheon writes: "parody can obviously be a whole range of things. It can be a serious criticism, not necessarily of the parodied text; it can be a playful, genial mockery of codifiable forms. Its range of intent is from respectful admiration to biting ridicule" (*A Theory* 15–16).

31. Eduardo Lolo explains: "Los hijos y los padres de *La noche de los asesinos* eran [. . .] los mismos personajes—tomados en épocas diferentes—pero semejantes—y yuxtapuestos en el tiempo por el artificio que la obra crea; eran, en fin, los jóvenes oprimidos de los 50 enfrentados a su propia imagen de opresores en los 60. En este sentido, los personajes de Triana se quedaron en una sola generación" (44) [The parents and children in *Night of the Assassins* were [. . .] the same characters—taken from different periods—but similar—and juxtaposed in time by the artifice created by the play; they were, in the end, the oppressed youth of the 1950s confronted by their own image as oppressors in the 1960s. In this sense, Triana's characters remained in a single generation].

Act II, Scene 1. Reimagining National Community: Performance and Nostalgia in Recent Puerto Rican Drama

1. See, for example, Jean Franco's essay "The Nation as Imagined Community" and the collection of essays on contemporary Latin American culture she edited with George Yúdice and Juan Flores.

2. Since 1956, the *independentista* vote has followed statehood as the third most popular status option (garnering between 1 and 4 percent of the vote). Factors involved in its loss of popularity include internal splits in the proindependence parties over whether to adopt a socialist orientation, the economic unviability of independence, and what Ramón Grosfoguel calls "the historical divorce between nationalist discourses and the Puerto Rican people" (70).

3. Aaron Gamaliel Ramos explains: "The initial phase of the industrialization process in the late 1940s relied mainly on the implantation of labor-intensive U.S. industrial enterprises. [. . .] as the colonial industrialization process became more tied to multinational capital, the program of industrial attraction was reoriented towards the highly mechanized capital-intensive industries that made little usage of the enormous supplies of labor" (267).

4. *Independentistas* Carlos Soto Arriví and Arnaldo Darío Rosado went to Cerro Maravilla allegedly to sabotage the communication system there. The fact that they were shot by police after they had surrendered became clear only when a 1983 investigation revealed that the police had committed perjury during the initial investigation.

5. See Arlene Dávila's book for an in-depth account of the 1980s culture wars (43–59).

6. As mentioned earlier, in the first plebiscite on the political status of Puerto Rico in 1967, statehood won 39 percent of the vote. In 1993, statehood garnered 46 percent of the vote, and in a nonbinding referendum in 1998 it retained the voter percentage it had obtained in 1993.

7. Important works by these authors include *Narciso descubre su trasero* [Narcissus discovers his backside] (1975) by Zenón Cruz, *El país de cuatro pisos* [The four-storeyed country] (1980) by González, and *La Carreta Made a U-Turn* (1979) by Laviera. Juan Flores's 1979 study of Pedreira's essay *Insularismo* also opened an important space for new approaches to Puerto Rican literature and culture.

8. Their best-known works of this period are Ferré's *Papeles de Pandora* [Pandora's papers] (1976) and Ramos Otero's *Concierto de metal para un recuerdo y otras orgías de soledad* [Heavy metal concert for a memory and other orgies of solitude] (1971). The works mentioned here offer only a cursory review of the rich pool of authors and works from the 1970s.

9. "Teatro fricción" is also a more inclusive label. Perales includes the theater of playwrights from earlier generations who continued to work in the 1960s and 1970s (Marqués, Arriví), playwrights such as Luis Rafael Sánchez and Myrna Casas who fit somewhere between the former generations and the NDP writers, and all the different variations of NDP playwrights. Similar to Ramos-Perea, Josefina Rivera Álvarez employs a generational model to study the new playwrights. These approaches tend to homogenize a theater that, according to Perales, "está regido por la fragmentación, por la atomización de sus creadores y sus manifestaciones, y lo que es peor, por los conflictos internos" ("Teatro" 75) [is ruled by the fragmentation and atomization of its creators and manifestations, and what is worse, by its internal conflicts].

10. An important aspect of this second cycle was the move to document and study the NDP movement. In 1985, Ramos-Perea founded the theater magazine *Intermedio de Puerto Rico* [Puerto Rican Intermission], and in 1988 he inaugurated a national archive of Puerto Rican theater. His 1989 collection of essays also chronicles the NDP movement.

11. Some of Puerto Rico's latest generation of playwrights also participate in dramaturgy workshops at the Ateneo Puertorriqueño, as well as work with the international theater organization Centro Latinoamericano de Creación e Investigación Teatral [Latin American Center for Theater Production and Research] (CELCIT).

12. Silén's *Hacia una visión positiva del puertorriqueño* [Toward a positive vision of the Puerto Rican] (1970) and Ángel G. Quintero Rivera's *Lucha obrera en Puerto Rico* [The working-class struggle in Puerto Rico] (1971) manifest this new historical focus.

13. Following are a few examples of the plethora of texts from the 1980s that implicitly and explicitly engage with the problem of representing history: *Seva: historia de la primera invasión norteamericana de la Isla de Puerto Rico, ocurrida en*

mayo de 1898 [Seva: History of the first North American invasion of the island of Puerto Rico in May of 1898] (1983) by Luis Lípez Nieves; *El día que el hombre pisó la luna* [The day man walked on the moon] (1984) by Edgardo Sanabria Santaliz; *Maldito amor* (1986) by Rosario Ferré (literally, "cursed love," but translated by Ferré and published as *Sweet Diamond Dust*); *Pasión de historia y otras historias de pasión* [Passion for stories and other stories of passion] (1987) by Ana Lydia Vega; *La renuncia del niño Baltasar* [The renunciation of young Balthazar] (1986), by Edgardo Rodríguez Juliá; and *La llegada* [The arrival] (1980) by José Luis González.

14. These phrases parodically recycle titles and phrases from an era characterized by cultural nationalism. The phrase "un tun tún de grasa y fritanguería" refers to the famous book of Afro-Caribbean poems *Tuntún de pasa y grifería* (1937) by the Puerto Rican poet Luis Palés Matos (1898–1959). "Por mi grasa hablará mi espiritu" [Through my grease my spirit will speak] refers to the statement "Por mi raza hablará mi espiritu" [Through my race, my spirit will speak] popularized by Mexican intellectual José Vasconcelos (1882–1959).

15. I interpret the fact that the exhibit was displayed both in New York and in Puerto Rico as a gesture that implicitly supports a conception of *puertorriqueñidad* that includes both island and diaspora communities.

16. According to Priscilla Meléndez, perhaps the greatest difference lies in the fact that the typical playwright from the NDP movement "alegaba tener respuestas a los problemas sociales y políticos de la Isla"[alleged having answers to the social and political problems of the Island]. By contrast, Meléndez argues, "El teatro de los 80 sigue siendo capaz de reconocer la monumentabilidad de dichos problemas, pero ya no alegaba tener y ofrecer respuestas para la solución de éstos" [The theater of the 80s continues to be capable of recognizing the monumental nature of such problems, but no longer alleges to have and provide answers for a solution] ("Teoría" 161). She draws this conclusion from a telephone conversation with theater practitioner Rosa Luisa Márquez.

17. Although García del Toro wrote numerous prize-winning dramatic texts and literary studies during the 1980s, his plays have received very little critical attention. An observation by Perales on the literary character of his plays may explain why they have not stimulated much dramatic criticism (*Teatro hispanoamericano* 281). Similarly, in his otherwise positive review of the 1989 production of *Hotel Melancolía*, Edgar Heriberto Quiles Ferrer points out that the play depends too much on narrative exposition, which results in a lack of dramatic conflict (287).

18. Although the piano itself implies that the Landrón y Rojas family is from the upper class, interestingly, no one identifies a kind of music that best represents *puertorriqueñidad*. In contrast, in *Los soles truncos*, Marqués uses music by European composers in several important scenes, and character references to composers and dances suggest that the Burkharts prefer classical music.

19. If the detective has actually committed the murder, then this is an obvious criticism of police corruption as well; given the events of the Caso Maravilla just a few years prior to the play, this is not surprising.

20. Since 1976, Ramos-Perea has written more than forty plays, many of which have been published and staged. In 1992 he won the prestigious Tirso de Molina prize for *Miénteme más* [Give me more lies], a play based on how scientists from the United States used Puerto Rican women in their experiments on the birth control pill in the 1950s. Other well-known plays based on Puerto Rican events include *Revolución en el Infierno* [A revolution in hell] (1982), *Módulo 104* [Module 104] (1983), and *Cueva de ladrones* [Cave of thieves] (1984). *Callando amores* premiered at the Centro de Bellas Artes in March 1995. A version for television was filmed in 1996. Unless otherwise indicated, my analysis refers to the dramatic text published in 1996.

21. Luis never appears onstage because he is in the United States making the land deal. His voice is only heard indirectly through the responses of Victoria and Gina speaking to him by telephone. His wife, Gina, is a more important character, but this study focuses on Mario and Victoria as the main proponents of the family conflict. A longer study might discuss further the stereotypic female roles in this play.

22. The relationship between Mario and Gina is the most problematic aspect of the play. I find the rapid development of their romance improbable and Gina's transformation into a more articulate and decisive person (thanks to the "guidance" of Mario) questionable. In my view, Mario's problematic treatment of Gina is part of his dubious politics.

23. Linda Hutcheon writes: "it seems reasonable to say that the postmodern's initial concern is to de-naturalize some of the dominant features of our way of life; to point out that those entities that we unthinkingly experience as 'natural' (they might even include capitalism, patriarchy, liberal humanism) are in fact 'cultural'; made by us, not given to us" (*The Politics* 2).

24. The repetition of the phrase "la tierra no se vende" can also be linked to the play's intertextuality, for it recalls the patriarch Wang Lung's exhortations to never sell the family land in Pearl S. Buck's *The Good Earth* (1931). Mario and his father certainly identify with Wang Lung's position on the question of land: "It is the end of a family—when they begin to sell the land" (Buck 307).

25. Undoubtedly, Sánchez's enduring influence has been aided by his enormous success as a short story writer, essayist, and author of the important post-Boom novel *La Guaracha del Macho Camacho* [Macho Camacho's Beat] (1976).

26. See, for example, the book-length studies on Sánchez by Efraín Barradas, Alvin Joaquín Figueroa, John Perivolaris, Gloria F. Waldman, and Eliseo R. Colón Zayas.

27. The collection was edited by Andrew Parker, Mary Russo, Doris Sommer, and Patricia Yaeger. See, in particular, the introduction and essays by Marjorie Garber, R. Radhakrishnan, and Rhonda Cobham. In his article on the dualities that structure *Quíntuples*, such as vibrant red/yellow and muted white/gray costuming, narrative and theater, expression and repression, and homosexuality and heterosexuality, Efraín Barradas links the deconstruction of such dualities to an implicit critique of the binarist thinking that has informed Puerto Rican politics ("Las dualidades" 289–

90). In an earlier article on Sánchez's short stories, Agnes I. Lugo-Ortiz makes a similar point but focuses more explicitly on gender and sexuality.

28. For studies on the metatheatrical levels and multiplicity of discourses at play in *Quíntuples*, see articles by Hortensia R. Morell and Johanna Emmanuelli Huertas.

29. His paternalism is further exaggerated by the absence of the children's mother. As sole parent, it is almost as if Papá Morrison gave birth to the quintuplets. Baby says: "Mamá no existió . . . quiero decir . . . Mamá murió dándonos vida" (23–24) [Mama didn't exist . . . what I mean is . . . Mama died while giving us life].

30. The erotic penetration of the house and the fact that his lover is a *mulata* who lives on the Calle de Cristo suggest that the whole episode parodies the repressed sexuality of the unmarried sisters in René Marqués's *Los soles truncos*. For more on incest, see Meléndez's article on farce and incest in *Quíntuples*.

31. It is important to note that these acts are obligatory: "Gender performativity is not a matter of choosing which gender one will be today. Performativity is a matter of reiterating or repeating the norms by which one is constituted: it is not a radical fabrication of the gendered self" (Butler, "Critically" 22).

32. The multiplicity of intertexts also underscores the play's theme of challenging authoritative texts. Sánchez mixes references to classical literature with Corín Tellado and comic book characters to collapse the boundaries between high culture and popular culture, as well as to show Puerto Rico's dependency on foreign texts in defining its own cultural voice. Furthermore, the narrative quality of the monologues blurs the generic line between drama and narrative (see John Kronik's article for more on this topic). In this sense, Sánchez challenges the authority of traditional generic distinctions. The fictionalized author identified in the prologue as L.R.S. further hybridizes *Quíntuples* by referring to it as an amalgam of popular theater styles: "un vodevil, un sainete de enredos. Es también, la parodia de una comedia de suspenso. Y, finalmente, una aventura de la imaginación, una obra dentro de otra obra" (xv) [a vaudeville, an entangled *sainete*. It's also the parody of a comedy of suspense. And finally, an adventure of the imagination, a play within a play].

33. Nelson Rivera recounts Antonio Martorrel's experience of designing the set for Marqués's *Mariana o el alba:* "Marqués refused to compromise on anything in his script, which had to be staged exactly as he had written it. He also attended each and every rehearsal to make sure things were done his way. His scripts were full of detailed stage directions for every single aspect of a performance" (64). See Barradas for a different reading of the stage directions in *Quíntuples*.

34. *El gran circo eukraniano* was first performed in 1988. This production, along with a mix of new and classic Puerto Rican plays by Jaime Carrero, Alejandro Tapia y Rivera, Roberto Ramos-Perea, and Francisco Arriví, toured eight different towns on the island. The play also has been published as *The Great USkranian Circus* in an anthology of Latin American women dramatists in translation edited by Teresa Cajiao Salas and Margarita Vargas. All citations in Spanish are from an unpublished

manuscript, and all citations in English refer to the Salas and Vargas translation. The published Spanish text is forthcoming from Girol Books.

35. See, for example, Juan Flores's collection of essays, *Divided Borders: Essays on Puerto Rican Identity* (1993), and *From Bomba to Hip-Hop: Puerto Rican Culture and Latino Identity* (2000).

36. The most recent images of the airbus, according to Sandoval-Sánchez, register the crisis of AIDS. The plane has become a floating cemetery for those who return to the homeland to die (Sandoval-Sánchez, "Puerto Rican Identity" 201).

37. For a comprehensive study on how Casas's theater posits Puerto Rican identity as uncertain and moveable through the innovative use of space, see Unruh's article. Her study encouraged my reading of the circus family as a metaphor for the Puerto Rican nation.

38. We discover a different version of this story at the end of the play when Gabriela believes she may have met her son. This recognition (or misrecognition) scene is a poignant reminder of the losses the circus members have suffered by choosing this lifestyle.

39. In his theorization of "mobile homes," Sandoval-Sánchez provides a more positive reading of migrant identity as portable, provisional, and a site of subject formation characterized by translation and resistance (*José* 197). (See especially chapter 7, "There's No Place Like Home.")

40. For an in-depth study of the film that includes analysis of the *Los soles truncos* intertext, see Frances Negrón-Muntaner, "Los dos sueños." My brief analysis of the film concurs with some of Negrón-Muntaner's points, but I view the film's ideological stance as slightly less conservative than she does. In my opinion, some of the film's conservative discourses are presented with an ironic twist that disrupts a purely nostalgic view of the past.

41. By national romance, I mean the love unions that metaphorically bring together different sectors of the nation in nation-building alliances described by Doris Sommer in *Foundational Fictions*. See Curtain-Raiser and Act I, scene 1, in this volume for more discussion of national romances.

42. One curious note regarding this relationship is Gustavo and Pilar's son, Tavito, who has Down's syndrome. Unlike El Nene, the encephalitic child in Luis Rafael Sánchez's *La guaracha del Macho Camacho*, and the similarly "monstrous" quintuplet progeny in *Quíntuples*, Tavito does not seem to be included for parodic purposes. While Sánchez makes fun of the discourses that present Puerto Rico as an infantilized and deformed colonial offspring, Morales might seem to fall back on this discourse by presenting Tavito as the outcome of his parents' failed union. However, the sensitivity with which the film portrays Tavito and his role in Gustavo's realization that, in order to retain a relationship with his ex-wife and son he must become more flexible, seems to encourage a less ironic reading of this character. Perhaps Tavito simply signals an understanding of difference in constructions of Puerto Rican collective identity.

Act II, Scene 2. Ties That Bind: Staging the New Family
in Revolutionary Cuba

1. See Act I, scene 2, for more on the transcultural (Fernando Ortiz) and translational (Gustavo Pérez Firmat) qualities that have produced a syncretic Cuban culture.

2. The United States expressed its displeasure with the revolutionary government by imposing a trade embargo on Cuba that continues to remain in effect today. Disaffected Cubans, in turn, emigrated to the United States. By as early as 1962, 195,000 Cubans had left the island (Pérez 335).

3. As Louis Pérez writes, revolutionary leaders "argued that communism required the creation of a new consciousness as a function of economic development. The development of the *hombre nuevo* and the attainment of economic growth were proclaimed to be one and the same process" (340).

4. Guevara was a medical doctor from Argentina who joined the Revolution in the 1950s. After serving as minister of industry from 1961 to 1965, Che disappeared from Cuba. He resurfaced as a guerrilla leader in Bolivia, where he was killed in 1967. Guevara's term "new man" implicitly refers to both men and women, but I prefer to use the more explicitly inclusive phrase "new Cuban," because some of the plays discussed here focus on how the formation of a new national identity demands changes from both men and women.

5. Some statistics from a study on the Cuban family between 1970 and 1987 reveal the inequalities of women's "double shift": men spend thirty-eight minutes per week doing household chores, whereas working women spend four hours and forty-four minutes; not surprisingly, working women have two hours and fifty-nine minutes of free time per week, whereas men have four hours and fifty-nine minutes (Reca Moreira et al. 132).

6. Some husbands and wives simply grew apart as they acquired (or failed to acquire) a revolutionary *conciencia*. These strains on the traditional Cuban family have contributed to a soaring number of divorces. Between 1959 and 1974, the divorce rate rose from 8.5 percent to 30.2 percent (Padula and Smith 84). In the period between 1977 and 1981, the divorce rate continued to grow annually by 9.3 percent (Azicri, *Cuba* 58).

7. Max Azicri points out that while Karl Marx, Friedrich Engels, and Vladimir Lenin addressed the issue of family, there is no centralized Marxist theory on the sociology of the family ("The Cuban" 187). Marxist positions vary from proposing that the institution should disappear altogether to theorizing on the development of the socialist family (which presupposes the death of the capitalist family).

8. I am focusing on the code's insistence on gender equality in the home. Other noteworthy sections cover divorce, consensual unions, and the rights of children.

9. The difficult task of changing the conventional views on sex roles is documented in a number of important films including *Lucía* (Humberto Solás, 1969), *De cierta manera* [One way or another] (Sara Gomez, 1974), *Retrato de Teresa* [Portrait

of Teresa] (Pastor Vega, 1979), and *Hasta cierto punto* [Up to a certain point] (Tomás Guitérrez Alea, 1984).

10. According to Guevara, young people are a particularly important educational target because, free of the prejudices and errors of the past, they constitute "malleable clay" from which to form the new citizen ("Socialism" 166).

11. For example, the party has allowed religious believers into its organization, and the constitutional amendments make it illegal to discriminate because of religious beliefs. The regime has also altered the constitution by dropping Marxism as the official ideology. For a review of systemic changes and shifts in social attitudes during the Special Period, see the article by Richard J. Planas.

12. Cuban literacy rates before the Revolution showed great discrepancies between men and women, urban and rural regions, blacks and whites, and upper and lower classes. Pérez writes, "In 1958, almost half of all Cuban children aged six to fourteen years had received no education. Only a quarter of the population fifteen years or older had ever attended school. Three-quarters were either illiterate or had failed to complete primary education" (358).

13. For more on the development of popular culture in Cuba, see Judith Weiss's article.

14. The Padilla affair is well known because it resulted in a letter of protest signed by important European and Latin American intellectuals. Padilla's conflict with officials began when he lost his job after writing an article favoring Guillermo Cabrera Infante's novel *Tres tristes tigres* [Three trapped tigers] (1967) over a revolutionary novel. He won a UNEAC prize in 1968 for *Fuera del juego* [Out of bounds], but the work was censored for its critical vision of the Revolution. In 1971, he was jailed but was later released after signing a long statement of self-criticism that he also delivered personally at a UNEAC meeting.

15. See Act I, scene 2, for more details on the early years of theater in the Cuban Revolution.

16. For more on the many groups representative of Cuban Teatro Nuevo, see Rosa Ileana Boudet's book-length study.

17. Cuban critics tend to favor the works of the Teatro Nuevo movement over other "*teatro de sala*" [auditorium theater] plays of the same period because they consider Teatro Nuevo to be more artistically innovative. Like many Cuban critics, Judith Rudakoff considers Teatro Escambray "a radical departure from the strictly propagandist theatre that was performed in Cuba in the 1960s, which relied almost exclusively on heavy didacticism. Teatro Escambray shifted the focus in Cuban popular theatre from dialectic and formalized structure to aesthetic concerns and highly theatrical, imagistic performance" (81–82). Other critics, in contrast, including Cubans who oppose the Revolution and some international scholars, would argue that the political purpose of Teatro Nuevo prohibits any of the works produced by these groups from possessing artistic value.

18. Terry Palls notes that economics also motivate institutional changes. In the economic crisis of the Special Period, the performing arts must seek financial au-

tonomy. To that end, the CNAE has outlined a marketing plan for the new theater collectives. This leads Palls to ask whether art at the service of the Revolution is nearing an end (128).

19. Structurally complex and philosophically dense works like Abelardo Estorino's *Morir del cuento* [To die from the story] (1983) and Abilio Estévez's *La verdadera culpa de Juan Clemente Zenea* [The true fault of merciful Juan Clemente Zenea] (1986) constitute two such examples.

20. Orihuela (b. 1950) started working with Teatro Escambray as an assistant director and playwright in 1972 and continues working with the group today. Many of his plays form part of the group's repertory, but *La emboscada* and *Ramona* are his best-known pieces.

21. This contrasts with the vision of the common people or the "folk" as the embodiment of tradition, characterized by timeless and unchanging beliefs, customs, and habits (Brecht 108).

22. It is important to note that this play dramatizes the crisis of the rural, peasant household. Zoila's defense of the family and negative response to the Revolution are different from the conservatism of the bourgeois, property-owning family in Estorino's *El robo del cochino*, for example. The play reveals how Zoila's lack of proletarian consciousness blinds her to both the injustices of the capitalist system under attack and the possible benefits of socialism.

23. For more on Estorino's use of realism, see George Woodyard's article and Act I, scene 2, of this study. Most critics mention Estorino's 1983 *Morir del cuento* as the piece that signals a new, less schematic and more formally daring phase of his work as well as a new period in Cuban drama. I would argue, as does Woodyard, that we should look to his earlier play, *Ni un sí ni un no*, for signs of an emerging new aesthetic.

24. This lengthy play includes more important life events for Él and Ella than I am able to examine here. One detail relevant to the theme of gender is the tension created by the fact that Ella has had more education (she is a nurse studying to be a doctor) than her husband (he is an electrician frustrated by being passed up for promotion).

25. Cuartas (b. 1938) wrote two very successful theater pieces early in his career. Many groups staged his play *Los ángeles no son dogmáticos* [Angels are not dogmatic], and in 1965 he received an honorable mention from the Casa de las Américas for *Llegó a la gloria la gente de los Santos Inocentes* [The people of the Innocent Saints arrived at heaven]. Since 1967, Cuartas is best known for his writing for the Cuban National Radio.

26. The regime's tourism policy is one example of how Cuba is literally prostituting itself. Enrique Baloyra writes: "prostitution, which Cuban officials had proudly declared extinct thirty years ago, has reappeared as a direct result of the upsurge in tourism and the increasing narrow employment opportunities" (35–36). Prostitution has returned in the form of *jineteras*, prostitutes who escort foreigners in exchange for dollars or consumer goods.

27. Variations of the word *gusano* [worm] refer to traitors of the Revolution. Any Cuban living in exile would be a *gusano* from Bururú's perspective.

28. Gladis la Jabá makes quite a return to her neighborhood. She interrupts Bururú's ceremony to erect the new bust of José de la Luz y Caballero with a raucous conga line. Gladis opens her suitcases full of gifts, and signs of North American culture such as rock music, McDonald's, and car ads magically fill the scene. As she leaves the plaza, some of the CDR members join the conga line. Given Bururú's inclination for fantasies, it is unlikely that the rest of the crowd sees the same splashy scene she did.

29. Pedro (b. 1954) may have had better luck with producing his play than Cuartas because of his long involvement in revolutionary theater. After graduating from the Escuela Nacional de Arte, he participated in two groups involved in the Teatro Nuevo movement, Cubana de Acero and Teatro Político Bertolt Brecht. He is now a member of one of Cuba's strongest theater collectives, Teatro Mío, directed by his wife, Miriam Lezcano. He has written many plays, including two hits from the 1980s, *Tema para Verónica* [Veronica's theme] and *Weekend en Bahía*. Pedro has also acted in the theater and in television and film.

30. In addition to the rusty cans and broken objects mentioned in the stage directions, in the performance Boudet describes, the apartment also contains a dusty bust of Lenin and remnants of sets from productions of Marxist plays ("Prólogo" xx). This production thus situates the play much more specifically within the post-Soviet context. Quotes in English with page numbers are from a translation published by Christopher Winks.

31. Pedro states that he was unfamiliar with Triana's play when he wrote *Manteca* and that "what's going on is a coincidence with Cuban reality, and in that sense Triana has the patent because I would in any case be demonstrating in another way what he has already demonstrated" (Martínez Tabares, "Theater" 61). Pedro's lack of familiarity with *La noche de los asesinos* leads one to wonder whether Triana might be the next Piñera, that is, the next Cuban playwright rediscovered by Cuban theater practitioners formed in the postrevolutionary period.

32. Informal methods of survival, meaning those outside the system, have thrived in Cuba since the late 1980s. Damian Fernández affirms that popular neologisms "express the ingenious ways that Cubans find to cope with the situation of shortages and adversity" ("Informal Politics" 72). *Sociolismo,* for example, a play on *Socialismo,* is a network of *socios,* or friends who find room for maneuver within the socialist system. This phenomenon will certainly influence the role of the family in contemporary Cuba.

33. The pig also recalls the Bay of Pigs invasion and could thus also be read as an ironic take on a symbol of the Revolution. The pig now embodies the heroic battle for food, not the fight against imperialism.

34. A passage in Pucho's novel also parodies the stereotype of the eroticized black male (176). The oneiric scene described by Pucho fits the white phobia of black sexual potency described by Franz Fanon in *Black Skin, White Masks* (157–209).

Exit. From the House to the Stage: Haunted Family Scenarios
in Cuban and Puerto Rican Drama

1. In developing his theory of theater and memory, Carlson cites ideas developed
by scholars such as Joseph Roach, Freddie Rokem, Elin Diamond, and Herbert Blau.
Recent studies by Diana Taylor on the Argentine "Dirty War," by Vivan M. Patraka
on U.S. Holocaust museums, and by Mike Pearson and Michael Shanks on theater
and archaeology also treat the cultural politics of memory.

Bibliography

Aguilú de Murphy, Raquel. "Hacia una teorización del absurdo en el teatro de Myrna Casas." *Revista Iberoamericana* 59 (1993): 169–76.

———. *Los textos dramáticos de Virgilio Piñera y el teatro del absurdo.* Madrid: Pliegos, 1989.

Althusser, Louis. "Ideology and Ideological State Apparatuses (Notes Towards an Investigation)." In *Lenin and Philosophy and Other Essays,* trans. Ben Brewster, 127–86. London: NLB, 1971.

Álvarez-Borland, Isabel, and David George. "*La noche de los asesinos:* Text, Staging and Audience." *Latin American Theatre Review* 20.1 (1986): 37–48.

Anderson, Benedict. *Imagined Communities: Reflections on the Origin and Spread of Nationalism.* Rev. ed. London: Verso, 1991.

Arango, Arturo. "To Write in Cuba, Today." Trans. Nancy Westrate. In Fornet, *Bridging Enigma,* 117–28.

Arias, Salvador. "Machismo, historia y revolución en la obra de Abelardo Estorino." Prologue to Estorino, *Teatro,* 5–26.

Arriví, Francisco. *Areyto Mayor.* San Juan: Instituto de Cultura Puertorriqueña, 1966.

———. *Vejigantes.* Río Piedras: Editorial Cultural, 1970.

Azicri, Max. *Cuba: Politics, Economics and Society.* London: Pinter, 1988.

———. "The Cuban Family Code: Some Observations on Its Innovations and Continuities." *Review of Socialist Law* 6.2 (1980): 183–91.

Baloyra, Enrique A. "Where Does Cuba Stand?" In Schulz, *Cuba and the Future,* 23–40.

Baloyra, Enrique A., and James A. Morris, eds. *Conflict and Change in Cuba.* Albuquerque: University of New Mexico Press, 1993.

Barradas, Efraín. "El machismo existencial de René Marqués." *Sin Nombre* 8.3 (1977): 69–81.

———. "Las dualidades de *Quíntuples.*" *Revista de crítica literaria latinoamericana* 23.45 (1997): 279–91.

———. *Para leer en puertorriqueño: Acercamiento a la obra de Luis Rafael Sánchez.* Río Piedras: Editorial Cultural, 1981.

Barthes, Roland. *S/Z*. Trans. Richard Miller. 1974. Reprint, Oxford: Basil Blackwell, 1990.

Bejel, Emilio. "La transferencia dialéctica en *El robo del cochino* de Estorino." *Inti: Revista de Literatura Hispánica* 12 (1982): 65–71.

Bhabha, Homi K. "Introduction: Narrating the Nation." In *Nation and Narration*, ed. Homi K. Bhabha, 1–21. London: Routledge, 1990.

Blanco, Tomás. *El prejuico racial en Puerto Rico*. New York: Arno, 1975.

Bonachea, Rolando E., and Nelson P. Valdes, eds. and intro. *Che: Selected Works of Ernesto Guevara*. Cambridge: MIT Press, 1969.

Boudet, Rosa Ileana. "Concreción de un Tiempo." In *Aire frío*, 11–17. Serie Literatura Dramática Iberoamericana 1. Madrid: Asociación de Directores de Escena, 1990.

———. "New Playwrights, New Challenges: Current Cuban Theater." Trans. Nancy Westrate. In Fornet, *Bridging Enigma*, 33–51.

———. "Prólogo." In Boudet, *Morir*, 9–34.

———. *Teatro Nuevo: Una respuesta*. Havana: Editorial Letras Cubanas, 1983.

———, ed. *Morir del texto: Diez obras teatrales*. Havana: Ediciones Unión, 1995.

Bourdieu, Pierre. *The Field of Cultural Production: Essays on Art and Literature*. Ed. and intro. Randal Johnson. New York: Columbia University Press, 1993.

Bravo Elizondo, Pedro. *Teatro hispanoamericano de crítica social*. Madrid: Playor, 1975.

Brecht, Bertolt. "The Popular and the Realistic." In *Brecht on Theatre: The Development of an Aesthetic*, ed. and trans. John Willet, 107–12. New York: Hill and Wang, 1964.

Brook, Peter. *The Empty Space*. New York: Atheneum, 1968.

Buck, Pearl S. *The Good Earth*. 1931. Reprint, New York: Harper and Row, 1949.

Butler, Judith. "Critically Queer." *GLQ: A Journal of Gay and Lesbian Studies* 1.1 (1993): 17–32.

———. *Gender Trouble: Feminism and the Subversion of Identity*. New York: Routledge, 1990.

Callando amores. Dir. José Orraca. Sección de Cine y Video del Ateneo Puertorriqueño. Puerto Rico, 1996.

Carlson, Marvin. *The Haunted Stage: The Theatre as Memory Machine*. Ann Arbor: University of Michigan Press, 2001.

Caro, Ana. *El grupo Minorista y su tiempo*. Havana: Editorial de Ciencias Sociales, 1979.

Carrió, Raquel. "De *La emboscada* a Electra: Una clave metafórica." *Tablas* 2 (1985): 2–8.

Caruth, Cathy, ed. and intro. *Trauma: Explorations in Memory*. Baltimore: Johns Hopkins University Press, 1995.

Casas, Myrna. *Cristal roto en el tiempo*. In *Teatro puertorriqueño. Tercer Festival*, 261–349. San Juan: Instituto de Cultura Puertorriqueña, 1961.

————. "El gran circo eukraniano." Unpublished play ms., 1988.

————. *The Great USkranian Circus.* Trans. Teresa Cajiao Salas and Margarita Vargas. In *Women Writing Women: An Anthology of Spanish-American Theater of the 1980s,* ed. Teresa Cajiao Salas and Margarita Vargas, 123–85. Albany: State University of New York Press, 1997.

Castagnino, Raúl H. *Semiótica, ideología y teatro hispanoamericano contemporáneo.* Buenos Aires: Nova, 1974.

Castro, Fidel. "Palabras a los intelectuales." In *Política cultural de la revolución cubana,* 3–47. Havana: Editorial de Ciencias Sociales, 1977.

Colón Zayas, Eliseo R. *El teatro de Luis Rafael Sánchez: Códigos, ideología y lenguaje.* Madrid: Playor, 1985.

Coontz, Stephanie. "Historical Perspectives on Family Diversity." In Demo, Allen, and Fine, *Handbook of Family Diversity,* 15–31.

Correa, Armando. "El teatro cubano de los 80: Creación versus oficialidad." *Latin American Theatre Review* 25.2 (1992): 67–77.

Cruz-Malavé, Arnaldo. "Toward an Art of Transvestism: Colonialism and Homosexuality in Puerto Rican Literature." In *¿Entiendes? Queer Readings, Hispanic Writings,* ed. Emilie L. Bergmann and Paul Julian Smith, 137–67. Durham, N.C.: Duke University Press, 1995.

Cuartas Rodríguez, Joaquín Miguel. *Vereda tropical.* Madrid: Ediciones Cultura Hispánica, 1995.

Cuba: Posmodernidad y revolución. Special issue of *Plural* (Jan. 1991).

Cuba Council of Ministers. "The Family Code of the Republic of Cuba of 14 February of 1975." *Review of Socialist Law* 6.2 (1980): 217–45.

Cypess, Sandra Messinger. "*Eugenia Victoria Herrera* and Myrna Casas' Redefinition of Puerto Rican National Identity." In *Essays in Honor of Frank Dauster,* ed. Sandra M. Cypess and Kirsten F. Nigro, 181–94. Newark, N.J.: Juan de la Cuesta, 1995.

————. "Women Dramatists of Puerto Rico." *Revista/Review Interamericana* 9.1 (1979): 24–41.

Dauster, Frank N. "Drama and Theater in Puerto Rico." *Modern Drama* 6 (1963): 177–86.

————. "The Game of Chance: The Theater of José Triana (Cuba)." In Lyday and Woodyard, *Dramatists in Revolt,* 167–89.

Dauster, Frank N., Leon F. Lyday, and George W. Woodyard, eds. *9 dramaturgos hispanoamericanos.* Vols. 1–3. Ottawa: Girol, 1979.

Dávila, Arlene M. *Sponsored Identities: Cultural Politics in Puerto Rico.* Philadelphia: Temple University Press, 1997.

Dávila-López, Grace. "Entrevista a Roberto Ramos-Perea." *Latin American Theatre Review* 26.2 (1993): 151–57.

Dávila Santiago, Rubén. *Teatro obrero en Puerto Rico (1910–1920): Antología.* Rio Piedras: Editorial Edil, 1985.

de la Campa, Ramón V. *Ritualización de la sociedad cubana*. Madrid: Cátedra, 1979.

Demo, David H., Katherine R. Allen, and Mark A. Fine, eds. *Handbook of Family Diversity*. Oxford: Oxford University Press, 2000.

Díaz-Quiñones, Arcadio. *El almuerzo en la hierba (Lloréns Torres, Palés Matos, René Marqués)*. Río Piedras: Huracán, 1982.

———. *La memoria rota*. San Juan: Ediciones Huracán, 1993.

Doggart, Sebastian. "Interview with José Triana." In Doggart, *Latin American Plays*, 82–84.

———. *Latin American Plays: New Drama from Argentina, Cuba, Mexico and Peru*. London: Nick Hern, 1996.

Donzelot, Jacques. *The Policing of Families*. Trans. Robert Hurley. 1979. Reprint, Baltimore: Johns Hopkins University Press, 1997.

Duany, Jorge. "Reconstructing Cubanness: Changing Discourses of National Identity on the Island and in the Diaspora during the Twentieth Century." In Fernández and Betancourt, *Cuba, the Elusive Nation*, 17–42.

Erikson, Kai. "Notes on Trauma and Community." In Caruth, *Trauma*, 183–99.

Escarpanter, José. "Imagen de imagen: Entrevista con José Triana." In *Palabras más que comunes: ensayos sobre el teatro de José Triana*, ed. Kirsten F. Nigro, 1–12. Boulder, Colo.: Society of Spanish and Spanish-American Studies, 1994.

Espinosa Domínguez, Carlos, ed. *Teatro cubano contemporáneo: Antología*. Madrid: Fondo de Cultura Económica, 1992.

Esslin, Martin. *An Anatomy of Drama*. New York: Hill and Wang, 1976.

Estorino, Abelardo. "Destruir los fantasmas, los mitos de las relaciones familiares: Entrevista a José Triana y Vicente Revuelta." *Conjunto* 2.4 (1967): 6–14.

———. *Ni un sí ni un no*. In Estorino, *Teatro*, 290–394.

———. *El robo del cochino*. In Estorino, *Teatro*, 47–103.

———. *Teatro: Abelardo Estorino*. Ed. Salvador Arias. Havana: Letras Cubanas, 1984.

Fanon, Franz. *Black Skin, White Masks*. Trans. Charles Lam Markmann. New York: Grove, 1967.

———. *The Wretched of the Earth*. Trans. Constance Farrington. New York: Grove, 1963.

Feeny, Thomas. "Woman's Triumph Over Man in René Marqués's Theater." *Hispania* 65 (1982): 187–93.

Fernández, Damián J. "Informal Politics and the Crisis of Cuban Socialism." In Schulz, *Cuba and the Future*, 69–81.

———. "Youth in Cuba: Resistance and Accommodation." In Baloyra and Morris, *Conflict and Change in Cuba*, 189–211.

Fernández, Damián J., and Madeline Cámara Betancourt, eds. *Cuba, the Elusive Nation: Interpretations of National Identity*. Gainesville: University Press of Florida, 2000.

Ferrer, Rolando. *Lila, la mariposa*. In Espinosa Domínguez, *Teatro cubano contemporáneo*, 294–344.

Figueroa, Alvin Joaquín. *La prosa de Luis Rafael Sánchez: Texto y contexto.* New York: Peter Lang, 1989.

Fletcher, Angus. *Allegory: The Theory of a Symbolic Mode.* Ithaca, N.Y.: Cornell University Press, 1964.

Flores, Juan. *Divided Borders: Essays on Puerto Rican Identity.* Houston: Arte Público Press, 1993.

———. *From Bomba to Hip-Hop: Puerto Rican Culture and Latino Identity.* New York: Columbia University Press, 2000.

———. *Insularismo e ideología burguesa (nueva lectura de A. S. Pedreira).* Río Piedras: Huracán, 1979.

Fornet, Ambrosio, ed. *Bridging Enigma: Cubans on Cuba.* Special issue of *South Atlantic Quarterly* 96.1 (1997).

Foucault, Michel. "Nietzsche, Genealogy, History." In *Language, Counter-Memory, Practice: Selected Essays and Interviews,* ed. and intro. Donald F. Bouchard, 139–64. Ithaca, N.Y.: Cornell University Press, 1977.

———. "Of Other Spaces." *Diacritics* 16.1 (1986): 22–27.

Franco, Jean. "The Nation as Imagined Community." In *The New Historicism,* ed. Harold Veeser, 204–12. New York: Routledge, 1989.

Franklin, Lillian Cleamons. "The Image of the Black in the Cuban Theater: 1913–1965." Ph.D. diss., Ohio State University, 1982.

Fraser, Howard M. "Theatricality in *The Fanlights* and *Payment as Pledged.*" *American Hispanist* 19 (1977): 6–8.

García, William. "Subversión y relaboración de mitos trágicos en el teatro latinoamericano contemporáneo." Ph.D. diss., Rutgers University, 1996.

García Abreu, Eberto. "Una tragedia en tono doméstico." In Espinosa Domínguez, *Teatro cubano contemporáneo,* 285–90.

García del Toro, Antonio. *Hotel Melancolía (Nostalgia en dos tiempos).* San Juan: Plaza Mayor, 1998.

García Ramis, Magali. *La ciudad que me habita.* Río Piedras: Huracán, 1993.

———. "La manteca que nos une." In García Ramis, *La ciudad que me habita,* 83–89.

———. "Para narrar el tiempo escondido." In García Ramis, *La ciudad que me habita,* 59–74.

———. "'Quiero pensar que mi oficio es la vida.'" In Vega, *El tramo,* 60–64.

Gelpí, Juan. *Literatura y paternalismo en Puerto Rico.* San Juan: Editorial de la Universidad de Puerto Rico, 1993.

Glissant, Edouard. *Caribbean Discourse: Selected Essays.* Trans. and intro. Michael Dash. Charlottesville: University Press of Virginia, 1989.

Gonázlez, Aníbal. "*La Cuarterona* and Slave Society in Cuba and Puerto Rico." *Latin American Literary Review* 8.16 (1980): 47–53.

González, José Emilio. "Aproximación a *Hotel Melancolía.*" In García del Toro, *Hotel Melancolía,* 7–9.

González, José Luis. *El país de cuatro pisos y otros ensayos.* 2nd ed. Río Piedras: Ediciones Huracán, 1980.

González Valés, Luis. "Towards a Plantation Society (1860–1897)." In Morales Carrión, *Puerto Rico,* 79–107.

Graves, Robert. *Greek Gods and Heroes.* New York: Dell, 1960.

Grosfoguel, Ramón. "The Divorce of Nationalist Discourses from the Puerto Rican People: A Sociohistorical Perspective." In Negrón-Muntaner and Grosfoguel, *Puerto Rican Jam,* 57–76.

Guevara, Ernesto. "The Duty of a Revolutionary Doctor." In Bonachea and Valdes, *Che,* 256–64.

———. "Socialism and Man in Cuba." In Bonachea and Valdes, *Che,* 155–69.

Guinness, Gerald. Introduction to *Puerto Rico: The Four-Storeyed Country and Other Essays* by José Luis González, vii–xvii. Trans. Gerald Guinness. Princeton, N.J.: Markus Weiner, 1993.

Halebsky, Sandor, and John M. Kirk. *Cuba—25 Years of Revolution, 1959–1984.* New York: Praeger, 1985.

Haliwell, Stephen. *The Poetics of Aristotle: Translation and Commentary.* Chapel Hill: University of North Carolina Press, 1987.

Hoeg, Jerry. "Coding, Context, and Punctuation in Triana's *La noche de los asesinos.*" *Gestos* 15 (1993): 83–98.

Holzapfel, Tamara. "The Theater of René Marqués: In Search of Identity and Form." In Lyday and Woodyard, *Dramatists in Revolt,* 146–66.

Hornby, Richard. *Drama, Metadrama, and Perception.* Lewisburg, Pa.: Bucknell University Press, 1986.

Huertas, Johanna Emmanuelli. "*Quíntuples:* Las máscaras de la representación." In *De la colonia a la postmodernidad: Teoría teatral y crítica sobre teatro latino-americano,* ed. Peter Roster and Mario Rojas, 285–94. Buenos Aires: Galerna, 1992.

Hutcheon, Linda. *A Poetics of Postmodernism: History, Theory, Fiction.* New York: Routledge, 1985.

———. *The Politics of Postmodernism.* New York: Routledge, 1989.

———. *A Theory of Parody.* New York: Metheun, 1985.

Ibieta, Gabriela. "Jorge Mañach y su *Indagación del choteo.*" *Revista de Estudios Hispánicos* 13 (1986): 71–75.

Innes, Christopher. *A Sourcebook on Naturalist Theatre.* London: Routledge, 2000.

Issacharoff, Michael. *Discourse as Performance.* Stanford, Calif.: Stanford University Press, 1989.

Johnson, Barbara. "Women and Allegory." In *The Wake of Deconstruction,* 52–75. Cambridge, Mass.: Blackwell, 1994.

Johnson, Peter T. "The Nuanced Lives of the Intelligentsia." In Baloyra and Morris, *Conflict and Change in Cuba,* 137–63.

Kershaw, Baz. "Performance, Community, Culture." In *The Routledge Reader in Politics and Performance,* ed. Lizbeth Goodman and Jane de Gay, 136–42. London: Routledge, 2000.

Knight, Franklin W., and Colin A. Palmer, eds. *The Modern Caribbean.* Chapel Hill: University of North Carolina Press, 1989.

Kronik, John W. "Invasions from Outer Space: Narration and the Dramatic Art in Spanish America." *Latin American Theatre Review* 26.2 (1993): 25–47.

Kruger, Loren. *The National Stage: Theatre and Cultural Legitimization in England, France, and America.* Chicago: University of Chicago Press, 1992.

Kutzinski, Vera. *Sugar's Secrets: Race and the Erotics of Cuban Nationalism.* Charlottesville: University Press of Virginia, 1993.

Landes, Joan, ed. *Feminism, the Public and the Private.* Oxford: Oxford University Press, 1998.

Lao, Agustín. "Islands at the Crossroads: Puerto Ricanness Traveling between the Translocal Nation and the Global City." In Negrón-Muntaner and Grosfuguel, *Puerto Rican Jam,* 169–88.

Lasch, Christopher. *Haven in a Heartless World: The Family Besieged.* New York: Basic Books, 1977.

Leal, Rine. *Breve historia del teatro cubano.* Havana: Letras Cubanas, 1980.

Linda Sara. Dir. Jacobo Morales. Cinesí, Inc. Puerto Rico, 1995.

Lolo, Eduardo. *Las trampas del tiempo y sus memorias.* Miami: Hallmark, 1991.

López, Adalberto, ed. *The Puerto Ricans: Their History, Culture, and Society.* Cambridge, Mass.: Schenkman, 1980.

Lugo-Ortiz, Agnes I. "Community at Its Limits: Orality, Law, Silence, and the Homosexual Body in Luis Rafael Sánchez's '¡Jum!'." In *¿Entiendes? Queer Readings, Hispanic Writings,* ed. Emilie L. Bergmann and Paul Julian Smith, 115–36. Durham, N.C.: Duke University Press, 1995.

Luzariaga, Gerardo. "Entrevista con Sergio Corrieri." *Latin American Theatre Review* 16.2 (1983): 51–59.

Lyday, Leon F., and George W. Woodyard. *Dramatists in Revolt: The New Latin American Theater.* Austin: University of Texas Press, 1976.

Lyons, Charles R. "Character and Theatrical Space." In Redmond, *The Theatrical Space,* 27–44.

MacGaffey, Wyatt, and Clifford R. Barnett. *Twentieth Century Cuba: The Background of the Castro Revolution.* Garden City, N.Y.: Anchor, 1965.

MacKinnon, Catharine. "Feminism, Marxism, Method, and the State: An Agenda for Theory." In *Feminist Theory: A Critique of Ideology,* ed. Nannerl O. Keohane, Michelle Z. Rosaldo, and Barbara C. Gelpi, 1–30. Chicago: University of Chicago Press, 1982.

Mañach, Jorge. *Indagación del choteo.* 2nd ed. Miami: Mnemosyne, 1969.

Manzor-Coats, Lillian, and Inés María Martiatu Terry. "IV Festival Internacional de Teatro de La Habana: A Festival Against All Odds." *The Drama Review* 39.2 (1995): 39–70.

Marinello, Juan. "Americanismo y cubanismo literarios." In *Literatura Hispanoamericana,* 95–111. México: Ediciones de la Universidad Nacional de México, 1937.

Marqués, René. *Ensayos (1953–1966).* Barcelona: Antillana, 1966.

———. *The Fanlights.* Trans. Richard John Wiezell. In *The Modern Stage in Latin America,* ed. George Woodyard, 1–41. New York: Dutton, 1971.

———. *Un niño azul para esta sombra. Teatro.* Vol. 1, 67–181. 2nd ed. Río Piedras: Editorial Cultural, 1970.

———. "Pesimismo literario y optimismo político: Su coexistencia en el Puerto Rico actual." In Marqués, *Ensayos,* 43–80.

———. "El puertorriqueño dócil (literatura y realidad psicológica)." In Marqués, *Ensayos,* 147–210.

———. *Los soles truncos.* In Dauster, Lyday, and Woodyard, *9 dramaturgos hispanoamericanos,* 7–58.

Martí, José. "Nuestra América." In *Ensayistas de Nuestra América,* ed. and intro. Susana Rotker. Vol. 2, 156–66. Buenos Aires: Editorial Losada, 1994.

Martin, Eleanor J. *René Marqués.* Boston: Twayne, 1979.

Martin, Randy. *Socialist Ensembles: Theater and State in Cuba and Nicaragua.* Minneapolis: University of Minnesota Press, 1994.

Martínez de Velasco, Javier. "La recreación de los mitos clásicos en el teatro del Caribe." Ph.D. diss., University of Kansas, 1998.

Martínez Tabares, Vivian. "*Manteca:* Catharsis and Absurdity." *The Drama Review* 40.1 (1996): 44–48.

———. "Morir del cuento: Aproximación a un texto teatral." In *Didascalias urgentes de una espectadora interesada (Aproximaciones al teatro cubano de hoy),* 35–46. Havana: Letras Cubanas, 1996.

———. "Theater as Conspiracy: An Interview with Alberto Pedro." In Fornet, *Bridging Enigma,* 43–63.

Martínez Vergne, Teresita. "Politics and Society in the Spanish Caribbean during the Nineteenth Century." In Knight and Palmer, *The Modern Caribbean,* 185–202.

Mateo Palmer, Margarita. "Cuban Youth and Postmodernism." Trans. Sophia McClennen Expósito and Candice Ward. In Fornet, *Bridging Enigma,* 157–68.

McLeod, Ralph O. "The Theater of René Marqués: A Search for Identity in Life and in Literature." Ph.D. diss., University of New Mexico, 1975.

Meléndez, Priscilla. "El espacio dramático como signo: *La noche de los asesinos* de José Triana." *Latin American Theatre Review* 17.1 (1983): 25–35.

———. "Lo uno y lo múltiple: Farsa e incesto en *Quíntuples* de Sánchez." *Latin American Theatre Review* 26.1 (1992): 7–22.

———. "Teoría teatral y teatro puertorriqueño de los 80." *Latin American Theatre Review* 25.2 (1992): 151–64.

Monleón, José. "Cuba y el Tirso de Molina." *Primer Acto* 257 (1995): 111–13.

Montes Huidobro, Matías. *Persona, vida y máscara en el teatro cubano.* Miami: Universal, 1973.

———. *Persona: Vida y máscara en el teatro puertorriqueño.* San Juan: Centro de Estudios Avanzados de Puerto Rico y el Caribe, Inter American University of Puerto Rico, Ateneo Puertorriqueño, Tinglado Puertorriqueño, 1986.

Morales Carrión, Arturo, "The PPD Democratic Hegemony (1944–1969)." In Morales Carrión, *Puerto Rico,* 256–307.

———, ed. *Puerto Rico: A Political and Cultural History.* New York: W. W. Norton, 1983.

———. "A Postscriptum: The End of the Consensus." In Morales Carrión, *Puerto Rico,* 308–16.

Morell, Hortensia R. "*Quíntuples* y el vértigo del teatro autorreflexivo de Luis Ráfael Sánchez." *Latin American Theatre Review* 28.2 (1994): 39–49.

Morfi, Angelina. *Historia crítica de un siglo de teatro puertorriqueño.* San Juan: Instituto de Cultura Puertorriqueña, 1980.

Morris, Nancy. *Puerto Rico: Culture, Politics, and Identity.* Westport, Conn.: Praeger, 1995.

Mosquera, Gerardo. "Los hijos de Guillermo Tell." In *Cuba: Posmodernidad y revolución,* 60–63.

Muguercia, Magaly. "The Gift of Precariousness: Alberto Pedro Torriente's *Manteca.*" *The Drama Review* 40.1 (1996): 49–60.

———. *El teatro cubano en vísperas de la revolución.* Havana: Letras Cubanas, 1988.

Muñoz, Elías Miguel. "Teatro cubano de transición (1958–1964): Piñera y Estorino." *Latin American Theatre Review* 20.2 (1986): 39–44.

Murch, Anne C. "Genet-Triana-Kopit: Ritual as 'danse macabre' (*La noche de los asesinos*)." *Modern Drama* 15 (1973): 369–81.

Negrón-Muntaner, Frances. "Los dos sueños de Jacobo: nostalgia y nación en el cine de Jacobo Morales (versión breve)." In *Saqueos: Antología de producción cultural,* ed. Dorian Lugo. Puerto Rico: Editorial Noexiste, 2002.

Negrón-Muntaner, Frances, and Ramón Grosfoguel, eds. *Puerto Rican Jam: Rethinking Colonialism and Nationalism.* Minneapolis: University of Minnesota Press, 1997.

Netchinsky, Jill. "Madness and Colonization: Ferré's Ballet." *Revista de Estudios Hispánicos* 25.3 (1991): 103–28.

Ngugi wa Thiong'o. *Penpoints, Gunpoints, and Dreams: Toward a Critical Theory of the Arts and the State in Africa.* Oxford: Clarendon Press, 1998.

Nigro, Kirsten F. "*La noche de los asesinos:* Playscript and Stage Enactment." *Latin American Theatre Review* 11.1 (1977): 45–57.

Orihuela, Roberto. *La emboscada.* Havana: UNEAC, 1981.

Oróñoz Echeverría, Patricia R. "La configuración de la historia de Puerto Rico en el teatro de René Marqués en la década de 1952–1962." Ph.D. diss., New York University, 1986.

Ortiz, Fernando. "Cubanidad y Cubanía." *Islas* 6.2 (1964): 91–95.

———. "Del fenómeno social de la 'transculturación' y de su importancia en Cuba." In *Contrapunteo cubano del tabaco y el azúcar,* 129–35. Barcelona: Ariel, 1973.

Padula, Alfred, and Lois Smith. "Women in Socialist Cuba, 1959–84." In Halebsky and Kirk, *Cuba—25 Years of Revolution,* 79–92.

Palls, Terry L. "A New Language for Today's Cuban Theatre." *Latin American Theatre Review* 31.2 (1998): 125–29.

Pánico, Marie J. "Myrna Casas: Nacional y trascendente." *Alba de América: Revista Literaria* 7.12–13 (1989): 411–18.

Parker, Andrew, Mary Russo, Doris Sommer, and Patricia Yaeger, eds. *Nationalisms and Sexualities*. New York: Routledge, 1992.

Pedreira, Antonio S. *Insularismo*. Río Piedras: Edil, 1971.

Pedro Torriente, Alberto. *Manteca*. In Boudet, *Morir*, trans. Christopher Winks, 166–98.

———. *Manteca*. *The Drama Review* 40.1 (1996): 19–43.

———. "Todo esto es una respuesta al fin de una época." *Primer Acto* 228 (1989): 72–78.

Perales, Rosalina. "Teatro de fricción o las nuevas corrientes del teatro puertorriqueño." In *Reflexiones sobre el teatro latinoamericano del siglo veinte*, 73–82. Buenos Aires: Galerna, 1989.

———. *Teatro hispanoamericano contemporáneo (1967–1987)*. Vol. 2. México: Gaceta, 1993.

Pérez, Louis A., Jr. *Cuba: Between Reform and Revolution*. 2nd ed. New York: Oxford University Press, 1995.

Pérez Firmat, Gustavo. *The Cuban Condition: Translation and Identity in Modern Cuban Literature*. Cambridge: Cambridge University Press, 1989.

Perivolaris, John. "'¡El cuento no es el cuento! ¡El cuento es quien lo cuenta!'": Terms of Subjectivity in Luis Rafael Sánchez's *Quíntuples*." *Revista de Estudios Hispánicos* 22 (1995): 337–57.

———. *Puerto Rican Cultural Identity and the Work of Luis Rafael Sánchez*. North Carolina Studies in the Romance Languages and Literatures 268. Chapel Hill: Department of Romance Languages, University of North Carolina, 2000.

Phillips, Jordan B. *Contemporary Puerto Rican Drama*. Madrid: Plaza Mayor, 1972.

Picó, Fernando. *Historia general de Puerto Rico*. Río Piedras: Huracán, 1986.

Pilditch, Charles. "Theater in Puerto Rico: A Brief History." *Revista/Review Interamericana* 9 (1979): 5–8.

Piñera, Virgilio. *Aire frío*. In *Teatro completo*, 276–398. Havana: Ediciones R, 1960.

———. "Dos viejos pánicos en Colombia." *Conjunto* 3.7 (1967): 69–70.

Planas, Richard J. "Political Changes and Social Attitudes in Cuba during the Special Period: Implications." In Schulz, *Cuba and the Future*, 83–96.

Quigley, Austin. *The Modern Stage and Other Worlds*. New York: Methuen, 1985.

Quiles Ferrer, Edgar Heriberto. *Teatro puertorriqueño en acción (dramaturgia y escenificación) 1982–1989*. Cuadernos del Ateneo. Vol. 2. Serie de Teatro 3. San Juan: Ateneo Puertorriqueño, 1990.

Quintero Rivera, Ángel G. "The Development of Social Classes and Political Conflicts in Puerto Rico." In López, *The Puerto Ricans*, 213–21.

Ramos, Aaron Gamaliel. "The Development of Annexionist Politics in Twentieth Century Puerto Rico." In López, *The Puerto Ricans*, 257–72.

Ramos, Julio. *Amor y anarquía: Los escritos de Luisa Capetillo*. Río Piedras: Ediciones Huracán, 1992.

Ramos-Perea, Roberto. *Callando amores*. San Juan: University of Puerto Rico Press, 1996.

———. "De cómo y porqué la nueva dramaturgia puertorriqueña es una revolución." In Ramos-Perea, *Perspectiva*, 41–58.

———. "La dramaturgia puertorriqueña: O como boxear con la derecha sin parecer izquierdista." *Revista del Ateneo Puertorriqueño* 3.8 (1993): 156–72.

———. "Escritura dramática en Puerto Rico: Hacia la reafirmación del contexto." In *Reflexiones sobre el teatro latinoamericano del siglo veinte*, 379–83. Buenos Aires: Galerna, 1989.

———. *Perspectiva de la nueva dramaturgia puertorriqueña (Ensayos sobre el nuevo teatro nacional)*. San Juan: Ateneo Puertorriqueño, 1989.

———. "Perspectivas de la nueva dramaturgia nacional." In Ramos-Perea, *Perspectiva*, 12–40.

———. "Teatro e identidad." In Ramos-Perea, *Perspectiva*, 90–91.

Reca Moreira, Inés, et al. *Análisis de las investigaciones sobre la familia cubana, 1970–1987*. Havana: Editorial de Ciencias Sociales, 1990.

Redmond, James, ed. *The Theatrical Space*. Vol. 9 of *Themes in Drama*. Cambridge: Cambridge University Press, 1989.

Reynolds, Bonnie Hildebrand. "La nueva dramaturgia puertorriqueña en el contexto del nuevo teatro latinoamericano." *Revista del Ateneo Puertorriqueño* 3.8 (1993): 139–55.

———. *Space, Time and Crisis: The Theatre of René Marqués*. York, S.C.: Spanish Literature, 1988.

Ríos Ávila, Rubén. *La raza cómica del sujeto en Puerto Rico*. San Juan: Ediciones Callejón, 2002.

Rivera, Nelson. *Visual Artists and the Puerto Rican Performing Arts, 1950–1990: The Works of Jack and Irene Delano, Antonio Martorell, Jaime Suárez, and Oscar Mestey-Villamil*. New York: Peter Lang, 1997.

Rivera de Álvarez, Josefina. *Literatura puertorriqueña: Su proceso en el tiempo*. Madrid: Partenón, 1983.

Roach, Joseph. *Cities of the Dead: Circum-Atlantic Performance*. New York: Columbia University Press, 1996.

Rodríguez, Ileana. *House/Garden/Nation: Space, Gender, and Ethnicity in Postcolonial Latin American Literatures by Women*. Durham, N.C.: Duke University Press, 1994.

Rodríguez Castro, María Elena. "Las casas y el porvenir: Nación y narración en el ensayo puertorriqueño." *Revista Iberoamericana* 59 (1993): 33–54.

Rodríguez Juliá, Edgardo. *Puertorriqueños (Album de la sagrada familia puertorriqueña a partir de 1898)*. Río Piedras: Plaza Mayor, 1988.

Rogozinski, Jan. *A Brief History of the Caribbean: From the Arawak and the Carib to the Present*. New York: Penguin, 1992.

Rubenstein, Roberta. *Home Matters: Longing and Belonging, Nostalgia and Mourning in Women's Fiction*. New York: Palgrave, 2001.

Rudakoff, Judith. "R/Evolutionary Theater in Contemporary Cuba: Grupo Teatro Escambray." *The Drama Review* 40.1 (1996): 77–97.

Ruiz, Ramón Eduardo. *Cuba: The Making of a Revolution*. New York: W. W. Norton, 1970.

Said, Edward. "Introduction: Secular Criticism." In *The World, the Text, and the Critic*. Cambridge: Harvard University Press, 1983.

Salgado, César A. "El Entierro de González: Con(tra)figuraciones del 98 en la narrativa ochentista puertorriqueña." *Revista Iberoamericana* 64.184–85 (1998): 413–39.

Sánchez, Luis Rafael. "Las divinas palabras de René Marqués." *Sin Nombre* 10.3 (1979): 11–14.

———. *Quíntuples*. Hanover, N.H.: Ediciones del Norte, 1985.

Sandoval-Sánchez, Alberto. *José Can You See? Latinos On and Off Broadway*. Madison: University of Wisconsin Press, 1999.

———. "Puerto Rican Identity Up in the Air: Air Migration, Its Cultural Representations, and Me 'Cruzando el charco.'" In Negrón-Muntaner and Grosfoguel, *Puerto Rican Jam*, 189–208.

Schulz, Donald E., ed. *Cuba and the Future*. Westport, Conn.: Greenwood Press, 1994.

Scolnicov, Hanna. "Theatre Space, Theatrical Space, and the Theatrical Space Without." In Redmond, *The Theatrical Space*, 11–26.

———. *Woman's Theatrical Space*. Cambridge: Cambridge University Press, 1994.

Shorter, Edward. *The Making of the Modern Family*. New York: Basic Books, 1975.

Silvestrini, Blanca G. "Contemporary Puerto Rico: A Society of Contrasts." In Knight and Palmer, *The Modern Caribbean*, 147–67.

Skidmore, Thomas E., and Peter H. Smith. *Modern Latin America*. 2nd ed. New York: Oxford University Press, 1989.

Smith, Lois M., and Alfred Padula. *Sex and Revolution: Women in Socialist Cuba*. New York: Oxford University Press, 1996.

Sommer, Doris. *Foundational Fictions: The National Romances of Latin America*. Berkeley: University of California Press, 1991.

———. *One Master for Another: Populism as Patriarchal Rhetoric in Dominican Novels*. Lanham, Md.: University Press of America, 1983.

Stevens, Evelyn P. "Marianismo: The Other Face of Machismo in Latin America." In *Female and Male in Latin America: Essays*, ed. Ann Pescatello, 90–101. Pittsburgh: University Press of Pittsburgh, 1973.

Tapia y Rivera, Alejandro. *La cuarterona*. San Juan: Universidad de Puerto Rico and Instituto de Cultura Puertorriqueña, 1993.

Taylor, Diana. *Disappearing Acts: Spectacles of Gender and Nationalism in Argentina's "Dirty War."* Durham, N.C.: Duke University Press, 1997.

———. *Theatre of Crisis: Drama and Politics in Latin America*. Lexington: University of Kentucky Press, 1991.

Triana, José. *Night of the Assassins*. Trans. Sebastian Doggart. In Doggart, *Latin American Plays*, 29–81.

———. *La noche de los asesinos*. In Dauster, Lyday, and Woodyard, *9 dramaturgos hispanoamericanos*, 133–201.

Umpierre, Luz María. "Inversiones, niveles y participación en *Absurdos en soledad de Myrna Casas*." *Latin American Theatre Review* 16.1 (1983): 3–13.

Unruh, Vicky. "A Moveable Space: The Problem of Puerto Rico in Myrna Casas's Theater." In *Latin American Women Dramatists: Theater, Texts, and Theories*, ed. Catherine Larson and Margarita Vargas, 126–42. Bloomington: Indiana University Press, 1997.

Van Der Kolk, Bessel A., and Onno Van Der Hart. "The Intrusive Past: The Flexibility of Memory and the Engraving of Trauma." In Caruth, *Trauma*, 158–82.

Vázquez, Liliam. "*Manteca:* La metáfora de la utopía." *Tablas* 3–4 (1995): 35–36.

Vega, Ana Lydia. "Cuento en camino." In *Falsas crónicas del sur*, 174–88. San Juan: University of Puerto Rico Press, 1991.

———. "En sus marcas . . . Palabras de inauguración." In Vega, *El tramo ancla*, 1–4.

———. "Madera y pajilla." In Vega, *El tramo ancla*, 292–96.

———, ed. *El tramo ancla: Ensayos puertorriqueños de hoy*. Río Piedras: University of Puerto Rico Press, 1988.

Vizcarrondo, Fortunato. *Dinga y mandinga (poemas)*. 3rd ed. San Juan: Instituto de Cultura Puertorriqueña, 1976.

Waldman, Gloria F. *Luis Rafael Sánchez: Pasión teatral*. San Juan: Instituto de Cultura Puertorriqueña, 1988.

Weiss, Judith A. "The Emergence of Popular Culture." In Halebsky and Kirk, *Cuba —25 Years of Revolution*, 117–33.

Woodyard, George. "Estorino's Theatre: Customs and Conscience in Cuba." *Latin American Literary Review* 11.22 (1983): 57–63.

Yúdice, George, Juan Flores, and Jean Franco. *On Edge: The Crisis of Contemporary Latin American Culture*. Minneapolis: University of Minnesota Press, 1992.

Index

munity in, 166; of *jíbaros*, 21; music of, 232n18; in NDP movement, 125; in Puerto Rican art, 128; in Puerto Rican drama, 214; subjectivities comprising, 120; symbolism of, 31, 48; translocality of, 156, 157, 166. *See also* Identity, Puerto Rican

Quigley, Austin, 8, 224n27
Quiles Ferrer, Edgar Heriberto, 232n17
Quinceañeras (birthday parties), 130
Quinquenio Gris (1971–76), 177, 187
Quintero, Héctor, 107
Quintero Rivera, Ángel G., 126, 222n4

Race: in Puerto Rican drama, 18; in Puerto Rican identity, 13, 21, 120, 123; theatrical representation of, 34; in works of Arriví, 224n20
Racism, 222n6; in *Lila, la mariposa*, 79; in *Manteca*, 210; Puerto Rican, 29–33, 38; in *Los soles truncos*, 52; in U.S., 224n20; in *Vejigantes*, 37, 38
Rafael Sánchez, Luis: *En cuerpo de camisa*, 123; "La guagua aérea," 157
Ramos, Aaron Gamaliel, 230n3
Ramos, José Antonio: *Tembladera*, 11, 76
Ramos Escobar, José Luis, 125
Ramos Otero, Manuel, 123; *Concierto de metal*, 231n8
Ramos-Perea, Roberto, 124, 234n34; national identity in, 13, 215; in NPD movement, 125, 146, 231n10; on Sánchez, 147; social themes of, 139
—*Callando amores*, 120, 131, 139–47; docility in, 143; family in, 139, 141, 144, 146; family romance in, 142; father figures in, 147; female roles in, 233n21; film version of, 140; house in, 140; intertextuality of, 233n24; land in, 141–43; national identity in, 143, 144, 146; nationalism in, 145; and *Un niño azul*, 143; nostalgia in, 143; productions of, 233n20; repetition in, 145, 146; self-reflexivity in, 144
—*Cueva de ladrones*, 233n20
—*Miénteme más*, 233n20
—*Módulo 104*, 233n20

—*Revolución en el Infierno*, 233n20
Readers: communities of, 9
Real Cédula de Gracias (1815), 19; proclamation of, 50
Realism
—dramatic: in American drama, 2; Brechtian, 156, 160, 181, 186, 188, 189, 203; *costumbrista*, 203; in Cuban family plays, 168; family in, 3; house in, 3, 214–15; of nineteenth century, 4, 219n2; in *La noche de los asesinos*, 114; of post-revolutionary Cuban drama, 203; Puerto Rican, 26, 214; stage techniques in, 4
—social: of Ateneo Puertorriqueño, 28; of Cuban drama, 174, 180–81; in Puerto Rican drama, 26, 28, 214
Reality: cultural knowledge about, 4
Refugees, Cuban, 172
"Relevo" (newspaper column), 130
Religion: Afro-Cuban, 167; under Cuban Revolution, 237n11
Republic, Cuban (1902–58): authoritarianism in, 67, 74, 78; Batista regime, 10, 74–75, 77, 106, 183; corruption in, 67, 74, 75, 87, 228n16; cultural infrastructure of, 73; drama during, 77–78; economic dependence of, 67, 69, 74; family during, 87, 88–89; Machado regime, 70, 74; national theater movement in, 68, 76; Zayas regime, 70
Retrato de Teresa (film), 236n9
Return, eternal, 162
Revista de Avance, 70
Revista de Estudios Hispánicos, 20
Revista del Ateneo Puertorriqueño, 20
Revolution, Cuban: artistic freedom under, 174; authoritarianism of, 106; children under, 171; *choteo* during, 114; crisis management in, 202; didactic drama in, 237n17; documents of, 12; in domestic sphere, 171; drama during, 77, 107, 167, 173–87, 237nn15, 17; economic changes under, 169, 172; education under, 171, 172, 237nn10, 12; in *La emboscada*, 181–86; experimentation during, 202; family during, 105–6, 115, 167–72; gender roles in, 102, 170–71; homosexuality during,

Camilla Stevens is assistant professor of Spanish at Rutgers University, where she teaches courses on Caribbean literature and Latin American theater.